Hornes Down Under

PART ONE

Hornes Down Under

Tony Horne

Matador
5 Weir Road
Kibworth Beauchamp
Leicester LE8 0LQ, UK
Tel: 0116 279 2299
Email: books@troubador.co.uk
Web: www.troubador.co.uk/matador

ISBN 9781848762008

A Cataloguing-in-Publication (CIP) catalogue record for this book
is available from the British Library.

Printed and bound in Great Britain by TJ international Ltd, Padstow, Cornwall

Matador is an imprint of Troubador Publishing Ltd

To Poppy Greta

Acknowledgements

God – this is where you leave someone out and they get upset.

Hearty thanks go to so many people, but mostly Wolf Blass, Jacob's Creek and Stanley Wine, all of whom accompanied me on this journey at various points. Stanley, for the nights penning away in the van; Wolf and Jacob for keeping me company over Christmas '08 when I was writing it all up again. Truly, I love the three of you equally!

To Harty - you're always there, whether it's dawn in Sydney and dusk in Corbridge. To Stonesy – I love you, you fat bastard. To Dogs – what am I going to do without you? You have been the best. To Chris Ryan – for all the advice, you retain legendary status!

To Chris and Jack – well, you're everything, and thanks for all the help from finding Troubador to re-reading for the fifty-eighth time. The mistakes are yours.

And to the Troubador guys – thanks for making it easy, and Claire Barber on PR....well you will find out how great you were whether or not you get a mention here in the next book! Final gratitude goes to Big John – King of the net.

Lastly, of course, enormous amounts of Scouse love to all the Hughes family and to Nat, Molly and Sam. This was simply the best thing that we ever did.

P.S. I haven't told Nat she is on the front cover yet and she is going to go nuts.

Cooktown
Port Douglas
Cairns
Townsville
Airlie Beach
Yeppoon
Rockhampton
Gladstone
Bundaberg
Hervey Bay
Fraser Island
Sunshine Coast
Brisbane
Gold Coast
Ballina
Nambucca Heads
Port Stephens
Sydney
Batemans Bay
Pambula Beach
Lakes Entrance
Traralgon
Port Fairy
Melbourne
Anglesea
Robe
Adelaide

QUEENSLAND

NEW SOUTH WALES

VICTORIA

TASMANIA

NORTHERN TERRITORY

SOUTH AUSTRALIA

WESTERN AUSTRALIA

Darwin

▲ Uluru (Ayers Rock)

Broome

Perth

(possible trip 2012?)

Let's turn the clock back to Tuesday 24th June 2008, when we undertook the biggest adventure of our life and without a clue what we were doing.

We are Tony (36), Natalie (34), Molly (8) and Sam (5), and if *you* are a burnt-out family, bitten by the credit crunch, bogged-down by nanny-state legislation, collapsing under the realisation that your life is flying by, with your kids growing up fast, together with the aching realisation that your career has positively stalled, whilst knowing that you only have the duration of the British school holidays to play with, then this is definitely the book for you.

If that's not you, hey read it anyway, because if you like wildlife, campervans, Australia, barbeques, arguments with airlines, theme parks, Steve Irwin, Kylie and Jason (of course!) and families who just limp from one cock-up to another, then it's all here too. In short, one mad family drive a campervan across Australia…Disaster ensues.

Let's be clear though, this is not a guide book. No way! We had one of those on our laps every day and we just looked at each other and shouted *fraud*.

After all, who is naïve enough to think that any editor has checked every detail in all those books, especially in a country such as Australia where the natives haven't even discovered all the land? Yet still we all buy them en masse as though we can't travel without them, when the reality is that you probably merely flick through a handful of pictures, barely noticing the text while the airport bookshop takes advantage of your pre-flight nerves and pickpockets you to the tune of £20 and some more.

No, that's not what we are about. This is a travel story of a family trying to re-introduce themselves to each other after many stressful years, following a route down the side of Australia dictated principally by campsites in the esteemed Big 4 group.

Being self-employed in the media, principally in broadcasting and in writing, my accountant says that this book is also the only way we could fund the trip. As a business expense.

There I've come clean. Now you know.

Day One

Unbelievably, I actually do my radio show on the morning that we fly. You see, that's self-employed syndrome. Work to the last.

My mind wasn't on the job of course, and my abiding memory of this morning is listening to a colleague slagging me off in another studio, something that was I able to pick up in my studio as his microphone was still on.

This is exactly why we had to take this trip. For the moment, I am done talking nonsense on the radio for five hours at a time and I am done working with the poisonous, talentless and insincere.

From here on in, we would leave the media and all its petty ways behind as we crave the lost values of time, family and space. We are on our way and we have a plane to catch.

Manchester airport is tough. Nat's parents, brilliant as always, are there. My folks hardly even know that we're off.

I knew it was eating John and Lynne, and I knew they would cope in their usual ways. John, marshalling the troops, triple-checking everything as if auditioning for security; Lynney wanting it over as quickly as possible because she didn't have that revert to bloke mechanism within. I knew that I would set her off if she didn't set *me* off.

We've all been there. Just like the scene at the start of *Love Actually*, but more sincere.

I need to mention this because anybody heading down under

has this moment. You dread it for days, and it rips your heart out at the time, particularly when you do that looking over the shoulder thing as you head through the x-rays and *they* head for the parking.

'I can still see them…I can still see them…that's it they've gone.'

And then you're ok again, and you know that you will be when you ring them as the 1825 lands at Terminal Five. It's just a moment in time. It kills you but it passes.

Something stupid shakes you out of it every time, whether it is an unpleasant airport worker whose jobsworthy nature collides with your emotion, or the laughable fact that my boss Trevor is trying to tell me about focus groups for my radio show even as late as I board, having promised that he would ring me back five hours before.

I like Trevor a lot, but I knew this would happen. I'm off the radio for two months, so he might as well have not bothered with the focus group in the first place. Radio people don't always think things through.

Plus, I'm officially on holiday, and that means that I have other things on my mind. I am duty-bound to spend £50 on stuff that I absolutely do not need before boarding. Lucky John Peel. I know you're dead, but I have chosen to buy you.

The fact that the air steward on the flight to London is called Floriano also helps to lighten the mood!

Terminal five is a shambles, and I quote the businessman in front, 'like it's a surprise that this flight lands here at 7.40 every night,' when there is no stand for us to park on, accentuated by our comic performer on the pilot's microphone ordering us to exit from the front, then the rear, then the front.

It's a comedy called *Carry On Up The Airport* except that we are in serious danger of missing our flight, particularly as all the transfer routes to T4 are blocked off, and eventually finding ourselves on the Heathrow Express line, we learn that our next train is fourteen minutes away. This is the busiest airport in the world where trains should run one a minute, but no, you will wait a quarter of an hour.

On the platform, paranoid at missing the flight, we talk to anyone. Nerves and adrenalin kick in. Our first victim is Steve, back home for his best mate's wedding. He is on the flight to Singapore too, but then direct on into Sydney where he lives now. He tells us straight. He will never move back to the UK. He works in telecoms and walks past the Opera House every day and thinks nothing of it. Well sold, mate.

We exit the Heathrow Express and find our flight is on last call. I am sure that I speak for so many people travelling through Heathrow – this is the most difficult airport in the world. We arrive at our gate sweaty, and we still have a dozen or so hours to fly through the night. Thanks so much British Airways. Thanks.

On board, you always look at other kids misbehaving. I delight in the rough Australian bitch in front of us hitting her son Daniel and his brother while their lazy English Dad ignores them all in his sleep.

I'm emotional all the way. I always am these days. I am thinking that this is a make or break trip for us, and I tell Nat so. She hasn't seen it this way. If it makes us, it will reverse all the problems of the last five years. If it breaks us, I will just come to a level of acceptance of what our life is – functional parents sharing a house.

Day Two

I remember nothing of the flight except that I didn't sleep. I always used to be able to, but post-kids, it is impossible. Molly slept diagonally across me the whole way. Somebody needs to tell airlines that the arm between the seats needs to disappear into a hole, rather than *almost* disappearing, so that it doesn't elbow you all the way, whilst your eight year old is snoring on your bollocks.

We land in Singapore. It is simple, clean, calm and unflustered, *so* the opposite to Heathrow that I am delighted to be here. Borrowing my father's gene, I have already decided that we will underground it to Orchard Road where we are staying, and Nat is already tutting that we can't get all this luggage and two kids there by public transport.

I am doing that vulnerable thing of pushing the trolley towards the exit, with no obvious plan, when suddenly this strange man befriends me. I resist at all costs, deliberately walking past. I am British. I don't make eye contact.

He follows me, and won't leave it. There is no way in the world that I am conceding to anybody pushy. No WAY. I absolutely hate being rushed into a decision. Respect my space please. My indecision against his pushiness causes the first row of the trip and it is suddenly my fault – yes, my fault – that we are now standing like lemons, easy targets with our luggage, in a city that none of us know. This is when Kenny enters our world.

'Everybody speak Engrish, I take you to the Night Jew,' he says, proving that everybody speaks English. In their own unique way.

For Jew read zoo by the way.

I resist all conversation. I do this. I leave it to Nat. I never talk until something clicks. He is taking us to Ocean Road. No, he is taking us to Orchard Road, but I keep thinking it is Ocean Road, which is a rather shoddy part of South Shields outside of Newcastle with lots of takeaways, to whom I broadcast in my day job. You see, it is not yet out of the system. I see things. I see work. I write it down.

Kenny used to be a tour guide, making sixty dollars a day. We are paying him forty to take us to the Marriott. Oh yes, he saw us coming.

When we arrive I laugh my socks off. A pianist is bashing out tunes from *The Lion King*. Oh dear, you don't get this at the Marriott in Gateshead. In fact the Marriott in Gateshead is a disgrace compared to this palace, with its funky outside bar, and its beautiful waterfalls, plus the fact that the nice young man on reception is upgrading us because 'I have a silver member.'

This is news to both my wife and I, though clearly not the Marriott rewards programme, which seems to have a file on my manhood.

We like Singapore immediately. It is efficient, seamless, tidy and law-abiding. It functions beautifully in a subservient way. It is difficult to call whether this is the simmering threat of communism or a throw-back to British imperialism. I am embarrassed to have come from such an empire. These people are wonderful, worth so much more than the *Jeremy Kyle* society that we have temporarily left.

It is expensive though. We head to a mall for a meal, and it is shocking in its content and price. The marinated chicken is vile, the bones in the soup leave you on the brink of vomiting, and the wine is £19 a shot.

It's a shocker and we are here for four nights. We vow to return via the 7/11 store. We'll do our usual trick of taking wine back to the room and not paying hotel bar prices. But it's £28 for a bottle of Jacob's Creek. This is a disaster. Is our alcohol problem so bad that we can't ride this out for four nights? Probably.

Shattered, we return to the room, and I am in trouble again for giving Sam big E numbers just before bedtime. Because bedtime and dietary requirements will be well observed on this trip. Of course they will.

I flick to CNN. They are running a story entitled 'Gender Bender In Virginia.' Their words not mine. I remember why I have embarked on this trip of a lifetime and I remember too the holidays where retiring to your room at night meant you wondered what the folks back home were up to. Nowadays, it is ruined by the fact that you know. The barriers of travel are no more. I figure it is time to put them up again.

Hey, Molly's best friend Robyn has even set up a blog so the two can keep in touch. Whatever happened to incognito and having a holiday and switching off? I vow that this will be the last TV that we watch for two months.

Nat is paying no attention to this. She is writing her own blog in the bed next to me. The plan is for us both to record the same experiences from each point of view and combine the book, or publish twice. Her account, and then mine – the one worth reading! Already, I am nervous at this concept. She keeps exuding secret smiles to herself as she writes, as though ten years of marriage frustration are coming out in the pen, as though she is having an affair, but with her script. This annoys me. Not only is this trip about to be a wonderful adventure. It appears to be a game.

I have no choice but to up the ante. Reluctantly, I ring Kenny.

Day Three

This place *is* expensive. I do not want this blog, these diaries, whatever you call them, to be a travel guide. BUT I have to give you this tip. Do not eat in any restaurants in Singapore unless you are a zillionaire. Go underneath the Marriott on Orchard Road to the Hawker market – wonderful pork skewers with asparagus for just a dollar. You can eat cheap and well, and it is clean too. So far! You won't find it in a gourmet guide, but trust me, the locals eat here and you should too. I make a mental note to self that we will eat here for the rest of the Singapore trip. The tight in me is smiling.

Today, though, is about Raffles. When we get to Melbourne, I am adamant that we are going on the *Neighbours* tour. Raffles is Nat's Ramsay Street. I appreciate that as an observation, this places me on higher intellectual ground.

I am led on this one, not particularly bothered, if I am honest. I'll let Nat fulfil her ambitions. So early in the trip, I am just so glad not to be working that she can do whatever she wants. Besides, this is the starter. Australia is the main course.

Of course, I am thinking *Tenko*, the eighties prisoner of war series, which filmed here. I am laughing all the way into the entrance about the Monday when we all went into school after the Sunday night programme, asking if everybody else had seen the tit. Yes Tenko showed a breast, and we were all fourteen. It was brilliant!

Nat, however, is strangely nervous. I can't understand why....
'Do you think we can go in?' (It would be well worth coming all this way to be turned away, wouldn't it?)

I am not for one for historical relics. Bloody hell, my deluded mother spent most of those adolescent years dragging me around Normandy cathedrals – no wonder the Tenko tit was landmark. Yet when you arrive, there is something truly magical about the place. It almost casts a spell in its imperial white. It exudes class and history. It makes a statement.

We pose for nonky photos outside the entrance. We even fake a picture by snapping the kids in front of someone's left-over meal, so that we can tell our friends that we ate in Raffles. This is the pathetic peer pressure that we have left behind, though clearly the desire to impress the Cheshire set or the Northeast radio audience has not totally departed our soul yet. I am embarrassed writing this, and re-reading this, that we could be so superficial, in the wake of such history.

The fans are rotating wildly above us. It is almost like an old-time movie where their spinning causes the director to cut to a flashback scene. This, though, *is* a moment in time, living in the past, and there are sadly, more tourists than residents, and how returning residents must frown at the obscenity that is the tourist shop, with a plastic bag at forty dollars, eleven for a postcard, twenty-nine for a mug and ninety-nine for a teapot. I am staggered at the influence of the East India Tea Company. It is everywhere. Can't stand the stuff myself.

And then we meet Archie, on his way to Horsham in Australia. His brother has days to live. This is his sixth visit back to Raffles. He doesn't directly say so, but he was clearly here in the war. He tells the story of how on the last time he came, they demanded that he have a tie in the dining room. An insult really to war heroes to be getting picky over dress sense. So his Aussie and Kiwi mates dined with their ties, not round their necks, of course, laid bare on the tables in protest.

We get chatting as we take his photo by the fountain, something that I always shy away from. I am just not a photo person though I know that there will be many over the next two months. I can't help but wonder though, as we gaze down the lens at him, what movies are playing in his mind, some sixty years on from when I presume that he came here the first time.

His story moves me. Though of course, he tells me very little of it. I am left to second-guess.

Nat's vile mobile breaks the moment. How often does that happen these days? The contrast between the two eras jars. Here is a man, coming to the end of his days, on the way to bury his brother, replaying his own tragic blockbuster movie in his mind, surrounded by the product of the generation that he fought to free and interrupted by a *Mika* ringtone.

I can only apologise.

It seems that Kenny has spotted us on the way to the Singapore Fryer. That makes it sound like a takeaway, I know. It's actually the world's biggest Ferris wheel thing, and possibly also the world's slowest!

From the top you get stunning views of beautiful Singapore. No, that's a lie. You see a city hell bent on constructing itself to oblivion. If you look out to sea though, you'll be tricked by the mirage. There aren't hotels in the ocean – it's just the angle of the flyer that creates the stunning illusion.

And yes, it is a flyer not a fryer but we have to write these things in the accent of Kenny. I think he told us that he saw us walking the long, tedious, ugly, hard walk from the MRT station to the wheel to make us feel guilty for not using him. By the way – and imagine this in London – the MRT has a recycling system for your tickets which refunds some of your fare, if you vow to save the planet. Some things just function better abroad.

The reality is that we shouldn't have bothered going at all, though the kids loved it. Perhaps this is an early marker. Their definitions and ours are clearly miles apart. It is only when you arrive at the flyer that you realise that there is a free shuttle bus there and back which, on return, takes you right up to the beautiful little cricket ground, something that I can only imagine must have housed some of the most pompous, snooty British imperial aristocrats of yesteryear, waited on by locals paid a pittance.

Are we just repeating this cycle with Kenny?

He seems to be on permanent call, picking us up a couple of hours later for the Night Jew and organising our every move as nature enters our lives for the first time.

Already just two days on from finishing work, I feel that I am returning to being a human being with a heart. I'm staring at animals that I have never heard of and wondering why we feel that *we* have the right to dominate the planet. I haven't felt like this for years. I can't remember *ever* thinking like this actually. If work comes uninvited into my mind, I just dismiss it with a silent curse.

We're literally so close to the animals as we ride the night safari train round Singapore Zoo that I can only assume that there have been accidents in the past. It is too close for comfort and despite warnings to keep the noise to a minimum, and flash photography non-existent, the Americans naturally break every rule in the book, with no respect for man or beast as they do their pre-heart attack microwave world tours, seeing the world in two weeks, ticking off the monuments before obesity gets them once and for all and they die.

Oddly though, since we are told not to talk, you still get a commentary.

We are convinced that Sam has night vision. We've always felt that he had some sort of ESP in the past, citing his pre-birth experiences as an angel flying into Mummy's tummy but now he spots everything – still or mobile – and can name it before it has been announced. Does my boy have some kind of animal kingdom autism?

I'm reeled in wondrously by the fusion of the dark and the straining sounds of the unseen animal in the jungle, yet even then the radio-trained cynic in me questions whether it is a night safari because the animals might in fact be models and therefore there is actually nothing dangerous at all going down here. Deceit in the darkness – it is all a trick!

Nat tells me that I always have to ruin everything.

I get her back in the bat sanctuary, which terrifies her. She taunts me with snake skin. I do not do snakes. We are both astounded that, if you pay the big bucks, you can go on the cocktail carriage of the train and have a meal. I just can't see that this could be safe, and worse, aren't you going to be eating a relative of what you are seeing? Vegetarians, are you still with me?

My good friend David (Harty) Hart and I always joke that we have early signs of Alzheimer's. I now proceed to tell Nat for at least the tenth time how I went to the house of the greatest distance runner in the world. His name is Haile Gebrselassie and he lives in Addis Ababa, Ethiopia. I was there on business for the Great North Run, of which Harty is the Communications Director. In the entrance hall lies a dead leopard or something from the tiger family. I am convinced that Nat is hearing this story for the first time.

The guide tells us that tigers sleep up to twenty hours, so maybe the big cat in Haile's house was just dozing and not dead. The male lion, I learn, is not a hunter. The female does the work. This is my kind of re-incarnation.

Sam wants to know why the otters aren't in wooden tubes like at Chester Zoo. Oh, let the journey of discovery begin, young man.

We are trying to work out why the horn is perceived as so valuable, as Nat, weight-paranoid as ever, asks me if she is as big as the rhino.

Surely the hunted horn must have some medicinal quality if it is so sought-after. I am convinced that it is sexual. I don't know the answer but I do learn that they do grow seventeen inches a year, so perhaps there is something in my theory.

Like many of these places around the world, they walk a fine line between conservation and commercialism. Of course, the selling your soul down the river mentality enables the good work to continue but it jars when I see the Ben and Jerry's ice cream for sale, not to mention the bongo burgers. Vegetarians, are you still with me, again?

I laugh at the well-meaning public attending conservation projects like this only to stuff their faces with meat while they are here. Should not all zoos only serve veggie food? Do we not have a contradiction here?

And then I am trapped too, in a moment of madness, splashing out on some ridiculous blue polar bear Singapore Zoo t-shirt that says it glows in the dark. At the point of purchase, I already know that, after the first wash, it won't glow, but I think I'm just giddy not to be working. I am holding it up like a prize clown, shouting to Nat.

'When did you last see me buy a t-shirt on holiday?'

The answer, of course, is when I wasn't xxx-large.

I think this is the first point, at which I began to lose Molly. Mentally we are drifting, and it is just a couple of days into the trip. Seven weeks lie ahead with embarrassing Dad and we hadn't even got to the confines of the campervan yet. She's thinking just one thing. My Dad looks a dick.

I will stop at paying five dollars for having my picture with a snake though, even if it is for some conservation project. You can throw as much aid-cash at places like this but you still won't be able to help the ugliest, strangest animal that I have ever seen in the world – and to lovers of the South American anteater – I'm afraid that that is you, you ugly bastard. Google it and see, it is very unfortunate.

Back at the Marriott, Sam finds a dead beetle in the room. My children have enormous respect for animals, installed in them by Nanny and Grandad. So we bury him tastefully.... after naming him Ringo. That's just our little joke.

We retire shattered but laughing at the prospect of the Greek entrepreneur Stelios expanding his brand to safaris on the cheap. We await the launch of *Easy Tiger*.

Day Four

Sentosa Island wants to be the new Disney. That much is clear. Kenny is now officially on our holiday with us and is taking us there, telling us on our way across the water that Singapore is the lion city. Thanks Kenny.

He has bought our tickets up front again. We have no idea where we are going, or what is there. Kenny just sorted it. I am wondering if he is fiddling us somewhere along the line, but either way, he has saved a lot of messing about, arguing over what to do and how to get there. It is roasting hot too.

We start today with the bamboo shark at Underwater World; then a stingray, evidently very friendly. I laugh to myself that it was this creature which finished off Steve Irwin when he would regularly be confronting much more dangerous elements of the animal kingdom. I have never seen his shows, nor did I understand the outpouring of grief at what seemed a tame death. In fact, I was on the radio when we got the story at 5.50 one morning. We all thought it was an entertaining way to go, and said so live on the air.

This place is an education however, and I mumble something toned down to the kids at what a load of religious nonsense the story of Adam and Eve is. Here is the truth – the hard facts. Forget all this 2000 B.C. nonsense. We are looking at fossils that are millions of years old.

The first evidence of man, yet zillions of people still fall for this religious thing. Face facts: we're all just passing through.

We ride the travelator around the aquarium. Being the clumsy family that we are, we don't get on in one piece. I have to backtrack there, don't I, because you don't know what a travelator is? I wouldn't have either. It's an escalator that is level. It is a word designed by Americans too fat to walk round the sights on show, or if I am polite, designed to keep those that can't move, moving.

The world's fish are on view. The swordfish through the glass looks like the Status Quo guitar, the rest frankly look miserable, as you might if you became a tourist attraction in a glass-encased surrounding when there was a big wide ocean out there.

It turns out, according to the book of Kenny, that Sentosa is actually a burial island for soldiers. What do you want to be when you're dead? Oh, a theme park? Like I said we are all just passing through.

Sam doesn't like the 4D ride. The 4D ride, I hear you cry? I can remember going to Cinema 2000 at Thorpe Park in the early eighties thinking how amazing and ahead of its time that it was. Nowadays, you actually get wet from the back of your seat and bugs fly out of the screen landing inches in front of your nose, as some Russell Brand-lookalike takes you on a pirate adventure. Let's face it, all pirates look like Brand, but who are these jobbing actors, who get the call from their agent to say that a speaking part has come in, and you're off to a desert island?

'Er, it's not a movie as such.....'

Except ironically you probably will be seen by Hollywood-size audiences if you play in a ten minute feature film at a place like this and at the Disneylands, though your self-esteem may be somewhat lower!

I was just grateful for the cool-off from the effects water. Nat, however, informs me that there is nothing more fun than screaming. And that's a direct quote sweetheart.

We're just different. She's a thrill-seeker and I'm the thinker.

No, I don't mean that at all! Though, I would say this. I am definitely becoming more Nat-like polite, just a few days into this trip, and the trip hasn't really begun until we touchdown in Oz. Clearly, simply removing yourself from all the idiots around work is the first step. God, I've probably missed out on twelve emails about somebody leaving, fifteen asking if anyone has seen my biro, forty-two from Brenda the P.A. demanding that you please clean up in the kitchen, and a whole hundred on 'please do not use the sales printer for the next half hour.' Oddly, none about radio though. That's the business I work in. Lots of people making a fuss, none with their eye on the real ball.

A mother is a full-time job though and Nat is still blaming me for deliberately not washing the kids' hair this morning. This is part of my cunning plan to ensure that I don't have to do it again on holiday. Her words, not mine.

We're off to the dolphins. By coach across the park – with half of India on tour.

They have never seen anything like Sam, patting him on his blonde head and chatting to him. Molly looks on wondering why him not her. They're not as polite as the Singaporeans though, pushing and shoving. Sam loves it, 'shaking hands,' Nat says, 'like Jeremy Kyle has just walked on stage.'

I am learning stuff all the time. So that's why the beds are unmade when I get home from work at 11am. She has been watching my old friend and colleague Jezza, as we know him, with his high-brow television show. The linen shall wait.

When we arrive for the dolphins we finally find a cheap place to eat in Singapore with Nachos at £2.50, coke a pound less – all a firm contrast to the £28 bottle of plonk that we bought last night in the supermarket. Is alcohol frowned upon here, or is it just damn expensive? Possibly both.

These dolphins, by the way, are not just any dolphins. They are not even M and S dolphins. These are the only pink dolphins in the world. Apparently.

Who are we to argue, with this the first of many inevitable and indisputable bold animal facts that will follow in the next two months? The kids want to get in the water with them but some pushy Indian youngsters get picked from the audience instead. Only two or three are allowed in.

The backing track is shocking. They could use my radio production mind here to liven things up. Jaws, the inevitable choice.

The show is cute without being spectacular. The Indians are in awe. We are left with time to kill before the Songs of the Sea, so we hit the souvenir shop. Remember I am a man under pressure here after the Night Jew glow-in-the-dark-fiasco. Ah, how could I possibly resist the 2005 IAAPA Souvenir of the Year, still available to purchase? (No, I don't know what those initials stand for – they could be anything.)

This souvenir is so must-buy that there are literally shelves of them untouched. Doesn't anybody want to buy anymore the orange Sentosa tour bus?!

Then, it is time. The big finale of a long day is here. The Songs of the Sea are in effect an Asian *High School Musical*, but not as good. Interestingly though, rather than a firework finale, we have waterworks, lighting up the night sky.

I am just thinking one thing. There's a drought somewhere in the world, possibly in this country or on this continent, and night after night in the name of entertainment tons of water are sprayed in the air as part of this show. This is bad. My radio brain – you see – is still trained to deconstruct.

After a long wait, the young actors mime but frankly, need better artistic direction, with better songs sung live and not mimed. It is some sort of fable with a cute story whose artistic merit is overshadowed by the water antics in the sky. The kids love it, of course. I am surprised that nobody at home has thought of waterworks over fireworks.

Then it's time to go, and Kenny picks us up at his little place in the know just outside the park. He is pressing us for movements tomorrow. He wants one big last Kenny tour but all I will give him is the flight time. My mind is turning to the big adventure. I can't believe it is nearly here and is actually happening. We started vaguely contemplating this trip in July 2005 whilst lounging in Menorca. We had been through a terrible couple of years treating each other like shit, drinking too much and fighting even more. Nat was reading *I Don't Know How She Does It* by Allison Pearson. I was reading the autobiography of Australian cricket legend Steve Waugh. I was Waugh and she was Pearson. That just summed up where our relationship was three years ago this summer. Tomorrow, the make or break trip would really get underway.

Day Five

Killing time for the plane. We've all been there. You could be having the most wonderful day in the most wonderful city but still that airport hassle and stress always lie ahead, and we were only arriving here just a few days ago, weren't we? Hence we're cool on Kenny today.

And in that moment we realise what a lifesaver he has been because we return to indecision, which leads to confusion, which leads to arguments. If you make a swift decision, then *we're* doing what *you* wanted to do. If *she* makes it, then all I hear is that 'you always leave it up to me.' Bring back Kenny.

We opt for Chinatown and Little India, on our own steam, but only manage the latter. Stepping out of the underground, it is a miserable sight. We stay half an hour and realise that this was a half-day destined only for the incredible Marriott pool. Incredible, in that it is the greatest pool in the world, but totally rubbish too in that there are building cranes and skyscrapers going up all round. There's a cacophony every time you bathe. Besides, we have done a lot already in a few short days and there are Chinatowns everywhere in the world, except presumably China. It's no great loss.

We all know it is time to go. We're dreaming of Jetstar. Don't laugh. It sounds like an Aussie Easyjet, but is taking us to paradise. That's our belief anyway.

I look for signs on days like this, when you are on the verge of something. It seems beautifully appropriate that the pianist in the Marriott reception entrances us with a dreamy version of *Somewhere Over The Rainbow*. Then I realise it's not that at all. It's a song of a similar name. *Somewhere Out There*. Looking for signs is clearly stupid and naive.

You talk yourself into ridiculous scenarios and find yourself saying nonsense like 'Oh I love that song – that has to be a good sign.' Only to discover that you built a belief on an error.

Either way, we are clearly very, very, very happy. Nat is noticing that, where normally my response to what I thought of Singapore would be that it is ok, this time I simply say that it's great. No elaboration, no negativity. It is just simply great.

We are way over budget, of course. Already.

It is true but I write that for the taxman too.

It could have been more as well, as the hotel overcharges me for children's breakfasts when any old fool knows that if you are on a bed and breakfast, the adults go in and stock up for the day and you smuggle grub out for the kids rather than pay full whack for what they will only abandon. They also fleece us for a late check out even though I had agreed it. I make these points and they reprint the bill with courtesy. However, I am sure it is routine hotel policy around the world to overcharge in the belief that in haste or failing memory, you will just sign and be done with it.

Anyway, enough of what *we* pay, how much did all those post-colonial middle-aged Brits fork out *on*, and *for* their thirty years younger Asian brides? The age gap is always huge. I have to question the sincerity.

There are so many of them and these are my farewell thoughts of a city that we knew briefly but warmly, and probably for the right amount of time, as Kenny drives us for the last time out to the airport. To stay any longer would wreck everything.

All roads lead to Darwin.

You do ridiculous things at goodbye. How daft is the concept that four burnt Brits, with a pile of eight bags in front of them, up against the backdrop of the glass front of Singapore's airport accompanied by one bonkers local taxi driver, should accost a stranger in the dark to take a photo? Just so we could remember Kenny.

Artistically, it is a shambles, and I know that the photos in our heads are better than something that will sit in a little photo wallet from Boots never to be seen again, but it is obligatory, isn't it? Kenny made Singapore happen for us. Both at the crack of dawn and late on a Saturday night, he was always there.

There is no doubt that a British taxi-driver may take you from A to B, but he won't go the extra mile, in any other sense than it is the long way round and you are paying more for it. This concept that Kenny was an ambassador for his country is something that you would never get at home, and we shall never forget. He is our first memory. He did go the extra mile and more.

Day Six

My, are we impressed with Singapore airport, once we had said goodbye to Kenny Horne. Well, not quite when we had said goodbye to Kenny.

First things first, nobody seems to know if we get off at Darwin or not. Everybody that we speak to gives us another version of the truth. Yes, we do get off. No we don't. Yes, we do get our bags too. No we stay on the plane. It's just for refuelling. Immigration wants to see you. You stay on the plane.

We check in none-the-wiser. And head for Burger King, in desperation rather than delectation. We're not starving, but we're craving cheaper food post-Singapore. Then the discovery of all discoveries – the rooftop bar!

Yes, really you can watch the planes take off and booze the night away in the very hot open air on the ceiling of the airport. It's a gorgeous spot, though I may say, somewhat fag-littered. Nat, therefore, is in her element.

I watch her through eyes that are over a decade old. She has the same look as when we met in the West Country in 1996. The kind of girl who would stand with a cool fag in the corner of the bar, radiating beauty and knowing that everybody wanted to talk to her, such was her presence. She was fun, cocky, and loved the banter.

I can't think what I saw in her!

And I can see it again tonight. Between these two points, and with so much water under the bridge, the passing years were staring back at me. I literally had worked too hard for too long for too many years, at the expense of everything. Seeing her standing there, with the most exciting view from an airport that I have ever seen, I don't recognise her as the person that I know now. I recognise the person that I fell for, and I think I could well fall again.

It's time to head for the gate, and it's already close on 10pm. We're flying on what I believe is a subsidiary of Qantas. It looks more like Easyjet, but I can tell you that it isn't. It is remarkably better.

Bev is my hostess, from Birmingham. I imagine everyone in Australia is. Not from Birmingham, but from somewhere in the UK. But she's nice, prompting one question: How did our cons make such great people? I feel this theme may return several times in the next few weeks.

Jetstar is excellent, but it is all relative, isn't it? The Aussies probably think that you are slumming it. You can just about afford to get to the promised land, but you travel in cattle class. I find the food, the blankets, the legroom, and the service a master class compared to their UK orange equivalent. Of course, I pinch the free pillows too.

I'm reading John Peel's autobiography flying into Darwin and I have Elbow on the iPod. I thought Peel was the most over-rated broadcaster ever to have made a living and I thought that he made a name playing bloody awful music, but I am moved by his story. It has extra meaning too, as he dies in Peru before the book is finished, and I know that one day, I will have to bring my Dad home from the same place, where he has been living since 1982. I mature over a handful of pages as it dawns on me that it is not the songs that you play on the air, or the nonsense that you talk, but the person that you are within. I would do well to remember. This, I had clearly forgotten over the last decade or so.

I am now so tired that I could cry at anything. We've been up for hours, and it is the middle of the night. Nat and the kids are asleep, but I have some strange determination to see it through, which is unlike me. I used to just drop off at take-off and wake up on landing but for some reason, I am not going to miss a bit, even though there is nothing to see and as far as time is concerned, this is the worst scheduled flight in the airline timetable stopping in Darwin at – what is it? – 4am for a refuel, immigration, and food quarantine check. I am not really sure exactly, but it plays havoc with the kids, who, of course, don't want to get off, channelled into a small room, in one of the most jobsworth ineffectual border patrols that I have ever witnessed. For Darwin airport read one room to the left and one to the right.

It's left to enter Australia, and right to delay the moment. We're in a small walkway off the plane that can't be twenty metres long. This is it then, the beginning of two months of everybody calling me mate.

Sam lies down covered in a black blanket in the holding area. He looks like a nun. I wander over to the quarantine bin, and dismiss it as naive. I'm already in the country, so anything on me now is alive and dangerous, or perhaps not, as the case maybe.

I'm doing that airport thing of pacing up and down without really doing anything. I decide, after all, to bin the apples that I stole from the Marriott. Welcome to quarantine part one.

I can't help thinking that I am at one of the world's most rubbish airports, though that is harsh. It's just basic. I watch the sun come up, against the dry background of the Northern Territories. It's already twenty-eight degrees and there is nothing but dusty orange on dusty orange. I stare out of the window and make a promise to myself to return on another trip, just to let the people of Darwin know that there is life beyond here. Many look like they have never left. In fact the whole stop seems an excuse to give the airport staff something to do, perhaps churn the tills of the economy.

On the approach to Cairns, I remain the only one awake. Nat, Sam and Molly are propped up by the free blow-up pillows that I stole from a previous flight. They don't seem to be mocking me now as they were when I pinched them. I am staying awake even though my eyes are sore. I am not missing this for the world.

Actually I am very excited and I don't do excited. I feel like I am embarking on a new life, a new world, but that is not really even on my radar unlike the many people who have made this journey before either by boat or plane. I just want to be free of work, of phone, of hassle.

Suddenly twenty minutes before touchdown, there's a rising sun and rocky landscape. Think Arizona perhaps.

I now have Elbow's *On A Day Like This* on repeat. On continuous. The line 'It's looking like a beautiful day' seems full of hope, and of the moment. I know instantly that whenever I hear this chorus, I will always see this flashback, and I only discovered this song by chance last week, yet already it seems perfect. If I had been directing the video of this song, there couldn't be a more apt place nor skyline to shoot it than this right now.

Up to that point and just like so many places in the world, the approach to Cairns leaves you asking where the civilisation lies. There's just nothing until these minutes before landing. You realise how damned cramped and ugly living in the UK is.

At touchdown, we're astounded. It had actually been raining. Worse – there's been a flood in the airport and a small part is damaged. I didn't necessarily come for the weather, I came for the experience, but I wasn't expecting this. Still, you can definitely feel the heat in that sweating tropical way, which you could never experience at home. You may have felt this in the Caribbean when you get the most violent fifteen minute downpour followed by bright sunshine and the speed of the recovery and the intensity of the heat that follows literally leave you breathless, as though the sky was burdened and needed to cry it all out.

This, I am guessing, would be what the Aussies call winter!

The queue at immigration is small. You still get nervous and feel guilty every time. Ahead there seems a long system of x-rays and conveyor belts. Either way, this is not an international airport. It seems a five plane a day kind of town.

Suddenly, we have a problem. You would think from the outside that anybody could slip through this border patrol, so sleepy is the airport. That would assume, of course, that you had done the paperwork.

This can rapidly become one of those 'I thought you'd done it – I thought *you'd* checked it – you always leave it to *me*' rows that spring up in public from nowhere. You are supposed to see other people argue like this, and then witness them check into your hotel later as you point in their direction.

'Oh look it's that couple that had the row at the airport.'

Now, it was our turn.

We had three big organising weekends before we left. We broke it down to a weekend per month from February to April to split cost over the credit cards when we were booking all the various bits of the trip. I was in charge of the Visa. Nat was in charge of the visas. Inexplicably, she had decided to move her birthday by a day. And today was the day that we discover this.

Actually this shouldn't matter nowadays with all the data that is held on you. Frankly, we don't look like the Taliban. Yet as we all know, a lie, even in mistake, starts the unravelling of your deceit and before you know it, the British embassy is on their way to prevent an international incident.

My mind is clear at this point. I am going forward whatever, even if Nat is going back. Oddly, they let us all through and tell us to wait on a bench while the head honcho disappears into a discreet room. Is he making phone calls, googling Nat, or emailing MI5? Is it such a big deal when she's already in the country technically?

I genuinely don't know what is going to happen to her – what a long way to come, only to go back again, though presumably this does happen to some people. Often, probably.

All I can think is that we are literally five metres inside the country and it is all going horribly wrong already.

Welcome to the *Hornes Down Under*.

Moments later, all is suddenly fine again with the visa. I know that, if this had been London, the treatment would have been, at best colder, at worst, involving a cell. If you're really unlucky pack your bags, you've won an all-inclusive trip to Guantanamo on the holiday that never ends. No fuss here – they recognise an error and move on. I am impressed.

Well... when I say move on, we only get another five minutes nearer the exit. Welcome to quarantine part two.

I have never seen a border staff so obsessed by food traffic. The sniffer dogs are all over our bags. The head scientist makes it clear to us on at least three occasions that there are severe penalties for transporting fruit and the like into the country. We're talking thousands of Australian dollars. I think he's paranoid.

Our bags go through three machines, and each time we are asked again if we are aware of the penalties. I'm laughing inside but concerned too. I am convinced that Sam has raisins on him. Is he really going to bring Australia down? Is Al-Qaeda no longer a threat? Must we now be on the lookout for a new type of terrorist – the food terrorist, often cunningly disguised in the unlikely profile of a blonde five year old who is knackered and had no proper sleep in the last twenty four hours?

In fact, in an insular kind of way, that seems to be the perceived threat at Cairns. It is a completely different mindset to fearing suicide bombers and hijacked planes. Beware the errant apple.

In the end I confess. We may have had some apples in the blue rucksack as recently as four days ago in Singapore. I keep quiet about the Darwin thing. If I hadn't put them in the bin a few hours ago, would I now face prosecution, fines, jail and exportation? Quite scary, and unnecessary too. Our bag is removed to a lab at the back. I thought this was one of the most popular points of entry into Australia. I appear to be part of a science exhibition.

Are they so proud of their country that this is needed? Is there genuinely a problem with fruit? Or are they just putting down a marker?

We're the last people in the airport when we are given the all-clear. The final few steps into Australia prove to be the toughest journey of them all. We're on our way with a smile and pleasantries. Sincere enough too. I know that in London, I would have heard a parting shot, reminding me to watch it next time.

Through the doors we fly into the great wide open. And there's nothing except anti-climax.

Everybody knows that feeling when they turn through the arrivals door to a million faces of different age and race. Normally, the cabbies greet you, and there is noise everywhere. The street of the outside world bustles and you are one step behind everybody else as you try to focus, laden with luggage, on the relevant sign or person that takes you onward.

We are literally the only people in the airport. There are no announcements as there are no planes for hours and our pickup bus isn't there. Presumably, because we're last out and therefore late. We have no idea if we are minutes or miles from our first destination. Nat has no choice but to call the Cairns Colonial Club.

It's one of those rubbish freefone phones that automatically connects you. It takes three attempts before anyone seems to be speaking the same language. Then in the same moment, the minibus turns up with a little trailer on the back, into which flies our luggage. Very Australian, I sense.

Our driver has a ridiculous tropical green shirt on – proving that wherever you work man has never yet mastered the concept of designing a uniform that would be socially acceptable to wear in public on your leisure time. His shirt does blend in with the tropicality and by the way it's pushing thirty degrees at 9am.

It turns out that we are just a few minutes away. In fact, that is Cairns for you, just a few minutes away from everywhere and nowhere. I would call this opening resort Butlins, but who were we to know when we began that blind process of trying to find a stopover hotel after the long flight, with only the internet to play with all those miles away back at home?

In many ways travel is easier because of the net, but it is worse too, because as soon as you take other people's recommendations as gospel, you can finish up in no man's land. If you take the public's advice from a travel forum, and it goes wrong, do you sue the travel agent, the website or someone masquerading under a funny user name? Imagine...next in court number three, the case of Horne versus Qantas versus Tripadvisor versus......Hairy Love Machine......

In the end we had plumped for the Colonial Club, because it is near the Maui depot, and tomorrow, the Maui would become our mobile home for the next forty days and nights.

Sensibly, they don't let you have the campervan until you have had a night's sleep, and sleep is first on the agenda when we check in, though the receptionist makes a point of telling us that check-in is normally 3pm, which is petty and power-broking of her, as she knew perfectly well that we were coming on an overnight flight and she had the room free anyway. It is just her little moment of self-importance for the day. After all, it is not busy. It is winter for heaven's sake. At thirty degrees.

It is like a jungle finding our room from reception: Butlins-style chalets and enormous leafy greenery surrounding them. Life is changing before us and an early warning arrives that we are now sharing this country with wildlife. A frog greets us as we enter our room. Two crushed snails are at the doorway.

It is basic but all we need is a bed. I do what I always do at home or in hotels. I turn the TV on. I must do this out of nerves or fear of silence since clearly I don't know what is on Australian television. It doesn't matter anyway. We're all so tired that we're flat out by 10am.

On waking, I just want to get pissed. I am alive now and ready to meet Australia. Let's get cracking.

We summon a cab. Colin from Colchester is our driver-cum-chatterbox. I am learning on the go so I dive in with the bog-standard relatives in England question. I promise myself that this will be my *Supersize Me* question, and by that I refer to the movie where the guy had to max his McDonald's order every time if prompted by the drive-thru assistant. I shall at all costs ask the England question when they detect that I am a Pom.

He follows the trend set by Bev on the plane with his potted life story, telling us that he has just been on the phone to his Mum in Adelaide, and that his daughter is moving to Canada. People in Colchester take note – there's a big world out there.

Significantly, I am aware that I am relaxing. I simply don't talk to taxi drivers, yet now I am thinking that it is not a bad gig at all. How much better would my life be if I dropped a few bags from the airport at the Colonial Club and went home for tea? A massive amount, I am already sure.

We wander the front, and yes, we've heard stories that people in Oz barbecue every day but we did not for one moment expect that your public park would just be lined with hundreds of free, well-kept permanent barbecue units.

I am staggered. Then row upon row of children's facilities. I am already convinced that this trip is the best thing that I have ever done and I haven't been here a day yet. These are facilities that a Brit could only dream of before a health and safety council pulled them down in some nanny-state legislative nonsense. Nat goes one step further, in tones of emotion that I have only seen her deliver as an actress on a stage in her professional world.

'I could move here now, my mind is made up.'

This – I was not expecting.

She is still too unadventurous however, to sample a roo burger so our first eat-out is at The Rattle And Hum. It looks ok, and has its own unique selling point with its see-through toilets and vibrating timers that go off in your hand when your meal is ready. The kids already think this is fun; Nat is eyeing it up as a pleasure tool.

In my world, I know Rattle And Hum as an album by U2. It seems that it is this strange timer device (that rattles and hums) that gives this eatery its name. Odd indeed.

'I felt that I would feel too far away from home. I feel more at home than at home,' Nat continues.

We agree in the nicest possible way that Nat's family are holding us back, if we wanted to move, though they wouldn't stop us of course. They love us very much and we them, and this, I am sure, is the first of many, many conversations about whether we could do it to them. Nat is dreaming way ahead of herself.

Despite these releases of British tension and our new-found carefree nature, I still refuse to tip on principal. I don't ever at home, but even in my new good-natured holiday spirit, I have to object to tipping a waiter who took your order but then left you to go to the bar to pick up the food when the rattle and hum rattled and hummed.

After food, it is time for our first Aboriginal experience, as we find a beautiful art shop called Mulliji. Nat assures me that we will be coming back and not to buy anything just yet until we know how big the campervan is. I make her promise that we will return and she agrees, but she is not really listening as she makes the first emotional phone call back to Liverpool pacing up and down talking Scouse at a million miles an hour. I can't even understand her.

I want to buy the whole shop but don't know where to start. I am probably being extremely nervous and getting first-day giddiness. Surely, Nat asserts, there will be other such shops.

Two items catch my eye. Firstly a work from Rowena May

Keating. I won't buy anything by R. Keating, I'm afraid. Not since the Boyzone split.

Secondly, and to my amazement, wooden bowls 'Commissioned By BT.' Is that why my phone bill is so huge? They are putting the money into art.

I am learning on day one proper that Australia makes you smile. I see a restaurant called Bushfire, which I think is brilliant. Even better though is one called Best Bloody Tucker. Is this the famous down-to-earth brash tell-it-like-it-is Australia, about which I have heard so much? Bluntness is something that I attribute to battle-hardy worldly people, and I respect that.

In contrast though, there is something very much thirty years behind about Cairns, and it is to be cherished. On the right hand side of the street is a sign. 'Toad Races Wednesday Night.' Directly opposite is the symbol of this 1978 feel. Woolworths is thriving – and sells the best food. I hadn't been to Woolies for years in the UK but I do associate it with growing up, and more innocent times, and I am delighted to see that 1970s Britain is thriving down under. It reminds me of an era when you could leave the pram outside the shop.

I feel like I am in a fairytale and this flourishing Woolies is the catalyst. Everybody talks about the ex-cons who came here, and my guess is that they were the lowest of the low. Cairns tonight looks like the England that I grew up in, a deconstructed England where the *best* bits remain and the nonsense is discarded. I am delighted, with just one reservation. Will I return here thirty years hence only to discover that the Britain of 2008 arrived in Cairns in 2038? I would rather hang to my original thought, that this is England, but a better England, the original England.

We retire with a glow to the Colonial. The clue to the above may be in that name. We're so tired now, and half-drunk that the kids rob us of all spare change. They have never seen pinball machines like this before, and we are stung to the tune of thirty dollars. Molly astutely observes that Mummy is doing that funny voice thing again that she does when she is drunk. Adrenalin, emotion, booze and fatigue are all in the mix.

It doesn't stop them taking advantage and it doesn't stop Nat doing one last thing before bedtime, sober or otherwise.

We are both in tears as she rings Auntie Celia in Adelaide.

Day Seven

We wake at 9.40. The travel and the booze have all kicked in. My radio discipline of having to eat when it is there, just to get through the show, means that I am the one up and marching off to breakfast. Molly comes too but there is no way that I am paying eleven bucks for each of us, especially when only the shrivelled stuff is left. Cunningly, of course, we smuggle some stuff out. I've stayed in hotels before, you know!

Checking out, we're told that we 'can hop a ride to Maui mate' as the airport pick up is heading that way. I imagine, that in the great metropolis that isn't Cairns, everything is going everywhere anyway.

Maui is the home of *our* home for the next forty nights or so. It's campervan central. Suddenly, it is reality time. Though, it takes forever. This has to be the slowest operation on the planet. We're there two hours, just doing forms, even watching a DVD on how to work the van with all its hidden tricks, as though that will be useful a week from now when I come to change that bog for the first time. They show you this twenty minute movie, but they don't think to leave the Hollywood blockbuster in the van, do they? Who, in their giddy expectation of the great adventure ahead, is actually taking any of it in?

Of course, we laugh at the line about all those people who have driven away with their main power still plugged into the socket on the campsite. That would never happen to us, would it…we'd always tuck it neatly away, wouldn't we? Wouldn't we?

There's so much to take in, but frankly I am more intrigued by my first 'mate' who has just from nowhere started talking to me about the fact that he went for a swim about an hour from here ten years ago, and liked it so much that he bought a hundred acres there and then and has never looked back. He's a mechanic, or a farmer, or something, and his name is, I don't know. Mate, I guess.

While we're waiting, my proper mate Harty texts me the cricket scores from home. Apparently, Colly – that's Paul Collingwood – is in trouble over some run out in the one-day internationals. Good, I am glad. I love Colly to bits but I am led to believe that I offended him in an article that I once wrote suggesting that he shouldn't have been awarded an MBE after his one appearance in The Ashes in 2005. So really, I am not bothered!

The cricket is the only information that I will absorb this summer. Other than that it is a self-imposed news blackout from now until late August. What bliss.

Finally the van is ready. Except, it's not.

There's no awning. And there's a chip in the windscreen. I am about to let the moment pass, when suddenly from nowhere I find a voice.

'Actually mate, I am not happy about the chip and lack of awning, mate.'

Where did that come from? I mean the *mate* comment, not the protest, but as Nat pointed out, we had paid twelve quid a day for the damn thing. And we're all mates after all.

I am not particularly bothered, barely paying attention when I get a demo of how to use the new awning on our replacement van. I just spoke up because I am trying to make it like the old days when I did speak up for my family, like on our honeymoon flight to Antigua, when I proudly used the word wife for the first time, informing the scraggy bird from BA that 'my wife doesn't eat fish, and I will require an alternative meal.'

God we've come a long way since then. None of it good, of course.

This was the re-addressing of the balance trip, ten years on from I do. As I am acutely aware. That's why I was suddenly speaking up on behalf of the awning population.

Finally, free to go in this town where everything is on the way to everything else, we get lost driving back to the Colonial Club, where we have left our luggage. It is a mile away. This is the dream start, obviously.

We hadn't really considered where our eight bags were going to go in the van. We just assumed. Already Nat is dismantling something that she shouldn't be and the kids are saying that the seats sway when they sit down. And we haven't even left yet. Oz row number one – and just six thousand kilometres to go.

We're heading north to Port Douglas.

Now, at this point we insert our rules of campervan travel. There are two: always fill up with fuel when you can and always fill up with food when you can, so we are barely out of Cairns when the lure of Woolies again means that we stock our tiny fridge for the first time. And parking the van for the first time is a disaster too. So, I let Nat do it.

This stop in itself is an education. You have to go to a separate store for booze. This seems positively Victorian to me, or perhaps they are such professional drinkers that only its own store will do.

I put this down as a one-off. It won't be like this all the way, I'm sure. We purchase something cheapo-looking called Stanley Wine. It claims that there are thirty-nine glasses in the carton. We had better get two or three in then. Obviously we buy cartons, because we are in a van that will rock so bottles are out. It in no way reflects any kind of chav status.

Already time is against us. It's three o' clock and we've done nothing. Eventually we are on our way but there are roadworks slowing us down. They are installing electric ants. That's cat's eyes to you and me.

Of course, I shouldn't be concerned about time, but we just have no idea how long things take in this country and we suspect that we have light until six o'clock. We pass Yorkey Knob. No, really we do. And many other staggering, beautiful, deserted beaches too.

Really, this drive is worth it even though it is a totally illogical thing for us to do to drive north before we head south, but then our whole route to get to Adelaide six weeks from now is wrong, isn't it? We should be driving from Adelaide to Cairns, not Cairns to Adelaide. That is what everybody else does. This is typical of the Hornes, of course, and is driven by price. Simply it was cheaper to get into Cairns and out of Adelaide than the other way round.

That said, I won't ever forget this first time that we just pull over about halfway to Port Douglas and stare at the sand. It is so still. I want to stick a flag in it, and claim it. Already we are miles from anywhere, physically and spiritually. Apart from the prospect of pitching up for the night there is no reason to leave. This is dream territory.

My affected Aussie accent is seriously winding Nat up by the time we arrive in Port Douglas itself. In return the all-knowing deity of trucking is reminding me that she forewarned me about the apples and quarantine in Cairns. A weak hand love, but you play it if you want to.

We barely have time to recce Port Douglas before we get a sense that night is falling. I am amused by some of the smaller campervans we see in the town. There's definitely a pecking order, a snobbery of van hire. The students are all in Wickedcampers.com vans decorated with anything Beatles or flower power on the outside. No room to swing a cat, mind.

We barely fit the four of us into a six berth.

Tonight we will rock up at the Big 4 Glengarry campsite. You can't miss it on the road out of Port Douglas. We do.

Nat's spectacular u-turn half a mile past the site brings us into contact for the first time with a big yellow 'Beware Crocodiles Here' sign. We don't quite know what to make of it, so I quiz our delightful hosts on arrival, who dismiss our fear, assuring us that we'll only see him at teatime tomorrow. Yeah, but what's he having for tea, I ask.

I know instantly that Mick Dundee on reception thinks I am some sort of British homosexual, especially when he backs Nat into our pitch and asks me why I am not driving.

He'll never understand that my job is the cooking in this relationship. He doesn't want to know that when I first met Nat in Bristol in 1995, all she had in her fridge were diet coke, mars bars and a pot noodle, and tonight the king of the barbie is back as we dine under the stars to burgers, salad and beer. I suspect too that we may be having this again several times.

Everyone else has gone to bed, and very early too, when Nat announces that she has never seen stars like this. You take it for granted at home that you never see them at all, but finally we are at one with the world.

It's our first night sleeping in the van. I venture to Nat how on earth anyone would attempt to shag in the van. I didn't have to wait long to find out.

Day Eight

We have been on the road a week. That is something that I struggle to believe. First things first this morning, we have to move pitch if we want to stay another night. Embarrassingly that means summoning the owner again to back Nat in. Oh, the Aussies are loving this. I am not having anything to do with this spectacle of comedy so I disappear to the tiny pool in the corner of the site, leaving Nat to take the applause for her parking and to the washing that is already piling up as I'm out of undies. I only brought five pairs with me. Perhaps, on reflection, an oversight.

It's thirty degrees out there but the pool is ice. I get chatting to June who has moved up for the winter. What?

Yes, she lives somewhere southern that I don't remember and every year they drive up this way to avoid the cold. She's English, surprise, surprise, but has been here forever since her Italian husband was told that if he didn't move somewhere hot, his bronchitis would kill him. So, they ended up in Oz, and now that they are here, they move up the coast every winter. These are eye-opening insights so early into the trip. I mean — they just get up in the morning, have breakfast, sit there and stay warm. Before you know it, it is night again and then the process repeats itself. FOR AN ENTIRE WINTER.

Lesson learned. Time is a meaningless device and this trip will teach me to forget it. Though, why they just don't move to the all year-round sunshine of Cairns is beyond me.

We make tracks down the road into Port Douglas for the day. Errands come first though. Nat has to take the morning after pill. I am not particularly bothered but she is adamant about not having any more kids. Curiously the chemist makes her sign a form to say that the sex was consensual. On this occasion, I believe it was, though I will let pass all the times that I was forced into it.

I'm outside chatting to the tourist information office, picking up millions of leaflets for whales and reefs. So much to do, so little time. We need a new travel plug too. Ours doesn't work, nor does the replacement it seems. It simply doesn't fit. It works, but the Maui doesn't like bulky things that stick out, so it doesn't. I can't work the hose either by the way. Welcome to the trip with no power and no water.

After so much messing around, we make it to the beach. It was Auntie Jenny who told us to come here. Normally I don't listen to a word she says but she got this one right. It is so clear and the sand is heaven.

We've bought Sam a cricket set, and set up three perfect sticks that I have found lying around, and make them into a wicket. Yes, you are correct, there is something extremely virile about finding things on the beach and making them into something useful. You just look like one of those cool, unflustered guys who can turn his hand to anything. Next I will be bringing Nat the perfect shell, or the message in the bottle that I threw in the Tyne before I left which has somehow made it to Queensland. No – that's not me at all. I just got lucky with three sticks of the same height.

Nat captures this whole moment on camera: fatty me bowling off two yards, Sam about to pull the ball to mid-wicket (the sea) for four and Molly, already bored, playing with a wedgie at wicket-keeper. It is the shot that neither Molly nor Sam want to see churned out at their eighteenth.

This is what the trip has to be all about. Father and son experiences. I am not sure what is in it for Molly however.

Nat, meanwhile is more concerned with finding the Versace Hotel where the contestants of the TV show *I'm a Celebrity* hang out when they've been kicked out of the jungle, so whilst I am serving up cricket expertise to the all-observant cricket crowd, she is being superficial and reading which stars have stayed there. We have not come all this way to go to Hollywood.

She insists that I google it when we return to the campsite, even though I tell her that this trip is over if she makes me go there. One google leads to another, however, and I already have six hundred emails from home, mostly spam.

Harty mails to tell me that Collingwood has a four match ban and that Laura in his office got married at the weekend. Still Laura, if you're reading, at least he told me the important stuff, hey!

Meanwhile, Molly's best friend Robyn has started a blogspot for the two of them to communicate, which is all very cute but I don't want to be logging on every night and my laptop is really here for internet banking, a bit of Skype and to catch up on five series of *Spooks,* which I have brought with me. This, by the way, is a change to the advertised scheduling as normally we always sit on the balcony of our common European hotel watching one of Michael Palin's series. This time, I am going to relax and for the first time in years, watch a TV show without the need to watch it for work so I can comment on the radio.

Already though it is clear that the less the laptop is on, the more we can slip away into oblivion. If I turn to watch a DVD, modern life tempts you to check your email too. On the plus side, I don't really know what day it is, except that my birthday is looming and I have no idea where we will be spending it. We notionally jot down a few days and dates of where we would like to be by certain days, but most of our sentences end with a place name, followed by 'wherever that is.' Safe to say, we are touring blind.

Burger, salad and beer again for tea by the way and four minutes of rain plus more emigrated Brits at the camp BBQ.

Ronnie Biggs type characters who, at a personal cost of £10,000, moved out here at the age of sixty. They make sure to remind me that you have one life, that it was the best thing that they ever did, and if family were the issue holding me back, then bring whoever wants to come and leave the rest behind.

I relay all this to Nat, struggling to see how she can do this to her parents.

Oh, and breaking news, they tell me, apparently our friend the croc made his daily appearance at teatime on the Mowbray Road today.

Truth or legend? Investigate at your peril. At some point you just know that we are going to have a real life croc experience, but for now, what to do tomorrow?

Port Douglas is a gorgeous little town, with the best beaches that I have seen outside of Antigua. (It is not located just outside of Antigua, you understand.) Yet, I am conscious that we have come north to go south and I suspect that this little gem often misses out on the tourist map for that reason.

I've already picked up too many leaflets and I sense that this van will be full of tours and trips that we will have experienced by the time that we reach Adelaide. There is so much to see. Everybody, and I mean, everybody, is offering reef trips, yet someone tells us that you can take them for miles up the coast. How big is this Reef thing? I thought that it was just a little lagoon off Sydney. Still, coming at these things from a point of total naivety can only lead to surprise and joy, can't it? As we were about to discover as we settle on tomorrow's destination, persevering north. All roads lead to Cooktown.

Day Nine

Or do they?

Our here-today gone-tomorrow camping buddies that you acquire so warmly and instantly, only to never see again, tell us that Cooktown is windy, and we'll be there in three to four hours. I am not sure why we are going. A sense of history perhaps?

I am not one of those people who goes around the world ticking off your Taj Mahals so that you can say that you have been there and done it, but strangely I am drawn to the place where Captain James Cook first landed to repair his boats after coming a cropper on the Reef.

Already, it is clear that Cooktown sets the tone for this country in that brilliantly Aussie way of always doing what it says on the tin. The road is the Captain Cook Highway and the town is Cooktown. It will come as no surprise to you to learn that we have just driven past Four Mile beach on the way out of Port Douglas. I'll leave it to you to work out how long you think that beach is.

I do have a lot of Cook questions oddly. Did Cook ever go back to Cooktown, what kind of job is an explorer, do Cooks exist any more both in his type of adventurer and indeed his family tree, and why are our stupid expectations of such figures all about finding treasure? I resolve to google him later as well. Interesting though, that they named a highway after a seafarer.

We're heading north, past the cane train. I have never seen one of these before. It's a train and carries cane. I hope I've cleared that up.

They run for miles by the side of the road. The process looks slow but fundamental. It looks like the cane train takes priority over the road. Who are we to know? I am not hanging around to get tangled up in one.

We pass through a town called Mossman. I don't like its name and I don't like *it*. It looks like a strange town in the mid-west of America where some cult might take siege. Indeed there are an extraordinary number of religious groups offering sanctuary. I may have it completely wrong, of course. Either way, it is the kind of town that you only ever pass through.

Next a key moment – the key moment. Just after Wanga Beach, we see a sign saying 'Ferry Crossing.'

Shit, is there a river? I prefer to come at these trips with zero research.

Nat screeches to a halt in a rundown truck-stop with no customers but plenty of people pulling in. We either go right to the ferry crossing or straight on. Nat is moaning that she had wanted to buy a map and now we don't know what to do. I wouldn't let her buy a map because we have sat-nav in the van. Have we figured out the sat-nav? Er, no.

In one of those moments where you know instantly that you have gone the wrong way, but you stay silent for four hours for fear of the steam that will come out of her, we head right to Daintree National Park. It's the wrong decision, and I know it. Moments later we are in line for the ferry to heaven knows where when there's a knock on our window.

'Hi mate, I'm Dave.'

And this sixty year-old just starts talking.

He's driving around the whole country in his 4 x 4. He doesn't know where he's going or where he's stopping or how long it will take. He will probably still be going the next time that we come back to Australia and we have only just arrived this time. He looks like he has never seen a watch and lives by the sun. We tell him that we're off to Cooktown.

'A few little creeks, a little bit of water, you'll be alright,' he says, patting the van. And off he goes.

We wait twenty minutes for the ferry, which lasts about thirty seconds, and includes the highly comical man on the tannoy announcing just these words.

'Welcome to the Daintree Ferry, please stay in your seats.'

He must utter this a zillion times per day, and looks like he has been doing it for a zillion days and some more. And that is all he says.

On the other side begins a jungle of tropical greenery. Beautiful, dark, mysterious and threatening all in one. So green but with dew-like juice dripping off every branch. Wet, and low on light but behind lies a burning sky.

We are guests in the rainforest. We twist and turn the narrow roads in our campervan, breaking for lunch at another near-deserted beach. If you wanted to hide, or murder, you would come here. Nobody would know.

The only man that we see hands us coconuts that he has fetched himself. He cuts them with his bare hands on the beach. This is the real deal, isn't it? Sourcing and eating your own coconuts on a deserted beach. He shows us where to get more, but warns that there are 'a few things moving in there, so be careful.'

We have to hit the road. Heading north, but seemingly going nowhere we become worried about time. Cooktown looks an inch away on the map but there are no signs, no indications. It must be just around the corner. We've been snaking our way through high don't-look-down-ledges for hours, all beautiful but inducing fear as you make no progress at all when suddenly, just after beautiful-but-nothing-to-it Cape Tribulation, there it is.

No, not Cooktown, the sign for Cooktown saying 106.

It's a big green sign, a proper, official sign. Not like some of these man-made roadside efforts that only confirm that you are on the road to nowhere. I am heartened though. It is a proper sign on a proper stretch of road. Brilliant – we'll be there in an hour. We're moving. For approximately two minutes.

We take a left, and there are a couple of vans pulled over. One of them is a Wicked campervan, on the opposite side is a Maui. The Wicked guys smile at us. I note to myself just how friendly everyone is, but I also recognise a knowing smile too. Were they smiling, or laughing?

The van is flying all over the place, the kids are scared, and we're probably within an inch of death over the edge if we get it wrong. Suddenly there isn't even a road now. The guy who erected the road sign must have known how many people he was going to piss off, when they turned that corner.

We're heading downhill fast. It's now a brown track and we are steep in the valley when we see the sign that we dread and thought would only greet us if we ventured towards Darwin. Simply it reads, 'Only 4WD Vehicles Past This Point.'

Now I know why Dave walked off patting our van at the ferry crossing, why the wicked students were smiling at us, and why the other Maui was facing the other way. We are in the narrowest boulder-like surface of the jungle. There is no road, or track. There is just a small creek on a turn and barely a trickle of water. We can't pass and will do very well to turn. Inside, I'm panicking. There are two vans ahead horizontally across the road, unsure whether to unload and cross the creek or attempt to turn and head back. Either way looks impossible and impassable. Ahead, no road and no certainty. Behind, back the way that we came if we can get there. Perhaps that's why the Maui was parked up in the other direction, after the exhaustion of u-turning here and revving all the way back to the top. This did not look good and there were already three parties in front of us. The sign saying '106' promised so much. What it didn't say was to not expect to get closer than 105 though.

You wonder how Dave got round. This was the only way, and his vehicle wasn't up too much. Probably local knowledge and a Mick Dundee attitude overcome all obstacles. There was no way a campervan was getting through there. In fact I wasn't sure whether we would get out of there today at all, or ever.

We can't ring Maui for assistance, even though we had bought the 'No Worries' insurance which pretty much gets you out of any creek or roadkill collision. It doesn't get you out of shit creek though if you have ventured off-road, and even though this was a road seconds ago, it is well and truly off now. Plus, we've already rung them about an aerial, loo detergent, sat-nav, TV remotes – all signs of first-time campervanners – and we'll be adding to that the toilet door which now has taken such a battering on this dirt track that it doesn't shut, and is blocking half the rear view. And I mean rear as in out of the back window, not Nat's arse, which I will never be able to lose sight of.

Her Dad would kill me. This is exactly what he feared. I am contemplating abandoning the vehicle. But where, and what do we do then? Yesterday was a gentle trot out to Port Douglas. This is day one of proper exploring and it's a disaster, and Adelaide, don't even mention Adelaide. That's nearly two months and six thousand kilometres away. Auntie Celia, you may have to wait.

Nat is trying to rev us out of trouble. It is an inch by inch manoeuvre, one step forward and two steps back, all the time with smoke coming out of the back. She's trying to turn in the dust, whilst avoiding backing into the orange cliff face behind. Stubborn cow that she is, she's ignoring any instructions that I offer. She's screaming.

'I can't rev any more,' and when I offer to help only shouts, 'get out of my way.'

I was merely supervising, darling.

'I told you we should have got a map,' the fangs are spitting. I offer the helpful 'I didn't like to say anything at the ferry crossing.'

As I explained in the beginning, this was a make or break trip for us. Right now we were broken.

Molly is screaming advice at me, and Sam just agrees.

'Yeah, Dad, you loser der-brain' is about the size of it. Life is full of irony. One day he will read this, on a tea break from his job as an RAC man. But only if he studies really hard of course.

She's trying to rev us up the hill, but you just know that it is going to roll backwards, though of course, it always feels that way.

The carton of wine is flying everywhere on the van floor. The loo door is banging like George Michael with the LAPD. We've probably wrecked the van before we've even got started. We level out after fifteen minutes.

The worst of the hill is over. Just the shocking stone road to deal with now, and a bridge with a twenty-five ton limit on it. We have no idea how heavy the van is. In one of those stupid moments where if it works you ask what all the fuss was about and if it fails you pay for it forever, I tell Nat just to go for it, 'like in the movies.' She tells me to get out to reduce the weight by a ton or two.

I am genuinely frightened, though I feel that Nat may have been hamming it up. When you live with an actress, you learn the signs. Either way, as she stops for a fag, she's storing it up for later. This is now baggage, and I will pay at some point.

I like the fact that we went at today blind, but I'm mad that, on our first real day of doing anything, we wasted the day, and got it so horribly wrong, and it's only 2pm but we know that the day is over. It's only 2pm but it's already 2pm depending on which way you look at it.

I'm watching the light, knowing that we still have to drive all the way back out of the rainforest the same way that we had come, and that we do not have a pitch for the night after I ring to cancel the campsite in Cooktown, having already checked out of Port Douglas. Cooktown is therefore a dream shattered. Daft really, as we didn't need to go. I just swept along on a cultural emotion. It was just a mental thing to make the connection, to tick off a Taj Mahal, and to have some laughs and bond along the way. There were no laughs today.

We can't return to the Glengarry campsite, tail between our legs. They already thought that we were clowns by the fact that Nat was driving. There is only one way to go. It's back to Cairns, which means one thing. We are now officially heading to Adelaide, and we won't be coming back this way – perhaps ever – not that we came this way at all.

As we gloomily greet the Woolies outside Cairns like an old friend that we don't really want to see with the fantastic Kuranda Skyrail looking down imperiously on us from high in the rainforest, I ring ahead to the Coconut Beach Resort, which looks the best Big 4 site in the book. I promise the resort that we'll be there by four.

Delighted, therefore, to turn up at six.

This is supposed to be the best campsite in Australia, fantastic for kids and home to the 'jumping pillows.' I think it has too much of a cheesy Disney touch. It *does* have great facilities, but it backs onto the main road, and has a touch of self-importance about it with its very own mini-petrol station, charging you considerably more than you get on the open roads. It has infinitely more than the Big 4 site in Port Douglas, but it has nowhere near the charm and warmth. Glengarry, from where we have just come, seems to work as a business because it gives you the air that you can come and simply park up in the family's big garden. The Coconut succeeds as a business because it is clearly a polished, clinical business, its reception packed with trips. One thing is certain already. There is no Big 4 standard.

Carolyn buggies us around the site to our plot in a way which is corny American rather than the down-to-earth Oz which we've come to love so far. Disappointment too, so soon into our epic trip, when we have to settle for a cabin for the night, as it is the only plot left. You might consider this welcome relief, but Nat and I are both gutted to have to sleep in proper beds with a television and a living room. Of course, the stupidity of this lies in the fact that the van is parked next to the cabin and we could have slept in it, but we paid for the cabin, so the cabin it is.

The kids only care for the jumping pillow so in my new holiday spirit of kids come first, I watch over them why they bounce skywards and wonder why we don't have these at home. There are so many kids here just playing while parents are off cooking, and you think to yourself just one thought: Madeleine McCann. Then foolishly, like so many before, 'it couldn't happen here.'

Nat is cooking a horrendous pasta concoction – our first break from burgers, salad and beer. I am due to change the toilet for the first time as it has been on the red, when it should be on the green and has been stinking for two days, and remember, the toilet door now doesn't shut either. She's screaming at me that I am using the wrong key but I get it open and somehow manage to glide through the process of dismantling the bog whilst depositing bits of Sam's soggy bog roll from the base of the unit onto the beautifully manicured greenery outside our cabin, proving to Nat that I am the useless piece of shit that she always suspected. In fact I am more useless than the useless piece of shit that I have just removed. I am absolutely hopelessly useless as pieces of shit go. I have so far managed to navigate us from Cairns....to Cairns.

Trying to relieve the tension, I tell Nat that I have a great line for the book and that was that line above. The cheery old tart informs me that I hadn't navigated at all. I had just told her to go north. Right, if she's going to be like that, it's time to tell her that, even though I said otherwise at the time, that pasta was vile. Utterly vile.

She's knocking back the Castlemaine XXXX longnecks and loving it. The kids are playing some rubbish card game that ohholy-Nanny has taught them. It's called Fish or something. I try to talk to Molly about the geography of the day but she's not interested and she *loves* geography. Just like Grandad John warned me about a decade ago, I am the least of her priorities, just the sponsor of them.

We'll start again tomorrow. We have to think about the route. Realistically we have to be in Brisbane in five days time. We're up against it. Townsville is where I want to head next. I've heard so much about it, and plus, it has a stupid name.

Lo and behold, I turn on the telly. Townsville is top story – a train has collided with a truck. They've also released a paedophile in Queensland. He is probably British, I guess. We're quite big on the paedo thing.

As Rolf Harris is collecting some award in Melbourne, I realise that we don't need TV any more, but I choose the moment to flag up a trip to the set of *Neighbours* when we get to Melbourne, and possibly too, *Home and Away*.

It dawns on us, as I utter these words, that people actually *do* run caravan parks in Australia just like in *Home and Away*, and we thought Summer Bay was just a work of fiction. I haven't seen either show for years but I do remember Alf's shop selling absolutely nothing that you would want to buy, yet being the most popular haunt in town.

Alf – it transpires – is based on a reality that I have so far seen in approximately two campsites out of two.

Day Ten

I think I was wasted last night. The usual traits are there. I sent Chris Ryan and Alan Shearer texts, and I rang my Dad in Peru. I had great pleasure in relaying the night time temperature and volume of alcohol consumed to Shearer. He once sent me a picture text of a pint of beer from his villa in Portugal. It's the least that I can do.

As for Chris, the man who single-handedly fled the Iraqi army in 1991, I went for an over-embellished 'stranded in the jungle in North Queensland, when is SAS recruitment this year?' He replied somewhat belatedly 'retrace your steps pal.' All of this I now regret. And that is the stuff that I can remember.

I would imagine half of the campsite is suffering. There was the big State Of The Union game on the large screen last night and all the Aussies went down with beer and blankets to watch Billy Slater be the hero. I've no idea what sport this is by the way!

Meanwhile in overnight breaking news, 'Mako,' Molly's teacher has read out Moll's email that she sent to all her classmates. We have communication from home to confirm this. So what, by the way, if we pull out the kids from school early? The head said that she approved, though couldn't authorise it. This is the Britain that we have left behind. A world where you agree silently but can't be seen to do so.

Today we discover how long it takes to do jobs. This process begins with packing up the van every time – there's half an hour gone already. Next we move out of the cabin to our pitch and unpack the van. Then we pack it up again to go out. Ridiculous.

We don't get far though as Ted and Pam get chatting. Pam is from Cornwall, once upon a long ago, and they have come up for two months from Melbourne for the winter. Just like the guys in Port Douglas. I tell them that's vaguely where we are heading. Yes, they do think it's funny that we are doing this completely the wrong way round and fill us with cheer by warning of the cold there. I laugh it off. Australia clearly has an all-round climate!

He wants to know what is happening in *EastEnders* which is six months behind. I tell him bluntly: Tania is doing Sean Slater.

It reminds me of the ridiculous state of affairs when *Neighbours* was eighteen months behind and we used to go into the prefects' room at school to watch it. Who the hell was Angry Anderson by the way? This is becoming a theme now, which is gathering some momentum, even though I know already that Nat will bin the trip to Ramsay Street when we get to Melbourne.

When we shake our new instant friends off, we're only parking up again a few minutes later just because we are on an alcohol run, and it's only midday. I remind Nat of the rules – always stock up and fill up when you can. But disaster – the guy in the liquor store says that Queensland is trying out new legislation that means that I can't buy wine in a carton before 1230. So I buy it in a bottle. I don't know what they are hoping to achieve. Did he think I would exit empty-handed in frustration at having to buy wine in a bottle?

On our way out, old habits die hard as I find Sea FM on the radio. In the nineties, Australian radio was perceived to be great by many British radio companies. They hired in lots of Aussies to show us the way. I thought it was awful and has never been the same since.

I can tell you that the best thing that I heard today was an ad for ejaculation. Premature, I guess, rather than just the act willy-nilly. I laugh to myself at how my MD would be disgusted if we were having an intelligent conversation about this on our show, but wouldn't think anything of taking the advertising dollar for the same thing. She has form, you see, with chlamydia. Not literally. Well, I don't know actually. I have never asked. I mean in a radio sense where exactly this very same thing happened on our show. We played the advert, but couldn't possibly discuss it, could we? So we did.

This one little incident encapsulates so much of what this trip is about. Leaving all that rubbish behind and flying into a land where they tell it like it is. Already I can see that this is a much better lifestyle.

That said, today we need to pop back to Maui to repair some Cooktown misdemeanours. I am driving and do not feel one ounce safe. We also need a new mop, a new door, and a remote for the DVD. Unless I mishear, the name of the guy running the repairs is called Shoddy. Can't think why.

The kids are delighted that the DVD is now working, though still with no remote. This seems picky, but trust me, the little things are everything in the van. *Charlie and the Chocolate Factory* and *Shrek 3* are first to play. I know what you are thinking. I should have let the kids have first choice!

We have decided that today is sport day. In short, this means Nat is doing the washing. Again.

For me, it is more go-karting, jumping pillows and mini golf. I get really mad if Nat ever comes close to beating me in mini golf. She can't even hold the club correctly. She calls it a stick. Thankfully, two holes in one early on the course take me to a two shot victory. I feel smug for the rest of the day. My particular highlight is when she has a nightmare hole, and hasn't putted on the fifth attempt. I'll stare into the distance shouting five....six...with the monotony of a chiming clock. This is good fun and winds her up for the duration of at least two loads of washing.

I find a sudden attack of deafness when I later hit a seven and she decides that she can count out loud too.

Back in the van, we make our first big call. The trip to the Reef is booked. We leave tomorrow at 6.20.

I do not feel much excitement. The clock is ticking again in my head and I want to get off this campsite and get moving. I feel guilty about the night in the cabin, like we broke a rule, as though we had cheated. Neither do I like this site much. It's too – I don't know – too polished, and doesn't that defy the rule of camping. I want to move on, but already am nostalgic for that first night along The Esplanade in Cairns, which reminds me... I am missing the toad racing tonight.

The picture of seventies Woolies that we saw that night filled me with hope that there is still a quality of life that a petty-rules-Britain has long since abandoned, and the fact that Nat is serving jacket potato for tea reminds me of those beautiful restaurants that we walked past on that first eve and the fact that I have still not eaten a fish, a roo, or an emu.

Her lack of culinary appetite has wrecked many a trip. I give you our regular trips to Nice and the usual snails fiasco as a perfect example.

We also have rung ahead for Townsville and Airlie Beach. They will be our next stops. Worryingly there doesn't seem to be anything after that for a long stretch. Nothing until Rockhampton. This makes me nervous as we still haven't done a long stretch on the road yet.

Nat, however has become a caravan anorak, wandering around the campsite, fag in hand, taking pictures of these fuck-off Winnebagos, saying '...ooh look at this one, it's got bits coming out of the side.'

She concludes that there *is* snobbery amongst caravan-owners. I put my head down for the night and put her straight. It's all about the man compensating for his small manhood. This is small knob syndrome.

Day Eleven

The Great Barrier Reef is overrated. I thought I would deliberately shock in my opening words today, though I am mellowing somewhat now as I reflect...

At hell o'clock, Matt picks us up and tells us that it is going to be a crackerjack of a day. As for all tours it seems, and he is not even the tour by the way, he gives you a tour and so much more. You get his life story. He tells us that it is twenty-three years since he moved here from Sydney and he has seen it go from two traffic lights to twenty-three.

I say he uses that line every day. It's a lovely little landmark stat though. Either way, Cairns remains tiny.

Our relationship with Matt is soon over. He just drops us at the Reef terminal, and we are soon on board Reef Magic, where the intense pressure to sign up for treats begins, as at least four different crew members visit you. I am tempted by the helicopter flight. Deep down, I know that this is a waste of money but I seem to be falling into Taj Mahal syndrome again. I want to tick it off and say that I did it.

To their credit, the journey to the Reef is taken very responsibly. Eric the on-board marine biologist is giving a talk at 11am. I wasn't expecting anything other than the trip to the Reef, least of all a school lesson on the way. Eleven days in and the work traits that I hoped to leave behind suddenly kick in, as I drop off during Eric's presentation. This is the normal time for me to feel sleepy after an early start. Nat, of course, hams up the public humiliation that my snoring has bestowed upon her. She has, naturally, been here many times before. That's the snoring, not the Reef.

I awake to overnight breaking news. Our friend Fiona is on a fortieth birthday party in Ibiza. Another friend Claire hasn't been invited. She has however just received a text from someone in Fiona's pink limo, which might be meant nicely though I would suggest has an element of nose being rubbed in it.

I turn to Nat and sigh. I wish our experience had such depth! What a delight to leave behind such a vacuous culture.

They're obsessive about their headcount on the boat. I think I have been counted eight times. Still, I am sure that every reef organiser has a story to tell about leaving somebody behind. They give name badges to everyone too, and I hate that level of Americanisation, where they shout 'good morning everybody,' followed by 'ok let's try that again, I said good morning everybody.'

Oddly, the slick polished staffing seems to have overlooked the fact that *Jingle Bells* is playing on the speakers, followed brilliantly by *Bridge Over Troubled Water*, and believe me, it is choppy out there today.

I start wondering about why TV-AM did a live show from Australia for the 200th anniversary way back in my childhood. I can see now Anne and Nick sitting there with a backdrop of Sydney Harbour Bridge behind them, and the more that I travel this land, the more I realise that random start-date for the beginnings of Australia is just a load of nonsense. Take, the Aboriginals, for example. Then think again about the two hundred years. Turning a blind eye to what went before.

Yet, as I understand it Captain Cook found land after running aground on this Reef, and so here it began. How bloody big is this thing? After all, we're miles from Cooktown now. The answer is soon served up in the stat of the day – the size of 70 million football stadia.

An early snorkel makes me nervous. I feel claustrophobic. I'm just not a deep-sea diver, even though this is the pre-school of diving. If we're honest, it is not even first week at nursery. We're parked up on a massive platform miles out to sea. How did they even build this platform? The Reef Magic staff keep shouting to keep off the coral. I am not sure why – there seems to be enough of it to go round. What's it worth anyway?

At lunch, which is a mass-produced, quite unappealing buffet, with its star attraction of barbequed chicken with the never-before tried sesame seeds on, Molly and Nat report that they are loving it. That's the trip, not the lunch by the way.

It has been one of the great moments of my life watching the two of them bond in the water, really having fun and with eyes full of wonder, made even more incredible by the fact that Nat, for all her practical skills, cannot swim.

Sam and I have been in the water less as I have decided to fly in the chopper but Damian from Helimagic – always calling me by my name of course even though I have only spoken to him for ten seconds previously – tells me that our pleasure flight will now be 12.30, or 12.45, or 1pm.

It turns out to be 1.40 and lasts five minutes. At the last second, however, to my utter delight, pilot Sam wants a piece of the action and jumps in the front with me, donning the headset and talking gibberish into it. Damian, in a casual attitude to health and safety asks me to sign for him, with my little man having missed the earlier safety drill.

This means that I don't get a repeat of his gag about there being weapons of mass destruction onboard that I have already forgotten and that I know he tells every day of his life. I do feel complete however that Sam is sitting next to me.

We glide across the Reef just up and down once, exposing beautiful marine colours and then it's over. We spot just two turtles. I think it cost £70 each, or dollars, or between us. I can't remember – the credit card is running away with us. Foolishly and uncharacteristically too, I allow Sam and I to pose for a photo, which we will later find ourselves in the embarrassing position of feeling forced to buy. I don't know why I have done this.

Was the heli-trip worth it? Er, no. Am I glad I did it? Yes, in a Taj Mahal kind of way.

Next we board the glass-bottomed boat-cum-submarine to explore the Reef in more depth. I am taking it all in. There are nearly three hundred types of fish out there. Or did she say three million? The pathetic fusiliers are so useless that they swim in a pack of hundreds; there's a butterfly fish to my right with three eyes.

I have never seen that before and I can assume it has evolved that way to somehow protect itself and see, if you like around corners; there's stag coral, which just sounds manly, and the big one, a shark.

I make a mental note to show the kids *Jaws* on our return.

I wonder why and how anyone began the process of cataloguing all this – surely a lifetime's work that someone else would have to continue, thereby making it a thankless task, and you would assume, an unfulfilling one. I am sure that millions of pounds worth of grant are available should you wish to go diving at the government's expense, casually noting the odd thing here and there.

All in all, I spend an hour in the water. That's enough for me. I am the only one in there without a wetsuit. The Aussies probably think I am crazy. I prefer to see myself as manly of stag coral proportions. Molly and Nat, however, are lost in the world of Wally.

Wally is something that has been dressed up in some Disney-like magic since before we even set sail this morning. Supposedly, it is a large, colourful whale that miraculously turns up around the same time that we do every single day and allows you to stroke it underwater while Lianne takes your picture. Funny that.

Or did Wally live on the ship and coincidentally get released into the ocean at the key moment on a daily basis? Either way, the myth of Wally is created.

Now, guess what, Sam and I didn't see this legend of the sea, but Nat and Molly did, and guess what – part two – Lianne got a picture of them which I now have to buy, and guess what – part three – Molly and Sam both want 'I Love Wally' t-shirts, even though the Wally that they saw is blue and the Wally on the t-shirt is green. Clearly there is more than one wally around here.

How on earth, did this Wally come to be, and what of its intellectual property rights, as its image gets bought hundreds of times a day and gets worn in all corners of the globe? Great technique this – create a legend and then flog it to death. I give you Loch Ness, King Arthur, perhaps Jesus Christ himself....

We buy the lot and with the three photos that you choose, you can also get Lianne's all time Reef favourites from her CD, which even though she is a skilled operator, seems a bit cheap to me. I mean, how do you go home and show off somebody else's holiday photos?!

The picture of Nat, Molly and Wally is wonderful but has such vibrant colours about it that it looks super-imposed. I revisit this theme that Wally is a figment of the imagination after all. Nat assures me privately that it is every inch the real deal. Better had be, the amount it has cost me.

We've nodded off again on the way back into Cairns, fatigued to the rhythm of the ocean waves, coupled with the experience as a whole. Only the voice on the tannoy wakes us as we dock, just in time for a final polished performance from the crew.

'Thanks to Captain Simon and first mate Dean...a big round of applause everyone.'

And everyone joins it. I'm astounded. You have paid and paid again for this trip. Why the applause? Do they not make it back to port some days?

Day Twelve

My birthday. What will this day bring? Well, the answer is our new game of what will be the last thing to break in the van? At the moment, removed from your bingo card are the shower door, an aerial, the loo flush, the DVD remote, the water nozzle for the hose and the step which has a chip on it. Did we break these or were they in some questionable state of flimsiness? Bit of both. We'd better get that DVD remote up and running. After all, yesterday's trip to the Reef means that this summer's in-van blockbuster movie will be *Finding Nemo*. Just two plays last night was all it took before the kids dropped off!

We were all shattered so had to forsake the marry-your-own-sister type of country and western do that was lighting up the campsite. Instead I met Bruce at the wash-up. He was on his way to Cape York, so I looked at it on the map. I lost interest though as soon as I saw Bones Knob.

My nickname at school had been Bones, though I am sure that some called me a knob too. In what is becoming evident as a typically Australian thing to do, there is also a place called Lookout. Your guess is as good as mine.

Then there was Guy from Sherborne in Dorset with a beard like a jungle, whose Dad left the UK to join the Australian army, bringing his nine kids over in the process. Quite why you would join the Australian army over your own and quite how your wife would take being left with nine kids while you go off to barracks or war or whatever you do, are questions that I simply do not have time to ask in this world of microwave friendships. You simply have a matter of moments, and no more, to get through an entire life story before the food is ready and the dishes are done and you move on again. And move on, we must.

We have a big drive ahead today. The first real, intentional, big drive. Lots of time, therefore, to contemplate, and already it is becoming clear to us that there is something in Australia that just works. It functions. I can't help but conclude that this has categorically something to do with the ex-con factor, a country built by petty thieves on the run, practical enough to survive on their wits, or perhaps it is the vast space that lies ahead of us today that gives people room to live and move. Either way, it seems like freedom to me.

I may mock the slightly Disney approach of the trip to the Reef yesterday, but I see the Reef Magic's pride in it too. Where else would you have a major international tourist site with a resident biologist on board? Perhaps this culture is also partially defined by a lack of history. Australia, of course a relatively young country in terms of non-Aboriginal people, though antique in terms of the natural world.

On the road today, it seems history mostly extends to towns where there was a mine or cane, and a railway in between. Just one mile out of Cairns and there is nothing. The Reef is keeping everything going. This is the road to Townsville.

I am drawn to Townsville by one thing. The alleged murder.

We don't often talk about Australian news stories on my radio show at home but I do remember this one. The allegation that, of two honeymooners diving at the Reef, only one surfaced alive after the other's breathing equipment was released. A picture on the internet captures the moment, her body on the ocean floor.

I am fascinated by the audacity of the story, and to find out as much as I can. This is the only reason that we are stopping at Townsville.

On the way we begin creek bingo, our second new game in half a day. To report that the highlight of this journey is ticking off the creeks is an accurate reflection of the vastness of this land. Oh, to work in the signs department at the council, and oh, the despair, should you find a creek that has already been given the same name as the one you intended. Your professional credibility destroyed!

At Frenchman Creek, I have to assume that one died there; at Double Barrel Creek I think I have the method. At Lagoon Creek, I am puzzled – is it a lagoon or a creek? Who was the tsar that lent his title to Tsar Creek and what was he doing out this way? Predictably Damper Creek is bone dry.

I am guessing that Mosquito Creek is some sort of warning, or it is a double bluff? Christmas Creek makes me wonder if people abandoned the festivities and found this land on the 25th December and named it thus, and when I see Stuart Creek, my mind is racing and I will not rest until I find Jonathan Creek, Jacobs Creek and of course, Up Shit Creek.

Post Cooktown, I just have this fear now of the road ending, simply expiring and coming to a grinding halt. Today it is banana plantations all the way, and the banter is good. Nat tells me, and I have no idea how she knows, but the bananas are called Lady Finger Bananas. Inevitably I ask if the lady does.

We pass through Mirawinni, home apparently to a world champion tri-athlete (they like to boast), and Murdering Winery! (They like to drink.)

We stop at Innisfall for a McDonald's, where I am amused to discover that they have a special African sauce promotion on. I am fascinated by how some big cheese in New York or somewhere thinks that this is the marketing win-win out here in the middle of nowhere.

It bills itself as a town 'As Green As I've Ever Seen,' ironic really as I am sure that it wouldn't be here at all if it weren't for the railway, which looks beautiful incidentally, even though it seems a one train a day kind of place. It's that sleepy, almost backward.

In McDonald's I view today's headlines in the *Cairns Post*. Should Queensland be a topless state... and the hunt is on for the region's banana-packing champion. It clearly is all happening here.

We drive on to Tully and Nat's driving is making me nervous. Mine makes me worse. We love the fact that Australia has a sense of humour about its road signs, perhaps unintentionally. Get this, can you imagine in England that you would be able to get free coffee for drivers at the roadside, let alone it being called the very catchy 'Free Reviver Driver,' and where we go for 'Take A Break, Tiredness Can Kill,' these guys spell it out with the rather blunt 'Rest Stop Dead Stop.'

We realise that we made a mistake stopping at Innisfall. If you happen to read this and follow our route, drive on to beautiful Cardwell. Trust me. Do not stop at Innisfall. You benefit here from what we found out after, and McDonald's know it too, because just before Cardwell, they have a sign saying the next McDonald's is forty-five minutes away. Desperation from the world's number one brand, recognising that this is a cute little town where the lure of the ubiquitous dish 'reef and beef' would be too authentic and too strong to turn down. Shame we had only just stopped.

We are tearing on towards Townsville with an optimism based on the sole logic that it just looks in bigger writing on the map. Plus, if one of the most extraordinary murders in Australia's history took place here, it must be a fascinating town.

We still fall out over the petty things. Nat takes offence when I say how stupid the Aussies are to drive during the day with their lights on. She thinks it is very sensible. The culture is rubbing off on us though. We salute every other Maui that we see on the road – something that we would never do at home....if indeed there were Mauis to salute.

We hit the metropolis that is Ingham. The writing size on the map is getting bigger, though the towns aren't. Though, it claims to have a twin town, so we must be going up in the world. Or perhaps not. Like all nowhere-villes, it still has signs up for events that took place two months ago! Still, Robinson's circus is in town today and accommodation downtown is just fourteen dollars. You get the picture.

We push on. Tomula Beach looks cute, and I am intrigued by a shop called Rusty Banana.

Sam makes us laugh all the way after reinventing his empty Pringles tube as a microphone so he can sing along to Shrek 3 which is playing again on the DVD. Against the monotony of the road, it is the little things that make you laugh.

Essentially though, stay on the Bruce Highway and you can't go wrong – as our hosts at The Walkabout Palms Roadhouse and Tourist Park put it when we ring ahead to book a spot for the night. The Big 4 book says our hosts are Rayleene, Ray and Max. Yes, I thought that too. Are we attending a swinger's convention?

Predictably stay on the Bruce Highway and you can't go wrong only means one thing. We get lost.

Nat is not interested in my perfectly legitimate protest that, Bruce Highway or not, it says in the book that it is on University Road, which you would think would be near the university and therefore, conspicuous. Sat-nav, or sat-twat as I am about to name it, has never heard of it.

We find it, of course, though not intentionally, with a massive, illegal, swing across the highway to what appears to be a service station. I doubt that this is the last time that I will say to Nat,

'Look, it's just for one night.'

The campsite has quite a lot of gravel; the pitches are low on grass. I don't like it. This is my birthday campsite.

You forget of course, that pitching up at a campsite late in the afternoon, with the sun going by six, you actually only have a couple of hours to do jobs before beer, burger and salad time again.

Consequently we divide the jobs evenly. Nat does the washing, I take the kids swimming. In the Big 4 brochure, it looks a cute little pool. In real life, it is right by the side of the highway. The camera *does* lie.

It claims that this place is four stars. I have always felt that England was the only place in the world where we took the star thing seriously. Everybody else always seems to over-grade by a star. That said, I rate this campsite two stars.

We take pot luck and head into town for my birthday dinner. No beer, burgers and salad tonight as it happens. We walk for an hour or so, sniffing out our guidebook's recommended restaurants, and looking out to Magnetic Island. By night, it seems a one street town. There *are* other streets, but it is youth hostel back-packer territory. One such establishment offers accommodation, breakfast, dinner and a pint for about a fiver. It looks like an old western saloon bar. Probably fantastic if you are in a gap-year; hell if you are in a family.

As it happens, it turns out that all of Townsville have been out on the booze at the races all day long. As a result, we pick the quietest place for dinner. It is called Bistro 1 but it's late and the kids are tired and hungry and whiney. We wait two hours for our food, just like the old days perhaps but no good with kids. It is just a reflection of the way that we live now that I even comment on the time that the food took to arrive. I can't remember the last time that I had real food cooked properly and was made to wait for it.

Of course, predictably our hostess is a Scouser with one of those modern degrees in travel journalism and ambitions to work in New York, earning money here solely to dive, and travel on. I can't stop staring at our waiter. He has an extraordinary limp, as though he had been shot.

I feast on Jamaican prawns and roo. I know that you think

that either sounds the vilest meal in the world, or a seat at the top table in Heaven. Try the latter.

Nat is not happy in the cab back because I am pursuing Bill over the Townsville reef murders. Extradition is on the cards apparently. The alleged is holed up in America and it is taking time.

Just like every taxi driver in the world, he times the whole story to finish just as we pull up back at the campsite, also throwing in bonus anecdotes about his daughter working for the BBC in Cardiff, that Errol Flynn used to live nearby and a restaurant was named after his boat Socorro, plus the fact that Nicole Kidman had been filming her movie just down the road. I suspect already that there is nothing *just* down the road.

I *can* see why you would commit a murder in Townsville. I can't wait to leave. Airlie Beach is our next stop. Bill puts this at between two and five hours away.

Helpful was Bill.

Day Thirteen

Delightfully I awake to some birthday texts. One of my oldest friends James Brokenshire has remembered. James is an MP and tells me that he may be going for Edward Heath's old seat at the next election. Wow – I've actually been to Ted Heath's old house in Salisbury just by the cathedral. I am delighted for him.

My best mate and best man Crossy texts to tell me that Daisy Cross has been born. John and I have known each other since we *were* the media in Swindon in 1995, and the boy has had a colourful life. I am absolutely delighted that his little one shares my birthday. This is a wonderful start to the day. I have yet to meet his current wife however, and perhaps I should hurry the rate he goes through them.

The day gets better as just outside Townsville, we hit the Billabong Sanctuary. Perhaps we did Townsville a disservice by not really seeing it in the day or taking the trip to Magnetic Island. The Billabong, however, just underlines what this trip is all about: a three hour visit, followed by another three hour road trip.

We glimpse scenes in Australian life then we're off again, but what a wonderful, cute, little secret this place is. Financially, I've no idea how it survives. Have you seen the price of gum tree lately?

Vince and Dan take us through the venomous snakes show, though I hadn't considered this as a form of entertainment previously. We're hand-feeding roos even though I had one of their mates for dinner last night, and we're becoming walking encyclopedias on all things wombat. There are just over a hundred of them left in the world apparently. I may have seen some of the last. Koalas are not yet threatened, though are perceived to be. One of these two, and I can't remember which, has a pregnancy that lasts just thirty-five days and pops something just the size of a jellybean. How they deal with premature birth is not worth contemplating. Worryingly, Sam seems to know what Naomi is talking about during this explanation. There is, after all, nothing funnier than a kid having an entire group fall about laughing as he shouts 'yeah they're sexing it,' unless of course, this kid is actually doing that ten years from now when he turns fifteen and happens to be yours.

Nat is furious at the five week pregnancy thing, and this, of course, is my fault for the next hour. My fault, because she had difficult births. Even though I didn't produce Nat, clearly it is my fault that she wasn't born a koala.

Snakes, you will be shocked to hear, are responsible for 1.6 deaths a year in Australia, probably less than vending machines. The point six figure is worth playing with.

I mean, do they actually kill one person but leave another three fifths alive, or is it the case that there were eight deaths in five years and they just did the maths?

Despite this lowly amateurish figure, Vince tells us that every Aussie has a snake story. They all include two elements, namely the phrase 'Oh mate you should have seen it, it was this big,' followed by '...yeah, and it chased me mate.'

They are either all liars or bad story-tellers, or both, and they all want to be Steve Irwin. Though alive, of course.

At every animal there is naturally a photo-op, and I think this is what funds the sanctuary. Molly becomes Veruca Salt, demanding a koala, but settling for a paid-for framed picture. Either way, Nanny and Grandad back home will have to raise their game from Chester Zoo and Martin Mere after this trip.

Do we *actually* have croc shows in the UK?

Before it begins, you wonder if there is any genuine danger. I think, in fact, that they are stage-managed and choreographed to perfection, though I am curious to know what goes wrong in the first few days when the croc-handler is just building a relationship and a show with the croc. Surely, it takes years to perfect it, and therefore, there must have been some close scares along the way.

Dan knows exactly what he is doing, but it could have been so different. He used to be a beach volleyball umpire. One career naturally moves logically into the other, I suppose. A quite obvious progression.

He teases the crocs magnificently with the food, but here's the skilled bit. He teases *you* too, timing everything to perfection with the food suspended in the air so that, on the third attempt, you get that million dollar photo of the croc snapping his dinner, enabling a generation of bullshitters to return home with award-winning photography of their *Crocodile Dundee* moment.

You just got lucky third time around. Dan is skilled and knew you would!

The turtle racing doesn't have the same lure about it. Primitive, by comparison. I argue with myself over the question of manipulation here. These turtles don't really want to race ten metres into the water, do they? Then again, there is tea for them at the end of it.

A note here, if I may, for the taxman. I hope that you are enjoying the book so far. You can see that we really are doing lots of things in lots of places, and that there genuinely is a book. However, I am unable to offer you a receipt for the twenty cents worth of birdseed that I purchased so that my kids could have the pleasure of feeding the Lord's creatures. I fully understand that you may now wish to investigate me, in which case, of course, I will have to fly back out in business class, on a business trip to the Billabong Sanctuary to obtain this important documentation. Hey, I may even take Nat and the kids, and do another book, perhaps this time down the middle or up the coast of Western

Australia. You let me know what you want to do. I'll keep the diary clear.

The road ahead is bleak. We head through Ayr, and there is a general Scottishness about some of the place names to come, though nothing of kilt ilk in the landscape. Instead it boasts that it is the birthplace of the one and only....Karrie Webb. No, I have never heard of her either. Apparently she is the best female golfer in Australia.

Then we pass a sign for Ashworth's world famous display. Of what I am unclear. But it's world famous anyway so you already know, I guess.

It seems an awfully long way from the tartan land as we sniff out Strathalbyn, Strathbogie, and Strathmore inland, and strangely Scottville. I am most amused though by a town called Claire, and instantly think of my neighbour Stonesy, or more significantly his wife of the same name, who at our farewell dinner already some fifteen days ago proceeded to remove her bra in front of everybody during Sunday lunch. Just for fun, of course.

It is odd how you can just be driving along and these random chuckles enter your thought process, and I am keen to stress that this little incident with the bra has happened to me once in my life, even though I report it to you as perfectly normal.

Similarly, but without the same derobery, I remember an old friend of mine from Inverness as we eye Mclean in the distance. So to my friend Gary of that surname, there... I haven't forgotten you, nor the day I decided on the spur of the moment to drive from Durham to Inverness, not realising just how far it was.

I think the significance of Gary here though is that my mind has been emptied of rubbish. I have the clarity and the space to recall dormant images of the past. I am awake and alive, and frankly, haven't been in years. I am ashamed to say that I had immense fun with Gary when we worked together in Wiltshire, and I haven't thought of him for a decade – until now.

At Home Hill we see consecutive roadkill. Our first. It is a massive bull. Must have been a hell of a hit. We thought we would have seen more by now, to be honest.

Ahead, a sign saying that Brandon Bridge is closed tonight and the road is subject to flooding. What do we do, if we find ourselves in these situations? Cooktown still haunts me. The certainty that we will one day come to a road from which there is no return is a constant already in my mind. Everybody always tells you as well that you shouldn't travel at night in Australia. A few hours later and we would have been stranded.

Next stop is Bowen, home of the Battle of Coral Sea. Such a title just doesn't sound butch enough to have been a real battle. In fact it sounds like it involved sea creatures and not men. A couple of divers or fishermen at best. It sounds like a cartoon, like a sequel to *Finding Nemo*. The reality is somewhat different, I learn. A four-day battle in 1942 with many men based here. Bowen, it seems, is also Queensland's oldest town.

There's really nothing to it, and far more entertaining is the Big Mango Tourist Spot, just down the road. There's no reason for it, and there's nothing to do there either, but if something in this book inspires you to replicate our trip, you too will fall off your car seat laughing as you pass the giant mango by the side of the road. You can't argue that it isn't a tourist spot. After all, who hasn't pulled up here and driven off in total amazement at the fact that they did actually stop? I know too that many a photo has been taken here, because it is just one of those things that make no sense at all when you get home. Who hasn't come to a grinding halt in a holiday photos slide show with the words, 'Oh, I don't know why I took that,' followed by an attempt to explain what it is, before hastily moving on with a quick 'you had to be there,' and of course, anybody who ends an anecdote or gag with those words has always failed in their delivery. Well, anyway, The Giant Mango...you had to be there.

We're tearing on to Airlie Beach. Nat is raging about something, saying that she'll be too tired to write up her version of events tonight. We have both set out to write the same story from each of our viewpoints. I offer to replace her and promise to slag myself off in appropriate amounts. She protests that I won't do it as much as her. This, I must read.

Embarrassingly, she still insists on calling every campsite a website. I laugh every time at how thick she sounds. There, my revenge.

We're in for two nights, allocated the pitch next to the wash block. If I had to summarise our different outlooks to life, then this is it. I think this is perfect, she thinks it is disgusting. I know that this particular explosion will pass in five minutes like the rest of them, and it does only for it to be replaced by some rant about a French woman hogging the washing machines at the laundry.

Life on the road is not glamorous. Practical things still need to be done. I leave her to earn her fare and do what I am best at. I invite some Dutch people for a game of cricket.

The campsite, by the way is a good one. If you like, it is a toned down version of the Coconut in Cairns, perhaps a little less showbizzy, and a bit more sincere. For most, it is the gateway to the Whitsunday Islands. We don't book however – that trip costs too much and leaves too early, and we've had a long, fulfilling day.

Then, suddenly, it finally happened and I had been wondering when it would. I meet a guy from Newcastle.

Newcastle, New South Wales of course. Had he been to the Newcastle on the Tyne? Yes, he had – on the way back from a mate's wedding in Airdrie. Intriguing.

I ask him if he knows the Angel of The North. We both laugh, in agreement, at the vile way that it looks like a rusted crashed aircraft. I ask him what he thinks of the outrageous claim from the development agency One North East that it has brought in £600 million to the northeast of England. He is not having any of that and rightly so, in my opinion. That obviously is a little piece of my work still seeping into this trip. Forgive me, I have a particular hatred for the afore-mentioned agency and monument.

That aside, I am beginning to master this nightly concept of getting to know everything about everybody at the cook area in five minutes flat, only to never see them again. It seems a fruitless exercise really, and it is unusual for me on holiday to get involved in any kind of conversation with anybody, but I am seeing myself changing in front of my very eyes, and I impose upon myself that I must keep this up when I return to the UK. Unlikely, I fear.

Similarly, I didn't really give much thought to this Irish chap who was cooking up next to me.

Day Fourteen

Sam's koala, which he bought at the Billabong sanctuary, is in pieces. Still we keep falling for this after all these years. I can't tell you the amount of *Tweenies* concerts at which we have bought nonsense that glows in the dark, only to find that five minutes after leaving the arena it glows no more. There are tears, of course.

The knock-on effect of this is that I have to replace the koala, probably twice, once to replace and twice to compensate. Something in the short-term to quell those tears, and something in the long-term-like another koala – to replace the afore-mentioned damaged goods.

So, now the kids are on an hour's karting, merrily driving round the campsite in buggies. Meanwhile at reception, I am being sold the merits of Dingo Beach. I'm wondering if this is where the famous dingo kidnap story took place and then come to my senses, realising that I am probably a few thousand kilometres off the scent.

Dingo Beach is about forty-five minutes away, the receptionist assures me. That's an hour and a half in my book. We decline.

Airlie Beach, though, is something else. We are back on track after a couple of grim days on the road. This is the Australia that we dreamt of. Summer Bay really does exist.

For the first time, we actually stop and look at houses, eyeing up a very affordable three-bedroom pad with an expansive entertainment area outside (naturally), with beautiful views across the bay. Six hundred thousand Australian dollars. There is absolutely nothing stopping me from buying it. I vow sternly that this book will be the bestseller to pay for it! No more miserable Aprils at Chester-le-street or Old Trafford, hoping for a peak of just acceptable weather and the cricket to start. It is not even a difficult decision. Simply, the life here is so much better.

In dreamland we go back three or four times past the estate agent Ray White's window, much to the annoyance of the kids. It is a beautiful little town with cute shops, not tacky ones, and a curved little beach with a couple of public swimming pools to the side. I can't help but think what a brilliant and novel idea the open air public swimming pool is. Then like Woolworths before, I remember that I used to go to one in Surbiton or Richmond in Surrey, near to where I grew up. It was a big day out in the summer, and Airlie Beach seems to me like the Bognors and Littlehamptons that we used to take the train to. This really is Britain in 1978. It is the only chance that I can get in life of seeing my childhood come alive in my present. I see glimpses of the future too. What price Molly and Sam boarding the *Greyhound* bus in the terminus, ten or fifteen years from now, and Nat and I sitting at home worried sick about where they are today? I shake my head at the two dozen or so student types waiting for the bus heading for Cairns. I would look a very old man on that bus right now, even at thirty-seven. This is backpacker country. Those days are gone too.

I wonder if this trip is passing the kids by, especially Sam. I think there was definitely a small element of a cry for attention when, totally out of character, he serves *himself* a slush puppy in an ice cream specialist called Cold Rock. Disgraceful behaviour, but highly entertaining too. Obliged to buy in embarrassment, I fork out twenty dollars worth of the most complicated make-your-own ice cream that I have ever seen, involving whole Crunchie bars and fizzy worms smashed up in a bed of toffee.

Molly is now in a mood, after learning that she has missed the hair-braiding at the Kermit Club back at the campsite while we have been looking at property that, let's be honest, we're not actually going to buy, are we? It is standard fare on a Horne holiday that hair-braiding will happen at some point, you see.

Nat is moaning that this is the hardest that she has ever worked in her life, so I offer to drive the mile or so back to the campsite. I wind her up even more as I reflect on that illustrious three-year career of hers before I casually impregnated her. Yeah, she is working hard alright. As hard as I say!

Back at base, I spot the Irish fellow that I had begun chatting to last night, as *Neighbours* airs in the background. It is going out at half six in the evening, which impresses me. We never quite had the courage to do anything with it in the UK other than hide it at half five or lunchtime, but we cannot let this moment pass without acknowledging the effect that this rather dodgy show has had on so many people in the UK. If the Ten Pound Poms ticket was the inspiration for the first generation of immigrants from the UK, Kylie and Jason were definitely responsible for the second. That whole Helen Daniels brings a casserole through your open backdoor thing, Lassiters and the coffee shop, the entirely new language of wagging school and rack off Bouncer, plus Mrs Mangel, and the ridiculous death of Kerry in a duck-shoot, the theme music with the cricket scene in Ramsay Street and Henry's car.....where do I stop? It was just a little piece of fantasyland, but now we are on its doorstep. I remind myself just how cross I will be if I do not get to Ramsay Street when we arrive in Melbourne.

I am surprised to see 'yer man' however, as they were going to leave for Rockhampton at seven this morning. That is all that I recall from speaking to him last night. It turns out that they didn't go and they are now in the next berth to us on the campsite. Still, it is an easy thing to do, decide to stay another day, and maybe another after that and before you know it, you are faced with miles to travel in a day to meet your end goal. Even on holiday in a land as big as this, you have to get some sort of routine and discipline to master it. As with many of these campsite relationships, I still don't know his name. We too are heading for Rockhampton in the morning. It's nearly five hundred kilometres away and there is nothing in between. We promise the kids that this will be the last big journey. This, of course, is a lie.

Day Fifteen

Nat has been having ridiculous nightmares all night long in the van. It has been this way every night since Cooktown.

I love the way that I say since Cooktown, the place that we have never been to, but has already assumed legendary status in that way that we all embellish our holiday stories.

She just lies there in the night, shouting 'help me, I'm falling, help me, I'm falling.' I wish I had filmed it.

I am sure that it is as much to do with the sleeping in the van thing as it is Cooktown. There I go again – Cooktown. We have never actually done anything like this.

I lived and worked in a tent for one summer as a campsite courier for Canvas Holidays but that was nineteen years ago. We as a family are used to alarm calls for my job and rowdy bin men waking us up at the crack of dawn, *not* natural daylight and whichever Australian animal happens to be chirping away in the forest. I can only assume that she is sleeping so badly because she is sleeping so well.

Now, you see that when I put things as simply as that, you know once again, why moving out here is not a difficult call. Ah yes, I hear you cry, but it's different when you actually live and work there. Need it be, though?

Embedded in my thought process is that we work so hard in an expensive, miserable country, so that our house becomes a priority. When outdoor lifestyle is the way to go, these issues and the desire to earn the maximum amount of money to provide the most amount of 'house' are less important. The world can be your garden. You need less money here. You therefore, carry less stress. Career is secondary. Life is first. When did that stop being so? Years ago.

But, I wouldn't want to live anywhere on this route today. This is the big journey, and the weather is awful. Our first really bad weather day.

Sam lightens the load by announcing that if Mummy and Daddy don't have any more kids, he and Evie will. Evie is five. It is the first time that he has really mentioned school. Though, of course he has had many lovers.

We've made the right call driving in the downpour, and we laugh at the Irish who we've left behind at seven this morning. They must have heard us go and they picked the wrong day to stay. This is a day to kill and I am prepared for a dead man's journey. Take Kuttabull, for example – a Shell garage and a butcher. That's it. Nothing else. And more roadkill than ever. We fly through.

The radio is no company either. Apparently, in Townsville they are looking for some truckie who has run down an eighteen year old in a hit and run. That's all we manage to pick up. I'm telling you that Townsville is cursed.

We push on through Mackay. It's a pain in the arse to get through, and deludes itself that it is playing on a world stage offering a Shakespeare Street, a Romeo and Juliet restaurant and, wow, an international motel. I'm overlooking something here, aren't I? At a guess Mackay was a thespian who tried to bring culture to Australia, and named the town after himself and all the streets after his first love. They built an international motel, waiting for tourists to flock. And they never came. Like I said, it is just a guess.

At Carmila we pass the greyhound bus, destination Cairns. I was right. It didn't look like the way to travel. We wish it well with a wave, but it is a mocking wave. They have a lot of the Bruce Highway to go. But so do we, in the other direction.

I'll tell you something here. You can find out where your relationship stands on a day and a drive like today. Nothing but open road ahead, there's a lot of silence to fill. We start speculating about Peter Falconio, the British backpacker who was murdered in 2001. My guess is that this comes up every time a British family undertakes this kind of trip. It has to be the emptiness of the road that prompts the conversation. I remember the case well, but I don't remember how it was resolved. I had heard of the outback and Alice Springs of course, but knew no more. I couldn't really name the girl in question, let alone the name of the murderer. I just remember that it shocked, and that there was something dodgy about the whole thing. I resolve to add this to my list of googles when we stop for the night, well aware that we could easily find ourselves in Falconio territory if we misjudge the light or the distance, emphasised by the incredible road sign that we see 'Ambulance Back 37km.' What are you supposed to do, if you have a near fatal ? Hobble back?

Nat flips when I suggest that we rock up at Yeppoon for the night, instead of Rockhampton. It looks just a tiny bit out of the way and right on the beach. It sounds perfect, but the red line on the map to get us there is worryingly thin, about as thin as the one to Cooktown. As it happens, we stop at neither. Rockhampton reminds me of Swindon in Wiltshire. An entirely functional place in the middle of nowhere, populated by relocated misfits. I will only remember this place for an appalling bag of chips and a nice waterfall on the way out of town. That's it. Oh, and I lived in Swindon once.

We'd come all this way, filling an enormous void on the map, relieved to have swallowed up that vastness of nothing, and really for nothing of note. Such is the nature of Australia though, that if we want to drive to Adelaide via Brisbane, Sydney, and Melbourne, you have to endure the odd Rockhampton on the way.

Rockhampton really should take note, fabricate some history or something, or build something amazing like *two* giant mangoes by the side of the road. It is such an obvious stop-off point for travellers (in that it is the only stop-off) that it could make a bit of an effort. Put some toad-racing on or something.

We're six hundred plus kilometres north west of Brisbane and Nat is moaning all the way, now convinced that the campervan is lopsided after we naughtily dumped the waste water by the side of the road, taking massive wind dents from passing lorries. She's hating me, having driven the whole day. If the campervan isn't lopsided, then she is convinced that they guess the road distances and just make them up. This is the kind of crackpot theory which frequents her mind from time to time, and whatever I say will be the wrong thing. There is also a rather gloomy sense that the best of the weather is gone, never to return. This is our worst day so far, by about five hundred kilometres.

We're now pursuing Gladstone – the pictures in the Big 4 book look fine, but the campsites are already starting to merge into one. We've broken the back of the coast in terms of miles covered, and some days you just have to tick off the miles. In reality, as long as the campsite is clean when we get there, we'll be heading off again in the morning anyway, but it takes forever to find, not because the route is complicated, but just because road travel takes time down under, and then with the fatigue of the drive, we start arguing about the fact that we've obviously missed the site, having come off the main road and now we're stuck with nowhere to stay, when guess what happens, we stumble across it after all.

It's sleepy. There's nothing doing. It's quaint, it's for old people. There's not even a rush for the laundry.

I feel like we have been travelling for ages, and I don't just mean today when we have absolutely caned it, but generally since Cairns, and we still have miles to go. In reality we've gone centimetres!

Consequently I'm now pitching myself at check-in as something of a Big 4 expert, offering the lady on reception tips and comparative prices on other Big 4 sites. You see, these campsites all join this Big 4 thing but there's no brand value in terms of uniformity, so they can't ever tell you about the next site. The brand, per se, is a supposed reasonable standard of site and a ten per cent discount for being a member, but that is as far as it seems to go, which is not helpful if you are moving from site to site, as presumably is their expectation.

We're off season now though, so there's no need to book, and it has been a damp, miserable day. We can have any pitch that we want, it's that quiet. We've been driving so long with no obvious visibility out the back of the van that I make a pathetic attempt to hose it down, but your seasoned Aussie camper Bill, who is just driving aimlessly around his country without going anywhere specific, seems to have everything that you could ever need in his van and produces a much better spray hose, and we have the van looking spick and span in no time, though of course, Nat moans that I shouldn't have bothered and I have left a wavy pattern on the back of the van. I think what she meant to say was thanks.

She practically disowns me when I tell her that I am putting my trainers in the washing machine, even though she has been bemoaning their stench for the last few days.

I take my laptop over to see if I can get on my email. I can indeed but already there are far too many – around two thousand and all spam – that my mobile broadband package can't cope. It gets to about six hundred emails at a fair old speed, then it's a snail's pace and I realise that I am doomed now in that my email account will have ten thousand or so on my return, and that I will never be able to keep on top of it whilst we are here. Of course, in five years time, I'll laugh that this was even a problem. How did things get like this though that email abroad was an even an issue? I cancel the whole download, having been at it for half an hour or so, choosing instead to google Falconio.

For the first time now, I can picture the scenario, though large parts of it still do not add up. I'm fascinated by the small detail, like a principle piece of evidence against the alleged murderer Bradley James Murdoch being DNA evidence from a Red Rooster restaurant, followed by his subsequent claim to be allergic to chicken; or the fact that Joanne Lees admitted to sleeping with a Nick Reilly character in Sydney during their travels. What became of his life, and what bad luck to be an incidental detail in one of Australia's biggest murder cases? If indeed Falconio is dead.

Naturally, he was supposedly spotted at a service station a week after his disappearance, and court evidence reportedly heard how he had rung home the day before his death and asked about faking his own death over a tax payment. There is so much to absorb - from their stupidity in travelling by night to the huge problem of solving a murder in this vast country, something that was only resolved with a large amount of luck.

I feel drawn to Barrow Creek, Alice Springs, the Red Rooster, even Joanne Lees' hometown in Yorkshire. Something is telling me that, even though this is all old news, it is not going to leave my system.

Or perhaps there is just nothing to do at Gladstone. I can't imagine what Bill does all day, except potter. We follow our noses down to the water to learn that we have crocodiles for company. There's a phone number to ring on the sign, but I just don't feel threatened by this anymore. Oh, it's another crocodile sign. Big deal. Perhaps this is the complacency that turns you into their dinner.

Suddenly, something mysterious and magical happens. We're so sodden and damp, and then from nowhere, the sky lights up in a magnificent orange, an unthinkable fusion of colours, that you would never see at home. After the dullness and dampness of today, it is a perfect tonic. Our spirits perk up and we rush for a camera, instinct telling us that we have five minutes to capture the shot. We're also well aware that it probably means that tomorrow will be a crackerjack of a day.

Day Sixteen

The weather has cleared and we're up and out in good time, cruising once again on the A1, this time to Hervey Bay. It has a bay in its name and there are definitely two Big 4 campsites there. At approximately five hundred and fifty kilometres north of Brisbane, it sounds perfect.

Everybody knows that Aussies tell it like it is; we've seen already so many examples of place names doing exactly what they say on the tin. If the beach is four miles long, they will call it Four mile Beach; if Captain Cook landed there it is called Cooktown. Examples are numerous from Rattlesnake Point to Policeman's Point, from Townsville to Ocean Beach.

So, what on earth are we to expect when we arrive at Gin Gin? I can find no confirmation that its origin lies in the booze simply that it survives as a town or perhaps a city by Australian standards, because it lies approximately halfway between Rockhampton and Brisbane. Such can life on the road be. This is bum country.

There is no reason whatsoever to stop. So, we do.

You couldn't spend an hour if you tried, but there is something rather naughty about the sign on entering Gin Gin, which proclaims it to be Queensland's friendliest town of 2003. You have to stop after that, don't you?

Presumably, it won because there are so few people to meet,

so the friendly percentages must be high, or maybe every town has a sign like this. It doesn't actually say who has awarded this honour and what the criteria were for winning. Did some bigwigs from Brisbane come and make meticulous notes for days on end, and did they therefore perform this task at all of its rivals? No, I suspect that they did exactly as we did. Stop at the Mobil garage for a Mrs Mac pie.

I tell you – these have looked so appetising on so many stops up to now and we have yet to try them, but they put the British trucker pies and Ginster pasties to shame as the temptation is too great and too tasty with lunch coming in at under a tenner.

I smell a conspiracy and by the way, they weren't over-friendly either. Presumably their warmth has been in decline for half a decade. They haven't won it since after all. Perhaps it went to their heads or they just couldn't live up to the pressure after 2003. Or maybe they just made it up.

Which awards await ahead at Wallaville, Childers, and Howard, all onwards in our path?

The answer is none.

Childers, for example, is cute and has a peanut van. That's it.

It is at Goodnight Scrub, however, that Nat loses it for the first time today. Yes, there really is a place called that.

The sat-nav, a new introduction to our daily routine in the van after taking a fortnight to get it working, is telling us at the same time to do both a u-turn and go straight on. It has Tourettes.

Most driving in Australia is about straight-on all the way so Nat's over-reaction couldn't have been more comic when she decides that the real reason is the posh English accent delivering these clear instructions. We pull over while she seeks a rough Aussie bitch to argue with. This at least cheers her up and saves me having to talk to her. Molly, as ever, sides with Mummy on all these rows in the van. I am officially an embarrassing Dad. Again.

But the sat-nav increasingly is a hindrance. When you are typing a campsite address, the location often covers four or five or more house numbers. After all, you couldn't fit a campsite on one house number, if you think about it. It doesn't like this one bit. Sometimes, the campsite is not technically a street, so beware your approach to Hervey Bay.

We have our usual routine now, namely to spot a Woolworths for a fill-up; next is the row that it takes to do the last five minutes of the route, normally accompanied by shouts of 'you said it was left,' and 'there's no point telling me after I've gone past it,' followed by 'I'm ignoring the sat-nav and going the way I think is right' (even though I have never been here in my life) finally accompanied by 'looks ok, oh now I'm not sure, well here we are anyway.'

The Point Vernon Holiday Park is a classic example of 'looks ok, oh now I'm not sure, well here we are anyway.'

Nat isn't speaking to me by the time we check in, so we're unsure, and embarrassingly can't agree publicly how many nights to stay. The problem has been that you follow the road beyond the road, taking a beautiful little circle down by the water's edge on your approach but then realising that the sat-nav is not helping you with its 'you are at your destination' when you are clearly not, so you go back on yourself to end up in just a normal street and you're thinking that there can't possibly be a campsite here, but there is and it's very tight. You wouldn't know it from an angle as there *are* houses either side.

Lisa, to whom I had spoken earlier, checks us in. She sounded so much fun on the phone. They all do. Nat says 'two nights' in a strop, but then is unable to park at our first pitch and we can't reach the water point at our second. It doesn't feel right. It feels like another Townsville. Again too much gravel and the grass is bare. We literally stop for twenty minutes before packing up and heading for Woolies but mistakenly leave our tables and chairs outside.

In getting lost on retracing our steps, we accidentally discover The Esplanade, and thank goodness that we do because this is where our trip changes forever. My heart is racing and my mind consumed with one thought – that there are two Big 4 sites in Hervey Bay and we just booked into the wrong one.

I'm on a mission to find Fraser Street, and can't resist wandering up to the reception where I spy a gem of a campsite and gorgeous lakeside pitches. Spontaneously, I tell Nat that we are checking in, and we're blowing the money at the other site, just about two miles away. Nat is scared that I will flip over the money but life is so cheap here, and it's only twenty quid or so, so we race back to the other Hervey Bay site and cancel our second night. This is unlike me.

Normally, if you're not happy within the first hour, then under Big 4 rules you can get your money back, so guess who turns up and hour and five after we've checked in and guess who finds that receptionist Lisa is not so chirpy after all? That will be the Hornes then.

There is always something embarrassing about reverse parking the van at these sites as all the blokes stand round in their vests swigging beer as the reverse noise goes off on the van, but worse than that is the rushed departure when you clearly have only just arrived, leaving everyone else on the campsite thinking 'well, we thought it was ok here.' Your departure says one thing. You are a snob and this site is beneath me.

Frankly, the owners at Pont Vernon must know in their heart of hearts that people only come to their site if they can't get in at the Fraser Lodge, an altogether better-equipped, more spacious site and genuinely a couple of hundred metres from the beach and a cute little parade of shops.

We secure the very last pitch for the night, and so popular is the site, even out of season, that we take an unpowered site on a slopey angle on the banks of the lake, but what an excellent decision to sacrifice mod-cons and the twenty quid or so from the other site, as our new home walks away hands down with the title of 'Best Pitch So Far.'

Astonishingly, as I am checking in and getting the drill from reception, you will never guess who walks in. It's the Irish guy from Airlie Beach.

I can't believe it. It's like seeing an old friend, except, of course, I still don't know his name. Last time we spoke, I wasn't really giving my heart and soul to the matter because I knew it was just cook area banter. Here today, gone tomorrow. Yet now, I feel a sense of comfort and security, though I didn't even clock him straightaway, and then it sort of dawns on both of us. I knew that we had a lot to catch up on, and I knew that we had been meant to switch sites.

'We laughed at you lot all day yesterday.' I begin.

'All we kept saying was ...the stupid Irish, it's pissing down and they are staying another day. We were literally hi-fiving each other at our genius.'

I start most friendships with a put-down.

He replies that he had heard us leave in the morning, and by 4pm they realised that they were beaten too and decided to hit the road, which is not the best time to do so in these parts.

'Did you see Rockhampton?' I ask.

'Ah Rockhampton, geez,' he replies.

'I know...Rockhampton...geez....Nat did 120ks all the way,' I confess.

'Well yer man on the sat-nav said it would take eight hours but we did it in six.'

There's a sense that you can get away with it out of the cities here. After all, if these huge road-train things can come tearing your way, carrying literally a train's length of vehicle and at enormous speeds, you have got to hope that you're going to be alright.

We chat for a glorious hour, and it turns out that they did the thing that you read about in books and which we haven't experienced yet. They just parked up at Yeppoon, and slept on the beach for the night. It sounds wonderful, doesn't it? If only I had mentioned it to Nat. Oh yes, wait a minute....

In the morning they sneaked across for a wash at the adjoining campsite, paying for nothing and then rang ahead to Hervey Bay.

I am so glad to see them and delighted that we hadn't been as organised in pre-booking as they had, or destiny would have meant that we wouldn't have met again. As the full-glowing orange sun goes down, and with it the heat, Molly and Sam are feeding ducks by the van, hunting for eels in the water, and look on in wonder as massive turtles roam the bed of the lake.

I couldn't be happier. Dan and Jo, by the way.

Day Seventeen

It was a cold night with no power and therefore no heating. As wonderful as our pitch is here, we are learning quickly and today's lesson is that it is going to get a lot colder, and even though everyone tells us that we can just turn up on spec from here on in on the way to Adelaide, the fact remains that we will die if we can't get heating overnight in the van. That would be unfortunate, as good a time as we are having.

I do recognise that camping was once always this primitive.

I slept alone too as Nat joined the kids after a horrendous row which ended up with me shoving my earphones into the laptop to watch an episode of *Spooks* after declaring that I was leaving. I meant it too, though, with no obvious plan of how to get home from Hervey Bay!

I don't even know what it was about but I recall a few classic lines from the rather niggled 'Nat, you said you wouldn't call home for a week,' to her critique of my navigation.

'There is no point spotting something and telling me to turn just at the last minute,' she roared. I knocked that one back.

'There is no point asking me where we are going when we are coming into a town that I have never seen before in my life.'

I'm sure the whole campsite heard, but we can't be alone in feeling the tension in such an enclosed environment. In fact, I know we are not, but the difference is that when we sat down and went through our campervan grievances with the Irish last night, the things that we had issues over collectively as one family – as two families we were laughing about. Clearly Nat and I are a disaster.

A member of the US navy once told me that he did some work at Sandals in Antigua and would laugh to himself when on the Monday of every week he would overhear conversations along the lines of 'so, you just got married this weekend...no way...so did we...what a coincidence...let's be friends for life.'

Well, first time campers must be like this as Dan showed me his van, and I showed him mine – not that I had driven it.

We have a Maui, they have an Apollo. We have a Playstation in ours, they have a crucial little hook for their ladder which we could really use. Oh how we laughed at how everyone's van clunks when you drive off over the speed bumps on every campsite; my did we chuckle at the 'if you want medical treatment go back 37k' sign – 'YOU SAW THAT TOO, OH WOW!'

Neither of us could believe that the campsites seem to just go to lights out at 6pm, and yes, wasn't it hysterical backing the beast into tiny pitches, and not funny at all, when you have to pull over for the vast quantities of enormous vehicles that come your way on the highway.

We both have the same thought – swap all our kids' DVDs. There is a long road ahead. We laugh at all the same things in a way that Nat and I have forgotten to. We see the same things and we think the same thoughts. We tell them that we are writing a book and if they are not careful then they will be in it. We are kindred spirits. We have found our 'stay in touch for life' friends. You don't have to have just got married in Antigua to know this feeling.

Today is washday but we have to move pitch first, reluctantly abandoning the lakeside dawn chorus of swans and geese at our door as the sun rises over the water. If it weren't for the cold through the night, I would never leave this pitch again, but with no option as someone else is coming in, we opt for the luxury of a pitch with our own ensuite bathroom, for a whopping £2.50 extra per night. Camping for snobs that breaks the bank!

We will be broke by Christmas at this rate.

I can't think why we haven't had an ensuite up to this point. You just park up and you have your own shower block on the end of your van. There just didn't seem any point. After all, why not mingle in with the riff-raff and pick up some athletes foot on the way?

For beauty, we are now on the worst pitch on the site, spoilt by the night before. That was proper camping – albeit in a van. Today, ensuite freshly cleaned, we're opposite the laundry and I can tell you – top tip coming up – forget the brightness of the morning sunshine or the zest for life after a shower and breakfast – 10.30am is the time to go washing because everybody is clearing off out of the campsite with trips planned or acres of ocean road to tackle. Nat, for once, couldn't be happier.

The bust-up is soon forgotten, and the kids are flying around on the go-karts, though Sam says his heart is hurting. The little drama queen. They are fleecing us left, right and centre for change at the newly discovered games room. We are robbed to the tune of fifteen dollars. This was change intended for the laundry.

I retire to the computers in reception, but I realise at this point that my email is at a point of no-return as a further two thousand messages await me. It's going fine until we reach the 200 meg mark and then it just grinds to a halt. You may think that two thousand is a lot but believe me, that's nothing. My email address being in the public domain, my life is a stream of communiqués from lost uncles in Nigeria and herbal salesmen in Nevada. So far, I have bought two degrees and a shitload of Viagra.

I only mention this in passing as in this world of eternal contact, most people that come to Australia will face that inevitable barrage of junk on their return home, so you have to make a choice to delete as you go, or shut the world off. If it's urgent, the real people know where to find me. Finally, I am making progress seventeen days in. My return to the real world is twenty years overdue. I do not need to be contacted.

Instead, I use my internet time more wisely. After the no-power show last night, I vow to look ahead more. The prices for flying into Alice Springs are astronomical. I return to the van to begin the process of letting Nat down that we won't be flying to the Rock after all, something for which she sold her car just three weeks ago. We just can't justify it, and it takes hold of both of us like a seizure as we instantly cancel our planned trip to the beautiful Fraser Island and utter those words for the first time. We *can't* do everything.

As we wander the two minute walk into Hervey Bay we are sure about a couple of things: We were absolutely right to change campsites and there would be no Hervey Bay at all if it weren't for Fraser Island.

But foolishly, it hadn't even occurred to us that Fraser Island was four wheel drive territory. How many times on this trip are we going to pass by in ignorance only to discover retrospectively how close we would have been to disaster. By logic, disaster must be just around the corner.

There's a Big 4 site there too, though clearly we would never make it in the campervan. This only just occurs to us now.

This time we miss out on what the Fraser Island website describes as forty thousand shorebirds, in that casual way in which Australian botany has to guess. I mean, has anyone counted them, and can you tell me, hand on heart, that it was definitely the round figure of forty thousand, and not one more or one less? With so much of this gargantuan terrain undiscovered and unpopulated, it is guesswork for the natives as well as the bumbling tourists too.

This afternoon therefore, needs alternative entertainment and encouraged by cycle lanes and dozens of others at it too, we hire a bike for four. Molly nearly crashes straightaway, and I can tell you this. Nat may have driven the Maui all this way so far, but when it comes to a 10mph bike carrying three other people, she's absolutely useless.

Up and down we go alongside the beach, and that is all you do. Pleasant as it is, I am well aware that this is one of the things that you just do on holiday. Hire a bike for four people at home? You have to be joking. I am using this bonding exercise solely as a scouting trip for dinner. We are not by rule, eating out, but we surely have to take advantage of the fact that we can actually walk to town without packing up and driving the van off, only to return later to unpack for bed.

We eye up a French restaurant called Aegean, but it looks like it is boarded up for winter. It has everything you could dream off, though little for the kids. I fancy snails, followed by crocodile. You see what I mean?

Back at the van, I ring ahead to see if they can accommodate children. As I am on the phone, a Scottish family move into the pitch next to us, and I take an instant dislike to them. There are three reasons for this. Firstly, I had already had one Scottish woman laughing at us in Woolies earlier today, informing us that you could always tell who had just arrived in town. I asked her when she had. Some thirty-four years ago, and not a twang of accent gained or lost. How very Scottish.

Secondly, the Irish aside, you *do* feel disappointed when you meet fellow home-grown travellers, though it was clear that these guys were now residents in Australia though nothing Australian had rubbed off on them. Lastly, they were camping anoraks – the very worst.

It wasn't the unloading of the bikes and all the extra bits which just announced that they were seasoned pros to our 4WD naivety, it was the fact that when they went off in the dark to a solitary BBQ, all alone, miles from the cook area, they wore head gear with a miner's light attached to it. Even the kids. They barely grunted at us. Parochial, insular, anoraky pricks. So, I said hello.

I couldn't understand how this Aegean restaurant ended up in

Hervey Bay, and why it was called *Aegean*. Of course French cuisine can be wonderful and Hervey Bay is a great spot, but I want to know more. How do people end up in places like this, and do they just wake up years later and realise that they are still there? I am thinking that this could be us, if I hadn't given myself the foolish security of signing a new contract to begin almost immediately on my return.

It is clear that I need to panic, that I need to be without guaranteed work and lifestyle, in order to appreciate a better one like this. As I stare into the darkened restaurant, excited by a break from beer, burgers and salad and the prospect of a superb meal ahead, I know that I have to change my life. I will do this contract and no more, and I will dine French and in style every night on the profits from this book.

So, we go next door to Sails restaurant.

It is empty. We have to remind ourselves constantly that we are out of season, when it is better than any season that I have been in at home. This is a simple restaurant with sports memorabilia on the wall, though it is not a sports bar. I think they are just proud to display genuine Allan Border and Steve Waugh cricket bats, plus a limited edition framed Elvis track. I contemplate where the journey began that concluded with these items ending up in Hervey Bay. The chances of anyone from here having run into all three of these characters in their lifetime seem remote. Yes, it is possible that a major cricket fan could have come into Border and Waugh stuff and settled here by the sea, but it doesn't explain the Elvis thing, and it doesn't look like the prize collection of a merchandise-hoarder as the collection stops at three items. I am confused. I settle in my mind for a big cricket fan who may have been mis-sold the Elvis record online.

Predictably the only people that seem to pass by the restaurant are... the Irish. At night and in the winter, clearly this is a ghost town, yet what treats are they missing out on as I have one of the all time great meals, modestly ordering 'The Great

Barrier Reef,' in that brilliantly talented way that Aussies have for naming anything. The meal is outstanding, putting Townsville to shame. And Townsville was a good meal.

I stress that it is not just outstanding because of the monotony of my cooking. This is steak, salmon and prawns all in one, with a great big bottle of red and a great big bottle of white. After all, white for fish, red for meat. Both, I presume, for both.

I know I will sleep well tonight, and I vow that next time at the Woolies counter, I shall pick up my prawns and replicate this dish.

We can't go to bed without the usual routine, but age and alcohol, almost pseudo Alzheimer's, mean that every night we live the routine like we are living it for the first time. It starts with more wine back at the van, a slump into the supposed double bed at the back of the van, the soundtrack to Blood Brothers on the laptop, and a vague peering over the map measuring inches with fingers and the bold declaration that we'll be there before lunchtime. Except that the Irish had bad news for us.

Day Eighteen

It is a beautiful morning, and I cook up bacon by the lake. This too, is part of our routine. Nat and Molly go off to the showers together, as do Sam and I on their return. She spends a ridiculous amount of time doing whatever it is to her face. I cook.

She says that she is not hungry, then eats it like a pig. The kids generally are nowhere to be seen.

Today we are heading towards the Sunshine Coast.

Curiously the Irish tell us that they have just come off the phone to the Noosa Bougainvillia Holiday Park, and were told that they had bagged the last pitch for tonight.

'He said that to *me*, just a few moments ago,' I protest, beginning another day in doubt. We had both been recommended the site at Maroochydoore. Anecdotal evidence all along the coast said this was the place to be. The Forest Glen resort also looked good in the Big 4 brochure. Yet, we could only get in – or could we – at the Bougainvillia in Tewantin.

I hurried Nat along – it might be between us and the Irish for the last room at the inn. Lifelong friends after two days we may be, but not at the expense of power for a night.

That said, with a pattern of beautiful mornings and cold nights after sundown, I am worried that we have panicked and gone too far down the coast too soon. Yes, this is a business trip in that it is a book; yes, this is a chance to get our lives back on track; but yes it is a holiday too and that means chill in the sun. Yet, of course, in our naivety, much of our time is spent on the road and hey, we have a month more than the Irish who have the van for just two weeks. They will be bailing out in Brisbane, where they will take a house with some friends of theirs from Ireland, whom we learn had emigrated, in an almost spiritual way, to a new life down under, after several personal tragedies.

The van is just like married life for its routine. We argue, and seconds later we laugh. The kids watch DVDs. We stop for food, snacks and diesel, and we do it all again. Molly is supposed to be doing a scrap book for school, but since Port Douglas any enquiry into its progress gets the response that she hasn't done much.....since Port Douglas. *Shrek 3* gets an almost twice-daily showing and whoever is not driving regularly tuts from the front as the mounted television once again swings round so the kids' only vision is the back of the unit. Such is the beautifully constructed Maui.

Noosa is our destination and like Auntie Jenny and Port Douglas before, we are only going there on recommendation, and it is not even the recommendation of anybody we know. One of my best mates is Stonesy. He works for the government in transport and like us all is still with his wife just to protect his assets and keep his kids.

He too is thoroughly fed up with his lot. Stonesy's brother Ian lives in Dubai and his missus has just left him for some Dutch guy we affectionately call Van Klonk. I have been getting regular updates on the state of the Van Klonkety Klonks by text.

Anyway Ian says we have to go to Noosa. We have to go to Noosa. It is the place that most Australians aspire to live in, in that way that we all make up facts and pass them on, when we know that recent experience, of course, tells us that is not true and the answer as to where most Australians aspire to live is actually London.

So, Noosa it is and the journey there is unexceptional, notable for just one thing. Matilda. Voted the best truck stop in Australia. The usual questions apply here. Did they survey all the truck stops? Do real people vote or is it a team of expense-fiddling judges on a jolly? Surely the truck driver's vote is everything, except do they not do the same journey every week, and can only therefore nominate a few? Why here and why so special? What are the criteria? We miss it, driving straight past, so I cannot enlighten you.

Google tells me that it is iconic. It's a fucking truck stop, it doesn't need a website. It is not even on the actual map. Perhaps, it is not called Matilda at all. That doesn't sound very Aussie. I think its full name is the Matilda Truck and Travel Stop at Kybong, the irony of the juxtaposition of travel and stop lost on the judges. Clearly.

Maryborough looks big on the map, and terms itself a city. We stop for a coffee and I don't know why. Gympie is worth a mention but only for its name. Both historic towns, in that limited way that Australia views history. In other words, about the last two hundred years and not much more.

Suddenly, for the first time on this trip, tied with already that sense that the best of times may have passed, we feel ourselves coming back to reality. I can detect a merging from country-bumpkin Australia where time waits for everyone into a more sprawling city mentality, the like of which I suppose that we had left behind in England, though clearly nothing as bad as that.

One particular element is the catalyst for this thought. From nowhere, Steve Irwin is everywhere. Signs for Australia Zoo are all over the place even though we are miles away. I have no knowledge of this man, though I know his image, and I know how he died.

I don't know what Australia Zoo is. All I know is that I saw the pictures of that little girl, his daughter, reading at his memorial service. I thought it looked awful. I know he fell to a stingray, when he fought crocodiles. I know that we laughed about it on the air when the story came in. That's it. The man, however, is very much alive and in our midst. My intrigue with the whole Irwin experience begins here.

But first we must pitch up and I prepare myself for the daily row that kicks in as soon as the campsite is in touching distance. You can imagine, can't you, the straight empty road of the Bruce Highway for miles upon miles, with no need to navigate, and then here it comes, the last mile. But, it is not my fault this time, as the sat-nav literally does the most stupid thing that a sat-nav can do. It sends us on a right, then on a hundred metres or so, then a left, and we are literally in a *Neighbours* type housing estate. I've a sense that we are here though, as my radar picks up golf in the distance, and the Big 4 book says that golf is nearby. Unfortunately the real radar is now taking the piss, like it literally does have a mind of its own. Next, we drive forward again another hundred metres or so.

Nat is screaming that this can't be right. The challenge is to reply even louder to make your point that you have never been here either. The kids pile in taking their usual sides. Now, we must take a left. I just wish the bitch would do what she says. No what I meant was that I wish Nat would do what the bitch says.

We're back on the main road, literally staring ahead to the point one hundred metres on, where the stupid sat-nav told us to begin a rectangular approach to the campsite for no obvious reason just a moment ago. It was there all along just fifty metres on our left. We had gone a mile to gain a hundred metres. We could have gone straight on. That sat-nav will cost me my already shaky marriage. I may be shacking up with either Stonesy brother sooner than I had expected.

We pull in, to the left. It is a Townsville type scenario in that there is a big service station at the front of the site. We are allocated pitch 72A, which tells you that it is probably us who got the very last pitch and the Irish probably got the real last pitch. We are in a makeshift pitch again. Not a 73, a 72A. An afterthought. And when we drive into the slot, we are once again the novelty act for the almost permanent resident fellow campers.

Now, of course, there is a penalty to pay for being the last allocated, so I trudge back to reception to explain that the hose doesn't reach anywhere near the water pipe. Most check-ins and park-ups normally are followed by the trudge back to reception to ask a totally thick question.

'You're in luck, mate, I've got a spare one. I'll bring it over.'

Or perhaps, as I like to think of it, *you're* in luck Mr and Mrs campsite. After all, I appear to have the pitch that nobody wants, though actually I think I quite like it.

We're just ten metres from the cook area, fifteen from the pool, and twenty from reception. Showers, oh they are miles away, something I discover as I peruse the site for the toilet dump, a traditional task on arrival, after Nat complaining that it stinks and it is my fault, which is a total lie as Sam hasn't hit the target once. I've only missed twice.

We don't use the shower in the van by the way. It's a token offering and probably real luxury if you are twenty, but for us it comes out as a piddle and most of the facilities on the sites so far have been excellent. Strangely, the site is not full, nor is there any sight of the Irish. Is it the case that everybody who rings ahead has just got the last pitch?

Well, no Irish, no point staying, so we head to Noosa, and in a beautiful irony, Molly nearly breaks the sat-nav getting out of the van, which sends Nat into the number one rage yet, showing all her drama queen skills, screaming that the sat-nav is one of the few things not covered by the 'No Worries' insurance. This covers everything, except of course, stuff that you break. Predictably, you will always break what is not covered.

'This will cost us five hundred quid, Molly, ' she says and I'm already making mental notes to embellish the figure when I tell the Irish!

It will be at least a grand by the time we get drinking later, but the thing is useless anyway, though Nat still trusts it more than me. It's hanging off its little stick in the front of the van, and I have never seen Nat so cross, since, well, about an hour ago actually. And of course, as always happens in the middle of such a theatrical performance, she is mid-rant when she miraculously fixes it, which then becomes my fault, for not ever having been likely to have fixed it in a million years. Sam gets off lightly.

Though he does refuse to get out of the van when we arrive in Noosa, and so is born a catchphrase on this trip, uttered here for the first time with sincerity, but as with all such sayings, surely to be heard later in mocking tones, as we ask Sam if this trip is a bit too much for him. He says yes.

Noosa is principally, right up at the front, a very tight street to drive on. Its approach reminds me of Walton-on-Thames in Surrey, not far from where I grew up and now with perceived wealth in the way that I had also been sold Noosa. Perhaps you would say that it has an irritating Chelsea culture. It has too many cafes and too many cars. An industry of people sitting and doing nothing. If there were one place that you would find an Aussie air-kissing and saying ciao, this were it.

Parking is a nightmare. Nat has already blown one manoeuvre where she illegally exits the tightest space in a miniscule car park and in the process bashes the side of the van to leave the awning adrift. She refuses to drive on, storming out of the vehicle with half the world watching. Never mind the crowd, it is the latest example of being able to drive into a space but being unable to go back on yourself to get out of it. I genuinely don't see a solution. It's an inch by inch process and we're just metres from the local constabulary. The tailback on the already compact road off the car park is now a mile long and some more. It is just an embarrassment but clearly when the Hornes hire a campervan, this is what we do.

Wherever we go in this town we'll be easily recognisable as the family in the van that smashed everything in its way in a bid to park. Finally she makes it out through the entrance and turns right over a roundabout only to head straight into the next nightmare, and a sign marked 'National Park – No Caravans Past This Point.'

This could be Cooktown all over again. I am literally scared to speak, yet my silence doesn't help either. I can see exactly what she is doing and the disaster to which she is leading us, insisting stubbornly that we are a campervan and not a caravan, and therefore not accepting that we are the bigger of the two and less likely to pass.

I hold my head in my hands and this just makes her madder still. If there were, at best, half an inch spare within the inside of the entry pillars to the car park, then she takes it, only to find after all that there is a not a space to be had and she has to reverse round and go back out the way that she came. How we have not had more than a scrape, or some kind of *major* disaster on this trip is beyond me. The *minor* ones seem to be accumulating.

We end up doing a full circle and driving all the way back down the main street, and on our left who should we see, with bits hanging off our van? It's the Irish!

There is a not a moment's hesitation as we honk majestically to everybody's embarrassment whilst flying over the speed bumps. I'm sure they were looking the other way, protesting that 'we've never seen them before in my life – honest.'

It is good news to see them though, and all self-consciousness goes out the window, as we rattle along, waving furiously, shouting out the window, as the van flies past. On day one, it was 'well, see you around' (never), then it became 'I've seen you before. Perhaps, we should chat.' Now I am thinking 'what good fun to see the Irish, I feel almost at home now.'

I wonder if at any point they will tell us that they are heading somewhere but miraculously aren't and we never see them again. Such is the fragmented nature of holiday romances.

Finally we park up about two miles from where we were, in a sort of rainforest car park. We're able to cut through to the beach, and the kids just stroll the surf with their clothes on, Nat insisting that they take a surf lesson tomorrow, and that she purchase a wetsuit which will cost about £100 and which she will wear approximately three times. Naturally, I see the sense in this and agree.

I detect there might be a creative air around Noosa. It feels different, aside from money in the air, and on the beach we stumble across the only kind of art in the world that appeals to me – sand art. Some budding Picasso has beautifully carved first a turtle and then a Formula One car, entirely out of the beach.

I think this is truly wonderful, and stand in awe for ten minutes. Naturally, as hundreds of people pass by this fine work with me motionless next to it, I feel obliged to take the credit! I am now that strange English guy in a hundred strangers' photos, who built the car on the beach, except that I didn't, of course, but I like the fantasy of being in somebody's holiday snap, without knowing anything of the journey that particular image will take, particularly in a digital age, where it will end up getting pinged all around the world, only for its path to cross an acquaintance of mine, and for it to be extraordinarily emailed back to me. Even the world is a tiny place these days, and we are well on the way to a thousand photos ourselves, some of which frankly, may come to haunt *us* in time.

Why, for instance, would our daily time-consuming trip to Woolies today take a diversion? To get to the drive-thru off-license, of course. It is called something like Liquor Land or Liquor Lounge. Either way, you don't have to get out of the vehicle, you just pull up and get served as though it were a burger. I think it is an exceptional idea, and wonder why the world hasn't embraced the drive-thru concept more. Medicine, I think would be a good addition to the drive-thru family. Just think, how much easier it would be to pull up at a window rather than have the pharmacist shout to the entire store.

'So Mr Horne, gonorrhoea, you say?'

Of course, we completely defeat the object of the exercise. By getting out. To take that photo.

I don't actually think we need any more Stanley wine. We have cartons of the stuff in the back, but it has just become habit now to stop, fill up and off we go again. I fear that we may be drinking it later with the Irish, so I stock up with even more. That is, of course, if they are still speaking to us after witnessing the whitest, skinniest, mankiest, sun-creamed-stained, scantily-clad pair of children walking the entire length of Noosa's principle street, in just their smalls. You would be proud to know our family, wouldn't you?

It is five miles back to the campsite. We can't even manage that without getting lost. Nat reminds me that it is the most sought-after place to live in Australia. Next to the campsite, however, is a sign proclaiming 'The World's Best Crematorium.' Australia simply loves handing out awards in the most unlikely categories. Clearly the best place to live *and* die.

Day Nineteen

Can I remember last night? Being just two pitches away was the fatal magnet which we could no longer avoid. In one single box of Stanley, I think we went from day one campsite conversation mentality of 'I'm going to tell you what I need to get through this conversation' to day three or four of 'I'm going to tell you everything about my life to the point that you will never want to spend any more time with us anymore.'

I remember that we told the Irish that we were writing a book for a second time, and this time Nat modestly read out certain chunks of hers. Of course, they said it was hysterical and that they would buy it. I remember pointing out too, that obviously they were now in it.

This, naturally, is most unfair. In that random moment where Dan first spoke to me at Hervey Bay – or was it Airlie Beach – his life became mine and yours. He happened to walk into our story.

They laugh a lot. Irish often seem too, or perhaps it is that musical lilt in the way that they talk. They are good storytellers and a good audience. For some reason, my receipts are a source of huge entertainment to them. I hope the taxman finds them equally entertaining. I had given Nat my usual drill of 'keep everything.' We wouldn't have been able to afford the trip if it hadn't been a business trip and my business hadn't been writing and broadcasting, but as hard as I have tried, some creative license may have to be allowed at next year's year-end accounts. After all, I cannot legislate for the world in which no receipts exist: table tennis, pinball machines, hell – even laundry sometimes. I'm sure that even if I am unable to provide documented evidence of the days when we inserted coins into a token-churning machine for the dryer, the Revenue does accept that we didn't spend seven weeks around Australia unwashed.

If however, there remains any dispute, as with the Billabong in Townsville, I repeat that I am more than happy to retrace the entire trip so far in search of the necessary paperwork, though perhaps we can all save time by arranging a meeting with my wife, who has an OCD in the field of laundry.

It turns out that neither the Irish nor ourselves opted for Fraser Island. In hindsight I wonder if we should have. I remember though, that we both convinced ourselves and then all piled in, in agreement, that you can't do everything and it was just another island. You see how blasé and comfortable we have become....it's just another Barrier Reef, you can't do them all.....oh that, that's just another Opera House, I can take it or leave it.

I recall that we also got talking to Dennis, who came to introduce himself from next door. Get this – he was here on this site for three months, and very much gave the campsite a sort of retirement village feel. He told me his life story in about five minutes; I told him I wanted to meet cricket commentator Richie Benaud. Then he buggered off. Nice guy, keen to sell his country. Or bored of his missus, on this most boring of campsites.

For some reason, I find myself asking this morning why the first aid kit is open. Neither of us can remember, though Nat sells it to me as bargain.

'Thirty dollars that,' she pipes up, 'though now we have opened it, it is ours.'

Oh yippee I jumped for joy. Of all the things to bring back from down under, you got.....a broken, green, first-aid kit. You'll love it. You can have hours of fun, after hours of injury. Wow, try these scissors out with my nephew baby Ben. A gift this good really says we missed you.

I am not a fan of those people who pretend that you got a bargain when you just got something cheaper, even though it was something that you didn't want in the first place. I can see Nat coming home now from Woolies when we emigrate to Noosa as she has been flagging up all trip.

'Honey, I'm home, they got cat litter three for the price of two,' she would surely say in a moment of American sitcom madness referring to me as honey.

I would have no choice but to reply as only I knew how to.

'Sugar, we don't have a cat.'

Stand back, flame well and truly lit.

'That's just typical of you.'

Followed by a three day silence. Or heaven, as I prefer to think of it.

Here's the best bit. No, I lied. Here's the saddest bit. I care not a jot for cars, unless they are made from sand on the beach. But, I do vaguely remember that last night we all anoraked each other's vans, and with it I felt a sense of one-upmanship beginning. We were a Maui, they an Apollo. We both wanted bits of each other's vans.

I awake, therefore, this morning particularly aggrieved at the added space behind the driver's seat, and their fridge, which, I have to say, wallops ours for six.

As you would expect, last night ended with declarations of undying holiday love, followed by the words, 'we're off to Eumundi in the morning.' And whoever hadn't said it first then said this second.

'Oh so are we, what a surprise.'

What a surprise indeed. We were now joined at the hip.

So, all roads lead to Eumundi, though as we were about to discover, not all of them lead out of there.

Eumundi is just a few miles away from the campsite but it was really getting a big build up as the place to be at the weekend. It was mentioned in the Big 4 brochure, there were leaflets at reception, Dennis next door had given it the thumbs up, and most importantly, the Irish had heard of it too.

It is a small market town, famous unbelievably, for its markets, one of which seems to be an all year-round Christmas shop. I am unable to decide whether this is business brilliance or business stupidity. Either way the place is heaving. On our approach, I am already thinking that this van in this place is a bad idea, especially as Nat misses a killer parking space right at the top end of the village that would have set us up beautifully for an hour or two of perusing the local tat.

The problem is that all the traffic is moving at five miles per hour, and you can't see ahead, and one of the reasons that you can't see ahead is that the road is about to disappear into two of the worst words in the English language. Overflow parking.

I feel us descending into a one-way street from which there is no return. Inside, I am having a mild panic. I don't like seeing one way traffic ahead, and nothing coming back the other way. The parking is full everywhere until one attendant says that we might want to try the field at the bottom of the street. I pause here, on the off chance that you are reading this right now and you too are on the approach to Eumundi. Whatever you do, stop, and don't do it. Don't take the field.

On the gate is one of the most uncouth, uneducated girls that I have ever met, who takes our three dollars and points in the direction of the bottom of the field. I question this to her and to Nat. Nat insists that if she says it is fine, it must be. There is no road at this point, just a dirt track lined by trees, and with field all around. I can see on most sides of me nothing but vast quantities of mud. I can see that only four wheel drives are here, and I can see that if she turns right five metres from here, as instructed to do, then we are in the sh.....Too late, she's done it. We're in the shit. Oh dear, this is Cooktown except worse.

We are now officially stuck. The wheel won't turn and vehicles are piling in behind us. This is a bog, and it looks like a bog that come rain or shine, remains a bog. We are bogged.

It is now eleven o'clock and I can still see us being here by nightfall. What on earth do we do? Is this then why we took out the so-called 'No Worries' insurance? Neither Nat nor I think that the no worries insurance covers stuff like this. Of course, technically it should. If after all, I had a nightmare last night about getting bogged, but then remembered that I had the no worries policy, surely the voice in my head would have said 'no worries' and I would have gone back to sleep unperturbed, but both Nat and I remember that the girl at Maui in Cairns had said that you weren't allowed to go off the road, and believe me this was no road. Cooktown, as we now referred to it without having made it there, had been a warning.

Guess what happens next? What may or may not be the owner of the farm is kicking off, demanding that we move. Now, let's be fair here to her. She is frightful, with a vile piercing under her lip, completely unattractive, and the kind of woman who looks, just looks, like she has had three kids by four different fathers, one of whom may be working the gate.

And yes, I meant three kids and four fathers. She *looks* like the kind of woman who doesn't remember one one-night stand from the next. Naturally, she has nasty dogs too. And a husband, boyfriend, whatever, in a checked shirt. Ah yes, this was the scene from our movie when all the clichés came home to roost. Whatever I say to her, she has an answer for. So far this has been a great country with great people. Today is the first time that I am called a whinging Pom.

I am somewhat taken aback by this, principally because I had expected this level of banter from day one and it never came. To hear it now, as I often reflect when people resort to stereotypical insults in the midst of conflict, just tells me that she is incapable of making a good argument without resorting to clichés or abuse.

In short, she knows that she is ripping everybody off. She has no argument. She knows that she is wrong.

Frankly, we *can't* move. She knows this but still the insults keep on coming. Here's the thing, though. Weighing up the situation, I am absolutely convinced that this happens every single day to somebody here. I tot up the sums of money that she must be making. Three dollars a time, two hundred cars, each staying for two hours, and then the spaces are refilled. And any for the taxman? I can only imagine.

She screams at Nat to just fucking call the FACQ. What the F*U*C*K is the FACQ? You learn quickly when you are bogged, believe me.

To make matters worse, the Irish, shopping well underway, turn up for a chuckle. Nat is on the phone for about twenty minutes. First to the Maui helpline, then to Maui Brisbane, back to Maui Cairns, then finally the FACQ national, then finally, finally, the FACQ local. They clearly must have zillions of freelance operators working under the badge, littered across Australia. I mean what are the chances in this vast unpopulated, road-shy land, that the FACQ can turn up within forty-five minutes?

Bugger all actually, as it turns out that they are called the RACQ, the first three initials of which suddenly look slightly more familiar. I think the FACQ blow people up in Columbia from memory. Or maybe that was the FARC. Either way add an e to the FARC and this is where we stood.

Now it turns out that the RACQ can't help us. The reason? We don't have an address for our bogging! That's because it's a field and not a road. That's why we are bogged.

Luck is on our side though, as the RACQ man has been here before, several times apparently. That's several times in the last week, and he advises us to meet at the junction of Napier Street and Albert Street. I am feeling better. Vindicated too.

This evil witch whose field it appears to be, clearly *has* seen this many times, and so has the guy from the Columbian military too.

You have to picture that we are parked at an angle in mud, the Maui attempting to turn but just spitting mud everywhere. Making life worse, is the fact that the field has tall trees at ten metre intervals which make margin for error...well, marginal.

Witch bitch has already wandered off, getting her story straight with her daughter-cum-helper on the gate, and we begin an inch by inch process of extracting ourselves from the bog. It literally is one step forward and two steps back, using anything like abandoned planks of wood to try and get the van on a firm footing. The wheels just spin, mud flying everywhere. The RACQ guy has a massive electronic tow on his truck, and keeps disappearing back into his truck to do some maths. Really, he is punching angles and distances into his computer and taking the scientific approach. I don't think that this is because he is a methodical German by the way, though he is. I think it is because he has done this before, many, many times, and the chance of failure is on a knife-edge. I look to him for guidance, nervously bantering in a 'will it be alright' kind of way that calms me and presumably irritates him.

I'm struggling to actually comprehend that his little truck can pull my six berth van, and sometimes it can't. And if he manages to get us moving, I don't see at all how he can swing our van behind him and make what was already the tightest of turns. Cars are still piling towards our end, and still driving into the bog. People do this though, don't they? They hear traffic reports on the radio, and assume that they know best, or it will be gone by the time that they get there, so they carry on and drive into it.

Our van, so cream with the green Maui logo just a couple of weeks back in Cairns, is now filthier than a Paris Hilton home movie. Nor, in its design fault, does it have a rear windscreen wiper. A colossal disadvantage for people intent on using the Maui for what it was intended – pegging it across Australia.

Between us, Nat and I reverse and advance, advance and reverse, and it is all guesswork, whacking a bush here, sinking into the mud there. We're going nowhere fast, inching just back and forth over ground that we have already covered.

A Japanese couple ten metres from us are now also bogged. I watched in slow-motion as they turned left off the dark track and I predicted to the second where they would become unmoveable too. I thought we might have trouble with snakes and spiders and the odd impassable creek when we began this journey but I wasn't expecting that we would be towed out of a bog.

It is a whole two hours after arriving before both vehicles are facing in the correct direction, and one rotation of the wheel will follow another. I fear permanent damage to the vehicle, Nat nervously awaits the bill.

It has been like one of those truck-pulling scenes from *World's Strongest Man* except with less success, but finally we make it out and the recovery guy confirms that he *has* been here many times before. Miraculously he claims that we are covered too and that there is nothing to sign for except to say 'job done,' though this doesn't comfort us, as we convince ourselves that there will be a bill to come later. It is easy for our German friend to reassure us now, never having met the man in Adelaide who could destroy us with a dreaded final bill.

Again Australia has proved to us to be a country which functions. Logic says that we should have been stuck here all day. As we pass that dreaded woman however, on the way back out, we both agree that we have had our first bad experience with an Aussie. She is the first to fall in line with the stereotype that we had been fed over the years, principally through sport but also in the many Antipodean clowns who had wrecked UK commercial radio in the 1990s with their bullying management style, and lack of creative flair. Many, many friends of mine had had careers interrupted by aggressive Australian incompetence, and therein lies the key, that the incompetent often overcompensate for their lack of ability – with aggression.

Bar that, I hadn't really thought about my career at all since landing here. This, at least, meant that the trip was serving a purpose. As we turn right out of the field, with much of the day still left, but with the desire to shop no longer there, we head back. Just on the right and at the back of the woman's house, is the police station. I am astounded. I can't believe that the police of Eumundi allow this woman to proceed with this money making scam, and I am sure that if they were to knock and ask for receipts and paperwork, they might find her lacking. I vow to write to them on my return to complain about this dreadful woman. I won't of course.

Day Twenty

Dennis came over last night and apologised after he heard me tell the 'fucking whinging Pom' story. He was genuinely apologetic on behalf of his entire nation, and didn't seem to notice that I had also bogged *his* pitch. I admit it. I have been taking a casual approach to waste dumping and I may have possibly let some of my excess water out on our pitch which may have possibly leaked onto his. Ok, it did.

You probably have to empty the portable toilet, dump the waste, and replenish the water every three days or so. Of course, that depends on how much you use and how weak your bladder is but it tends to be a bit of an afterthought for us, hence the random dumping underneath the van. The Aussies are more systematic about the whole thing, with enormous pipes that just stay permanently connected to their vans while on site. I have a pathetic curly hose that barely fits into its tight little unit, that doesn't always connect and rarely recoils compactly into its cupboard. You understand perhaps, my aversion to using it. You cannot, of course, drive off, with these things hanging out. The water hose, for example is stored on the outside of the vehicle.

Again, though I am piecing together this conversation. I believe we began drinking with the Irish at 4pm last night.

Now, look at how much trust and how free-spirited we have become. Dan suggested that our kids join his in their van, while they come over for a drink, but first could he have my laptop to whack some fun stuff on it for everybody for the long miles ahead?

Now, clearly this trip has gone to my head. As Nat will tell you, I don't even give her my laptop at home. Yet I had become all-trusting and without fear in just a few weeks. It shows essentially one thing – how bad for your mind your job is, and what suspicion it arouses.

So what potentially was on my laptop? I had my contract, my accounts, my two previous lawsuits (against me), a whole load of personal stuff and loads of nonsense that, in the wrong hands, would embarrass me. So I gave it to him.

Strangely, he was gone for some time but let me assure from the banging head that I have this morning, his wife Jo more than made up for it.

Beyond that, I remember only these four things from last night.

Firstly, Dennis, somewhat intriguingly told us that he had been making a 'five year blueprint for a secret, electronic engineering government department.' Oh Dennis, you silly fool. As kind as you have been, that has to be in the book.

Secondly, dinner. Oh yes, dinner. Well, it was on the barbecue of course, and I do remember blowing away a couple from Tasmania by telling them that I used to drink with David Boon occasionally in the years 1996 to 2000.

Boony, legendary Tasmanian, more impressive drinker, had been cricket captain at my beloved Durham, and by nature of the fact that their wicketkeeper was living in my house, I was always in the bar with them and sometimes, hell, even in the dressing room. This remains a highlight in my life.

As any cricket aficionado will tell you, he is noted for breaking the all-time record for number of tinnies consumed on the Sydney to London flight, something which is incredibly mean as he was a top drawer player and even better bloke. My memories of D.C. Boon are him saying that the marketing department at

Durham had been 'fucking useless' and that my radio show was effectively it, and that if he had been back home he would have been on the side of every milk carton at the start of the season, and if it hadn't been for me on the air, nobody would know that there was cricket...Or words to that effect. Which I, of course, loved.

Next, when I asked him how his family were, he replied,

'I just gave Pip half a million fucking dollars and she has bought some land near Launceston. I haven't seen it yet, mate.'

Who wouldn't want to drink with a guy like that?

Well, my new found Tassie friends loved that and I admit I told it to impress. But I had been in shock, you see.

Just minutes earlier, it was nearly two disasters in one day.

I like generally to make my move on the barbie when there is nobody around, just in case there are some embarrassingly tricky obstacles to overcome. Like turning it on.

Equally, if I could avoid clearing up after myself, that would be a bonus.

So, it was dark last night, and the cook up area was free. Nat was making some notes for her epic masterpiece of her version of the book (I doubt it), whilst having the usual fag and early wine, and I had gone off to cook. I turned the big dials on the grill and nothing happened. I turned them again and nothing. Well, what would you do in this situation? Beautiful meat awaiting warmth, and only a matter of time before you look useless, I started really yanking the dials as though pressing harder would invoke life. As you do with a remote control pressing harder and harder when it is actually the batteries which have gone.

Still nothing. There seemed to be no obvious reason why the barbie would not light for me. I couldn't get help because obviously, the law of sod would mean that any Aussie wandering over in their shorts and hat, already laughing at me, would gently twist it and depart chuckling some more with a mocking 'there you go mate, easy, you Pommie poof.'

I looked around, I recall, and with the coast clear, decided to go for it. I knelt down, placing my head level with the gap between the metal surface of the barbie and the dials, just to the point where you can see in for any potential flame. This gap is about the size of my hand. In one fell swoop, I threw a match into the abyss. This is why this morning I awake not only with a sore head, but with only one eyebrow. Parts of my hair are also missing, though I am liking the style.

In the same way that when kids on *You've Been Framed* run into the patio doors, and their parents carry on filming to get their £250, I had been watched after all. I picked myself off the floor to raucous laughter coming from outside our van where Nat had seen it all, and was already describing it as the funniest thing that she had ever seen. Bear in mind that on our first date, I had pulled down my yellow underpants, and said,

'There you've seen it now, so let's get on with it.'

This apparently was funnier.

Never mind that I had had the cheapest haircut and lost an eyebrow, as long as Nat was entertained, then that was fine. My hair feels somewhat dry this morning and with a gassy smell.

Still, it clearly set the tone for the evening. Nat, somewhat encouraged, blew me away somewhat more with the classic, 'so what do you Irish do about contraception?'

Sadly I don't recall the answer, though she too was now so into Australia that her inhibitions were departing her soul. Or she was pissed.

As ever, the only other thing that I can remember was the 'best friends forever' declaration at the end of the evening...

Dan: 'We're going to park up just outside Brisbane tomorrow.'

Nat: 'So are we. Wow!'

Jo: 'We're thinking of going to Australia Zoo.'

Nat: 'No, you'll never guess what....'

And so, off we head this morning, in search of Steve.

I have never watched his shows. I remember his daughter at the memorial and thinking what a precocious child, feeding the world's media and not even ten years old. This is not natural behaviour for one so young, I thought. I remember finding his death hysterical on the air, that he had perished to a stingray. I remember interviewing Australian rugby world cup winner Matty Burke in Newcastle and egging him on about Steve and he just straight-batted me with total sincerity that it was a sad day for every Australian. I couldn't understand our country grinding to a halt like this over Johnny Morris. Clearly he was the classic Aussie mate in a world where mateship was king.

I see roadside images of Steve the closer that we get. I remember Jo and Dan saying last night that sometimes in the holidays Bindi appeared at the zoo. Yeah right, I thought. That's the kind of great myth that brings in business, only for busloads of tourists to depart uttering the words 'guess we didn't see his daughter then, maybe next time.'

We were heading to Beerwah, itself an unusual name. It is the first time really that we have not tried to hug the coast, coming inland off the A1. Ahead lay the M1 to Brisbane, our first motorway, as we would think of it.

We have driven to Cairns and are nearly at Brisbane, and we haven't seen a proper motorway. That gives a fair picture of the isolation of some of these places and Beerwah, believe me, is remote, but then zoos have to be, I suppose, by definition.

I am driving too, and it is a stress swinging blind off the A1 onto the Beerwah road, or as they call it here, Steve Irwin Way. God, this man owns this land. He has been dead, what two or three years, and he has a road named after him. You have to have been dead a century or two in England to get that honour and then someone will probably complain. Nor, is there anything else on it. This is not unusual in Oz but the location adds to the drama and the star quality factor. And then suddenly we're there, parked up just two spaces from the Irish inevitably, though arriving at a different time.

I know as little of this zoo as I do the man. I am surprised that it is not some poky little zoo. It is a fully-fledged tourist attraction, not easy to get to, hence buses laid on from Brisbane, easily an hour plus away.

Once we're in we find ugly Tasmanian devils, dingoes, and Aggro. Aggro is a crocodile. Such is my Irwin ignorance that I don't even realise that Steve caught these crocs, often relocating them for their own safety. I am astounded with the little notices by the croc pools. 'Caught By Steve' or 'Caught By Steve And Wes' or something equally heroic.

Then I realise the name Wes rings a bell. I remember hearing Terri Irwin flogging her book on Simon Mayo's show on BBC Radio 5 Live, possibly the Christmas before last. She came across well, though I still thought the total commercialisation of Steve, the whole writing the book cash-in, the entire Bindi being a star with a fashion label was just not right and signs of an abnormal family. I remember too that Terri mentioned this chap called Wes. Wes is Steve's best mate, for whom the show must go on.

My radar says that you can see Terri's influence in the Hollywoodisation of the park. First evidence of this is at the elephant feeding, all beautifully choreographed with entertainment manager Mike turning up standing in the back of the jeep. My first thought is that perhaps Steve had the vision, the balls, and the passion; Terri might have brought the American Disney magic.

I take a moment to feed the elephants, and I don't normally do stuff like this. Back at the Billabong sanctuary, I had been the one taking the photos while the kids whored themselves to every koala, kanga and croc, and this is no different in that it is not so much about the slimy sensation that you get in your hands when you feed the elephants, it is, of course, about the photo op that you can purchase later. Terri. Disney. Magic.

I'm very glad that I came at this blind though, and that is rare in this day and age. If I had come as a massive Steve fan, what would I make of all this? If I arrive with nothing but a gutful of negativity, then the only way is up perhaps, though Nat jumps to the Irwin's defence when I say that they have clearly sold out, reminding me that it takes a lot to run a zoo.

I am now so relaxed at being an Aussie that I think nothing of approaching the ice cream vendor and asking him if he knew Steve. Unfortunately for him, his warmth and generous conversation still doesn't make him a sale!

We're en route to the Crocoseum. What a ridiculously brilliant name, conjuring up an image of Roman gladiatorial conquests in a modern day sporting stadium. Absolutely stunning, and to get there we pass now abandoned show areas of a previous Steve era. Once the crocoseum came along, that was it and the goalposts were moved. I hear it can seat five thousand.

I am still unsure of what we are doing or seeing, except that there is a croc show at eleven. We take our seats high in the stadium and Steve videos play constantly on the big screen. I don't think that there has ever been a dead man who is more alive than Steve Irwin. He is what I refer to as a brand within a brand. The zoo is one thing but Steve Irwin is an altogether different beast, and you cannot help but think that in a John Lennon way, his death was and is good for business. I can't decide if the ever-present images of Steve are a family in denial, their way of keeping him alive, or business is business and Steve remains at the core of that. Perhaps both?

They must have so much archive, unused footage that will keep the Irwin shows playing forever, but what of the next generation of Irwin product? Well, unbelievably, I am sitting five metres from it. To my right I recognise Terri and Bindi and deduce that that has to be Junior Steve. I didn't even know that there was one, let alone his name. Movingly, though to him it is probably just normality, young Robert Irwin watches his Dad on the big screen, as the tape counts down with an awesome production piece into the croc show. This, genuinely, is one of the most exciting beginnings to a show that I have ever seen.

So, it really is true, Bindi and the Crocmen are about to perform at the Croc show. She already has her own TV show, and every July 24th you can come and have a birthday breakfast at the zoo for Bindi's big day. I am astounded, in fact star struck. I can almost touch them.

It dawns on me that it was here that Bindi did *that* TV memorial. At the time, I couldn't understand how there had been footage of such a personal event, and why oh why she was on it and then I see that there are TV cameras all around, and that in fact, as I had wrongly judged before, she hadn't been appearing before the world's TV cameras just days after her Dad died, but she was on home territory, and that, naturally, they were in control of the image at all times.

Then, I overhear somebody in front talking – this apparently *is* their home too. The Irwins actually live here, and I never knew. They roam the park freely unbothered and at one with their animals, and so from a remote corner of Australia was built an international phenomenon – a million times the *Crocodile Dundee* story, and with conservation at its heart. And you are welcome in almost every day of the year.

So, here's the bit that everyone struggles with – thrusting Bindi into this spotlight singing with the Crocmen that 'they don't want to save the world by wearing tights, they'll fight the animal world with human rights,' or something like that.

She is almost political in the ad-libbed conservation messages that she delivers, though she must be too young to see the ironic juxtaposition of Australia's four campest men prancing around on stage with such a serious message at its heart. Hey, I get that they are making environment and wildlife fun, and for the kids too, but frankly it is all a bit unheterosexual for me. Bindi, I must observe, is an absolute pro, and possibly the cutest kid alive. I pray for just one thing – that she doesn't grow up to reject the fact that this life was pre-determined for her, and you wonder if somewhere along the line young Robert who must know his Dad as much through the TV image as time spent with him, may move away from the zoo and reject the whole thing, when surely the script dictates that he inherit it.

I am uncomfortable with the force-fed environmentalism served through the eyes of young Bindi but I suppose it is her generation who will have to save the planet, if you believe in all that stuff.

Again, we have high cheese production values, as microphone Mike makes a second appearance of the day, and there's the dreaded audience participation in the bird show, but all this birds and snake-handling is tame stuff compared to what is to follow – the main event, the croc show.

Wait a minute, that's Terri down there in the Crocoseum and Wes is actually doing the croc show. This is like playing football with the Beckhams in their own back garden. My ignorance is such that I didn't realise that they *themselves* did the actual show, and there are two of these a day. It just never occurred to me. I work with so many people in radio – programme controllers mainly – who can't cut it when it comes to broadcasting themselves, and I have no respect for them, so to see Terri getting her hands dirty and nearly eaten is the kind of management with big bollocks attitude which can only command respect.

Today Wes and Terri are baiting Mossman, and with brilliant camera work you can see from wherever you sit the precise moment when Mossman is released from his holding area outside the arena, and all the way up to the point where this terrifying beast is seduced into the main pool. The camera work and camera positioning are second to none.

All the while Terri is educating, selling, cracking gags. The only fact that I retain is when she says that Steve had a vision and spent nine million dollars of his own money to build the Crocoseum, at the back of which lie all the crocs, each with its own residence if you like, and on a given day, anyone of them could be doing the show. Nine million dollars, everybody!

I assume that nothing has ever gone wrong. Surely we would have heard about it, but knowing that nothing can go wrong in the hands of these seasoned experts in no way takes away from what we are about to see, and the slightly dark hope that it might, as Terri takes enormous pieces of meat while still commentating, and Mossman performs on cue, jumping high for tea.

The Billabong looks pathetic in comparison, and at the time I thought it was awesome. Wes goads the world's great survivor from the animal kingdom, a predator that has outlived them all. He's being backed up by a team of four or five, and then suddenly Mossman death-rolls, and Wes shouts 'cut it now' as the mighty croc makes its move on the huge block of meat hung to the end of a string. And they do this every day – twice a day!

Is it cruel to make sport and entertainment out of the animals that the Irwin Zoo love so much, or is it the method through which they educate? Either way, at just fifteen metres from the croc, it is breathtaking.

After, it's down to the shop where the full range of the Irwin product is clear, and there's a special guest appearance from the Crocmen signing their CDs, prompting me to ask the assistant if these guys are really famous, or just within the bounds of the zoo. Fool that I am, it was unclear that they were megastars!

I repeat to Nat that the Irwins have sold out and she is denying it, reminding me that all the profits go to the Wildlife Warriors conservation charity. I won't let it rest, saying that you could still pay yourself zillions before giving what's left to a good cause.

I am, of course, being completely harsh here on the fact that they have done incredible work but I think the thing that swayed it was leaving the store with a good few hundred dollars on the credit card, the principal purchase of which was the full attire from the 'Steve Lives' collection. Yes, the Steve Lives collection.

Oh boy, was I looking forward to telling the Irish this. Is it a piss-take or the ultimate in positivity, or self-denial? Either way from plastic Bindi things to the Terri Cougar collection (clothes), Irwin was a brand, and it proved you can put your name to anything.

After lunch, in the shape of the highly nutritious themed-park hotdog, we wander the park. I am swayed by the Irwin attitude. Their enthusiasm and attitude is total, their commitment genuine. The difference between you and I and them, is that they didn't just think about it, they did it – with their natural instinct thrown in.

I learn that when the tigers are just two weeks old, their handlers begin to virtually live with them so the relationship of no fear and compatibility is formed. I watch Sam now so totally at one with nature feeding the kangaroos incessantly. I can't pull him away. I stand in front of Steve's old tree house that they apparently turned into a TV suite. I stare as the elephants play football. It is inspiring.

This is a key moment that confirms both my naivety of the Irwin story, and my absolute belief, in this context, that naivety is bliss. Behind the elephants are the Irwin houses. This is their home, their business, their passion, their entire world. The public *could* just wander down and knock on the door, but I think we all understand the rules of engagement. I would be surprised if anybody at all *had* over the years.

As the day has worn on, I have become fascinated retrospectively by Steve and the entire family. If I weren't normal and the commute from the UK to Beerwah had been shorter, I would now be a stalker. I am immersed in guilt over everything that I have said on the radio about his death, and my cynicism towards everything Irwin including a nation's collective grief at his demise. I remain astounded by his ironic death – at the hands of a stingray.

Australia Zoo is a wonderful experience, enhanced of course, by the tragedy that has propelled its fame, and the bright shining hope that is Bindi. We bale out around half three in the knowledge that we have done a day's entertainment but must make tracks for the night. Plus, the heavens open and it is pouring. My lasting memory? The incredible tributes paid by the public that now form a permanent part of the zoo underneath the main concourse.

Left out of Beerwah we must go, and ominously Nat nearly heads down a road defying the van's height clearance, and then we hit traffic on our first motorway. Traffic? This is new stuff to us.

It is clear, as Nat remarks that we have only been in the van for two weeks, that this is a landmark journey on our trip. Firstly the Steve effect and secondly, it is cities all the way from now on.

And so the face of the campsite changes too as we rock up at the Northside Caravan Village just twelve kilometres out of Brisbane. We're literally a couple of turnings off a motorway, and depressingly this site has permanent residents which I think tells you something. The skies are grey, and the site is purely functional. They can put a pool in the Big 4 brochure if they like, but this site is only for people who want a cheap option outside of Brisbane. Still, you learn to make your own fun, don't you, and the fun soon begins when two Scots in a small Maui park adjacent to us, and I befriend them after they walk on my already stretched power-cable bending its pins forever, throwing my power connection into chaos!

They are Gary and Linda, two teachers on their delayed honeymoon, and I invite them for a drink as the Irish haven't turned up yet. As they are Scottish they naturally agree but fail to bring any booze to the party.

I tease them about the size of the Maui which they have for a couple of weeks before flying to New Zealand. I am a Maui expert now, and confirming that you learn as you go, I am happy to point out to them that their water port is hidden behind their sliding door, something which has troubled them so far, as you can't actually see it when the door is open! Me, the overnight expert!

They are so young, and probably in love, and so obsessed with their new iPhones, which have just been released. How can you tell me in one hand that you have come from the Glass Mountains and then in the other give me a twenty minute demonstration of your latest apple technology? They're fun though, and I play the radio knob for a bit after they tell me that they listen to Robin Galloway on Real Radio in Scotland.

'Ah yeah, here's his number,' I said, having done an outside broadcast with Robin in Hong Kong in 2006!

Well, this was high excitement for them which meant that they couldn't resist outstaying their welcome, despite the detour offered by the Irish who have booked a table at a local steakhouse, which we decline, though, on their return, some two hours later, we are still drinking which means that the Irish pile in for their last night booze up. The jocks finally take the hint, and retire, though I think our vehicles were too close for them to shag in confidence.

We finally abandon the booze just after midnight, way past the camp curfew. It has been a long day, with lots of driving, but lots of real life too. Apart from for Steve, of course, long departed but not forgotten.

Day Twenty-One

That was a heavy night. Perhaps Steve-inspired, or egged on by the Irish who told us that their plans were to visit some friends in Brisbane having left Ireland after some intense personal tragedy, we found dark humour last night discussing wakes!

We also had the Kate McCann conversation.

I think everybody who has children and has been abroad since May 2007 has had the Kate McCann conversation with a complete stranger on holiday. The irony being that one assumes that a stranger is at the heart of the McCann story.

It is time to say goodbye this morning, though my gut is that we will meet them again. They are about to bin the Apollo and hire a car. How normal.

I feel, even though we never sought this relationship, that a security blanket is gone, that something special is no more, that a cherished memory is about to become just that. Despite the fact that we are both heading in the direction of theme parks in Brisbane, I am convinced that for the rest of the trip we are on our own now. This wonderful family, apart from being great drinkers, outrageously funny, and truly laidback, seemed to have escorted us from the great weather of the Reef and Cairns through the shocking Rockhampton trip, abandoning us only now as the journey was about to change again. From here, we only had Sydney on our mind.

Before we part, email addresses exchanged, they can't resist revealing a cunning layer of storage space in their van that the Maui just didn't have. Petty, stupid, manly, oneupmanship. Like I said, I never warmed to them!

Dan's last words, as we left, were, 'whatever you do, don't drive through Brisbane.' My plan, when I vaguely sketched out a time frame and a route was that we would spend five days here. I would say one hour is closer in the end.

The sat-nav takes us straight into the heart of Brisbane!

It looks a cracking place, at times a mix between San Francisco and Singapore, but we are so genuinely frightened at driving the van in one of three tight lanes twisting and turning through the heart of the city that all I notice is the Gabba cricket ground and the road signs *out* of town, which come as an utter relief. My apologies to the people of Brisbane for expressing a mere token few lines on your city but if you are doing Beerwah, and you have only a certain amount of days to do a huge amount of miles, you can't waste one driving just twelve kilometres from the campsite into the city centre.

We also have zero on the diesel. First panic of the day. Therefore, first row of the day. Others follow of course, from the toilet stinking to the inevitable and daily 'which way is it now' as we cruise into the Treasure Island Holiday Park.

We are on the Gold Coast, just one mile out of Surfers Paradise. Now, of course, I didn't realise that this was actually the name of the place. I thought it was a description, as in the Gold Coast is a surfer's paradise, but no, it is the bloody name of the place.

My instinct is that this is a good campsite. You get a radar by now as soon as you enter reception. You get to sense the practical sites, the family ones, the really beautiful ones and those like the Coconut in Cairns that just seem to print dollars.

This is the gateway for all the theme parks each within fifteen minutes of here, but it is cute too, despite, as so many inexplicably are, being once again just off the main highway. Maybe this is the norm, because if you go any further off the beaten track, then the words beaten track are very generous indeed. Roads just end here. In England, you would expect to disappear miles down a country lane before stumbling on your campsite. In Australia, just follow the highway. That's all there is.

Today though, is a day of practicalities. Nat is washing to excess and I am trying to meet a time zone so I can call my Dad who lives in Peru, where it is still the day before. We have not had much contact on this trip but today....or yesterday, if you like, he becomes a pensioner. Now, he doesn't really care for birthdays, having spent so much time so separated, but I care, and I am beginning to worry about the years and the distance.

He has been trying to get answers out of the pensions department in Newcastle upon Tyne for about two years regarding his pension and they appear to be slightly useless. This makes me feel doubly awful as I could easily go in and see them when I am at work in the Northeast. However, when I get through to him in the middle of the day in Australia, it emerges that they have actually rung him in Peru. After years of not getting the right person and always the wrong answer, they pull one out of the hat and phone him to apologise for all the cock-ups. Well, what are the chances of him being in? Perhaps that was their plan. Alas for them, he took the call.

I feel moved talking to him. Guilt too. In that single phone call, I put all my valued relationships into context, and mentally discard so many people with whom I have just an acquaintance or a flimsy basis to proceed. I wouldn't have this clarity at home.

Nothing highlights this more than this following episode.

For three weeks we have been travelling. During this time, I genuinely have no idea of when we give the van back in Adelaide and when our flights to Hong Kong are. All I know is that I am back to the shallowness of work on Monday 18th August.

Today, we decide, as it is a practical day, that we will get everything out of the safe and sketch out a plan for the rest of the trip. Now the safe in the Maui is hidden at the back of the van and under what is either a seating arrangement or a double bed, depending on what you have done with it. We have chosen to travel the entire journey with the bed down, and chuck all the bags on it at night.

Hence, we only really want to get in the safe once. The kids are playing so we choose our moment to dismantle the van.

Now, like most people, our passwords or key codes are predictable. I think normally we would use Molly's birthday. So I punch it in, but I make a mistake and nothing happens. So, I have another go, at which point Nat starts screaming at me, that there are no second chances with this safe, that if you do not get it right first time, you can't ever get it right again. I tell her that this is nonsense, and that no safe in the world operates like this, and to stop being so pathetic. She doesn't seem to realise that every time she starts world war three, that everybody can hear her, especially all four vans parked less than ten metres from us. The number of times that we must have already driven off and people surely have said 'thank God they are gone' must be...well, at least one a day.

There is absolutely no sign of life in the safe. I do what most guys do in this situation. I yank it, I bash it, I try the code again, and then I give up. It's time to phone Maui again. My mind is working overtime now and I genuinely convince myself that we are not going to leave Australia at all at this rate. In my head, I am picturing racing to Canberra to get new passports or wherever it is you get them from. I am thinking cost. I am thinking panic. I am always thinking the worst in these situations.

Then a voice in my head says that surely this is not the first time that this happened to Maui. Even in a shit-hole like England they would have a plan B, and this is a great country where everything functions.

Oh you should hear the drama in Nat's voice on the phone to Maui. It is now the daily Maui call. They must be laughing their heads off about us on their internal email.

'Hey guys, watch out for this mad British family coming south – they've got disaster written all over them.'

Unfortunately for Maui, I am now about to blow one of their safety secrets, because they do have a plan B. It just happened to be rubbish.

Apparently there is always a master key hidden and tied to the pipes underneath the sink in the van. Well, on about the fifth search, it turns out that there is. I feel better now, calmed that this little drama is passing until....it doesn't work. The master key that opens everything is the wrong key. How useless is that? This is obviously another Cairns issue. You can't dispute the fact that they clearly overlooked trying both keys in preparing the van. Is this our fault for demanding a van change at the last minute when they tried to fob us off with an awning-less vehicle? Well, yes and no of course.

We now do not know when we leave Australia and we have no passports. We are fucked.

The Maui phone operative asks if we would like to go back to Maui in Brisbane. Er no – not going backwards and not driving into Brisbane. Not ever. There is only one possible solution. We will somehow find and call in at Maui Sydney in the next week or so.

Then the usual abuse follows...

'I want to go home and leave you, you can have everything. I've had enough, even the kids are killing me on this trip.'

Actually it was me that said that! Molly has developed a cocksure cheek and Sam has become a nutter in every games room on every campsite shouting 'die, die, die' at every video game. At home, he just doesn't play these things.

Then I wonder, still thinking of my Dad, what there actually is to go back for. Just my mate Stonesy over the road, Nat's family, and the money. That's it.

I feel at the lowest point. I can't bear the thought of going back on the radio. I dread the idea of opening the *Daily Mail* in the studio at 5am reading about some latest health and safety nonsense where taxi drivers are not being allowed to display tinsel in their cabs, or a father has been arrested for taking pictures of his son in the school play, or the EU says this man's ladder is one centimetre too short. I loathe the call centres ringing the home phone during the soaps. I am already angry about the clowns at work sending mass emails to all staff with subjects like 'has anyone seen my biro, it's my favourite one?' And worse, I absolutely detest every one of the ten people who feel the need to reply. Plus, I am very nervous about the safe.

It takes me three hours to just about get over it, and even then I don't have a plan. I will call a locksmith or buy a pickaxe or something. We have to get this safe open. Violence has to be considered.

Nat won't tell her parents for fear of panicking them. Suddenly the heart has gone out of the trip, though ironically it is the one thing that could prolong our stay.

We are booked on this site for three nights. I am not sure why. My *guess* is that we have twenty-four nights left and I am probably wrong, but it could be more, indeed many, many more if we don't get that thing open. I'm starting to panic about almost everything now. I try to focus my mind by totting up some receipts but they are all over the place and I can't believe the money we've spent. Ten dollars tonight on some nachos when we have chips and dip in the van twenty metres away from the restaurant is ridiculous.

Tomorrow – another big expense awaits as we head to Movieworld. I know in my heart that we will run into the Irish who said that they might be there. I bloody hope they are.

I await our next disaster. Stranded at the top of the highest ride in the world would seem a good place to put your money. On a positive note, I take a picture of my arse and show it to Nat. She still finds that funny. Maybe there is hope after all.

Day Twenty-Two

Of course, the kids want to go to Movieworld, Seaworld, and Dreamworld, but not only can you not do everything, nor do you want to! Our campsite is, of course, brilliantly positioned for all three, some fifteen minutes away, though that still doesn't stop us making a hash of things getting there, and in the cold light of day, it dawns on you, the Gold Coast is Benidorm.

We're at the park for half nine. I've learnt the routine by now, and effect it to everyone's annoyance. We make butties before we enter, or we don't go in at all. Clearly the ten dollar nachos are on my mind.

I seemed to have momentarily parked the safe scenario too, though I can't quite shake it off. What if nobody in Sydney can help? Should I phone ahead? Are we just drifting needlessly towards Adelaide beyond the point of no return? If we were to get proper help, surely the last possible port of call would be Sydney. After that, the world diminishes. It is making me tense.

The kids are hyper, and the first ride is *Batman*. At the entrance, there's the real car as used in the *Batman* movie. I have such poor knowledge of the movies despite having studied Italian cinema for a year at university, that I didn't even know that there had been a *Batman* movie out, nor did I believe that it was the genuine car. As if they would leave it here at a theme park! Come on, who are you kidding?

The ride meets the first criterion. Can Sam get on it?

As rides go, it is bollocks. It is one of these indoor rides where it is all in the motion and graphics and to get to the actual ride bit of the ride, you have to walk through about five different nancy-boy scenarios that wouldn't scare a newborn baby. I walk off shrugging, and get criticised for my cynicism straightaway.

I am thinking that, in a shock move, I may actually be in the mood for danger today, and right next to the ride is the Batwing Spaceshot, an altogether more exhilarating prospect, made worse by the fact that, as you stand in the queue, you watch everyone go before you and change your mind several times before you reach the front, and the speed of *that* can easily be increased if you listen out for the shouts of 'do we have a spare two on their own?'

I have never seen this before, and am impressed that you can ethically queue jump with help of the staff. Equally as you board they have built in boxes on the ride for your valuables, probably an Aussie thing for all the sunglasses that could fall off and injure the queue. A totally unique approach to a near-death experience! Very Australian. Molly accompanies me – she has no fear, and as with all these things it is all in the anticipation. On this occasion a fifteen minute wait and then literally less than ten seconds blasting at speed into the sky, followed by one bounce down and bounce back up and down again. Then, it's over.

And therein lies the secret of the theme park – six or seven great rides, each generally with a thirty minute wait, all over in seconds...quick turnaround and business keeps moving and you can make a day out of it.

In the interest of the Sam factor, next it is time for 4D cinema at the *Shrek* show. When I look back again at seeing Cinema 2000 at Thorpe Park in the early eighties, I can only laugh at how far multi-dimensional TV has progressed, yet curiously not really to the home TV.

Just like at Sentosa Island in Singapore, you're sitting there watching *Shrek* with big Timmy Mallet glasses on when suddenly you get a soaking. You can't get this on your plasma at home though can you? Nat thinks this is hysterical. I tend to see it as slightly damaging to my day's entertainment.

She once went on a freebie outside broadcast to the opening of Animal Kingdom in Florida, and this is the benchmark for her, and even though, this is no Disney, by midday she is already trying to panic us into position for the 'legendary' parade.

I am eyeing up the Spiderman ride which seems to disappear through a wall. I am unsure whether to risk decapitation, so instead I take an amazing photo of the exact moment that the corkscrew-like rollercoaster goes through the side of the building, knowing that I can claim that I was on the ride should I bottle it, in the same way that back at Noosa, I built those racing cars out of sand on the beach.

Instead we take the family decision to queue for the *Scooby Doo* ride. This is the longest queue of the day and we pass the time by watching a feature about the making of the *Scooby Doo* movie....again and again and again. I think we have seen it four times by the time we reach the entrance. Again, I didn't even know that there was or had been a movie.

Now, this ride looks innocuous. After all Sam can get on. But I think it is the most lethal of the day. Firstly I am too big physically for this, I am sure. I can feel my weight steering the little Scooby car, and the very skinny Sam crashing into me all the way. Secondly, it is inside, so naturally, mostly in the dark, and this means that you don't see the twists and turns, nor do you see the height, and I swear that if I hadn't ducked it would be all over for me. However, the key ingredient is that we discover here that Australia has a passion for reverse rollercoasters, that just stop and then send you hurtling backwards. I have never experienced this before in my life, and when you don't know that it is coming, it is a shocker, whether you are five or thirty-seven. Molly loved it. Sam was not impressed.

It seems the log flume in the wild west section of the park also fancies the 'spin you round and send you into reverse' technique, except that this is worse – or better depending on your viewpoint – as you are doing it in water and believe me, if you ever find yourself on this ride, only a second or third go will show that position in the boat is key to your enjoyment and wetness!

This is a brilliant ride that leaves you soaked in a much more fun way than a few squirts at the *Shrek* show, and of course culminates with a massive descent into the water. Again, it is not the drop, or the resulting splash, it is the anticipation at the top as you hang over agonisingly waiting to take the plunge. When you have your fifth or sixth ride on the log flume, it is only then that you master the cool, laid-back pose for the rip-off souvenir photos that appear so quickly in the shop as soon as you exit the ride. We don't buy any on this occasion.

Whoever was the first person to recognise that you could only exit a ride by doing so through a gift shop has made zillions for the theme park industry, and I bet never received a word of thanks.

The much touted parade is tame – a few characters wander Main Street and wave a lot. The Austin Powers is poor, and in this respect, it is a poor man's Disney. Deep down, I think it is an excuse to sell balloons that will blow away and fizzy drinks that will make your kids obese.

Strangely though for an eight year old, Molly Horne has never had a fizzy drink in her life. She hates the stuff, even though she has never touched it, and while Sam spends his pennies downing pop after pop, Moll fulfils a Horne holiday tradition of getting her hair braided, and she looks cute too, though doubtless school will demand it be cut out on her return.

At 3.30pm, disaster strikes. From nowhere the heavens open, and I don't mean some tame little English shower when cricketers come off the pitch for days, I mean torrential rainforest weather. We get soaked just legging it to the van, and the whole world decides that this is the cue to leave. Nat is almost in tears – she's left the washing out at the campsite.

There is no talking to her when she is in this mood. So I don't, and when she tells me that she knows the fifteen minute route back, I turn the sat-nav off only for her to miss the turning, turn off the engine, storm out of the car, demanding that I drive in the downpour only to change her mind, before she takes us through every back road back to the site only to turn up an hour later. Remember, that's a fifteen minute journey.

She is distraught at the washing, angry too that nobody took it in for her. This sets us back time-wise and financially too. When you are on a journey like ours, you do the chores when you can, after a long drive. You don't have time to waste to do them twice. We are flooded in the pitch and that brings problems too. You normally have to do most tasks outside of the van, but of course, you are always in and out of it and that means you take the flood into the van. You get to a point where you are so soaked that you don't feel it anymore, and you laugh at it. I have no choice but to make a mad dash out of the campsite and across the highway to a parade of shops in search of a brolly – well, we didn't think we would need one in Australia.

Crucially too I pick up cartons of Stanley as I know that we are out of wine and when we have made some sort of sense of our bogged world tonight, we will have to drink the night away. I must have run two miles in the most lashing rain I can remember. I am drenched but I somehow look a hero, as though I was doing something helpful in Nat's eyes after having made the foolish mistake of allowing it to rain!

By 8pm we are absolutely exhausted. Soaked and exhausted. The van is a mess, soup is all we can muster for tea and the electricity looks suspiciously dangerous in the side of the van nestled in a flap outside which doesn't even shut. We have nowhere to put the wet clothes, and we are still booked in for another night. Our plans have been thrown to sea, and this, all in Surfers Paradise.

And we didn't see the Irish either. I think they truly are gone now. This campsite, as much as I really like it, has brought us bad news. Only a very loving cuddle from Molly at bedtime makes the day worthwhile, especially as I thought she had been slipping away on this trip into a frumpy teenager.

Day Twenty-Three

It is still wet in the morning. You can look at the sky and convince yourself that after the rain there must be shine, but I could only see doom ahead. I make a carpet of a spare bedding sheet in the van, so that anyone going in and out doesn't bring too much filth in with them. This is tricky, of course, because, life on the road is a process of pack up and go, unpack and live, and that means while we were sleeping the four chairs and fold-up table outside took a battering too, despite being under the shelter of our lopsided awning.

The morning, therefore, is slow.

I think we are both in two minds about what to do, though really we are of the same. We don't want to be sticking around here if it is going to pour down. Rain means road in our world.

I turn on the radio. It seems that the Pope is heading to Sydney. I find this quite exciting and amusing too, not being religious. I think nothing more of it because suddenly there is a scream from the bed above the driver's seat in the van as the same little gorgeous Molly Horne whom I was cuddling last night has kicked her brother Sam in the head. Another day, another disaster.

It really was classic brotherly-sisterly love but it starts Nat off for the day, demanding that a head injury means hospital. I really can't be bothered with this drama, and suggest that we wait. Where the hell are we going to find the hospital, and do we really want to spend half a day sitting there waiting to be discharged?

Surely it will pass, won't it? This is my standard response, you understand, to medical dramas.

Molly – if you read this some years later – you were very upset by the way, and I know that Sam *was* being a monster.

Finally, and reluctantly, with bruised boy in tow, we push off to Surfers Paradise for a drive, parking up just by the beach. There is a small commotion just a hundred metres away. I have noticed that this tends to happen in Australia and suddenly a crowd is formed with nobody really knowing what they are looking at. We join in and, in the choppiest of waters, point the camera seawards despite having no idea why.

Then a few moments later, hundreds of metres out to our left, we can see what all the fuss is about and what a fuss too, as a school of whales are making their way up north caressing the ocean, then disappearing, re-emerging seconds after, before teasing again with their disappearance. This is a truly wonderful moment, and how lucky are all Aussies that they can just run into random acts of wildlife, animal life and sealife while just going about their business. They are blessed really but I think they know it. You begin to understand that 'no worries' is not a cliché, simply a permanent state of being.

If I drive into Newcastle, I get the bloody Angel of the North. If I drive into Manchester, well there's nothing at all. Wander along the beachfront and you happen to wander into gorgeous whales. I am truly impressed, though my Gold Coast pleasure ends there as we head in from the beach to the concrete jungle that it is the vilest place in Australia. Benidorm indeed, but without the worst Scousers, Geordies, Brummies and Cockneys bringing it down. Buildings are sky high, shops are tacky. What am I to say to Molly and Sam as we stand in awe and disbelief outside of *Condom King*?

Having arrived here with a mental state that all Aussies were ignorant and chauvinistic but having learnt quickly that everyone is your mate and the culture is the richest in the world, I do not expect to find myself outside a shop full of johnnies. I can only blame the English.

Nat and I have exactly the same thought: We live not far from a woman who was once our friend but proceeded to get horribly drunk and make a very offensive error in our house, for which she refused to apologise. She is a loud Scouser, with an apartment or villa somewhere near Benidorm and she seems to sell things from her house, the origin of which I cannot be sure. In the period after said event, many of our mutual friends unbelievably ceased to talk to Nat.

From our point of view, it looked like some backstabbing stirring had gone on. It was definitely clear to me however that some of the wannabe wags in the world of playground politics just didn't have the bottle to stand up to this woman for fear of social exclusion. She is the kind of woman who natters at the school gate for ten minutes, while her kid runs off in the playground, only to let out a deafening scream for him moments later that echoes around the school when she has finished her networking. Know the type?

We both agreed. She would love this place.

After an hour Nat and I both know we have to get out of here. Eighteen year olds on their surfing gap year may find this staggering. We however, have a bit too much class. We decide to make a punt for it. Let's hit the road and get as far as we can. But first we have to get back to camp and pack up all the stuff that we have left out in the wet, which means we'll be travelling with all that damp stuff in the van.

Infuriatingly, we can't even make the simple journey back.

'We did not cross this bridge coming,' Nat roars.

We seem unable to retrace our steps on just the shortest of journeys. Plus, it turns out that with all this rain around, we've been driving with all the flaps out on the side of the van. These give various access points to the hose, the toilet, the waste, the electricity. Shit, the electricity!

'That could kill us, ' she screams.

Whatever, love.

After an eternity we are on our way, checking out early. We write off the money that we had spent on an extra night, and drive down the Gold Coast but just slightly in from the beach road. It remains vile. For me, you would have to be of low social standing, a property developer, or a belief that this really is the greatest surf in the world to stay even five minutes. It's just not for us. Sorry.

Our journey is changing all the time in front of us, and you can see this through simple items such as the quality of the road to roadside branding. I think I prefer, on instinct, from where we have come to where we are heading.

We pass another Big 4 site. It is difficult, even with a map to gauge which Big 4 site is the right one for you, geographically and socially, until you get there. We learnt this, of course, at Hervey Bay.

Some sites are written up the same but have vastly contrasting facilities; some like the Coconut in Cairns are simply fantastic for the kids. However, Hastings Point is not one of them this time around. As we fly past, we notice that it is Priscilla night. Ok, so the entertainment is hotting up and the Aussies really do like it in drag. At this stage I'll not be encouraging Sam to wear women's clothes. That pleasure can wait.

We just push on, only conscious of the time and the light really. It *hadn't* been our intention to stop at the next Big 4 site but we're nervous about our ultimate choice because even though the star ratings are a bit of a farce, almost you suspect self-awarded, the Ballina Lakeside Holiday Park doesn't have any at all.

It is about an hour up the Gold Coast and probably three days from Sydney. It is also a fiddle to find, unless we have gone the wrong way. Furthermore, we have crossed the border into New South Wales. Not that it is a chore but we are starting to break the back of our trip.

The site is good, with a beautiful lake, and eighteen holes of bonkers crazy golf. I am reminded too that I have a date with the Great North Run two months from now and it is at least a month since I have run. There is a gym here, which I choose to ignore despite a text from my mate Harty informing me that he has just bashed out a 10k in forty-five minutes and the bastard isn't even running the race. I mention this only to underline the fact that the goalposts of our reality have moved. Despite the rows, and the daily disasters, I've forgotten all about the shit, the very functional things and the petty nonsense that controls my life. Routine is no more and I'm watching my kids grow and be at one with nature – unless they are killing that nature as Sam has just done with a mozzie whose demise was greeted with those video game words 'die, die, die.'

Nat and I are having a laugh too. I just don't tell you about the good bits.

Unfortunately, as is proving to be a regular event, we don't get to appreciate fully this cute little site. On days when you have to drive, you drive hard from first light to last, so the campsite could be the Ritz but essentially it is only a safe place to park, before you move on again. All that really matters here is how quickly we can get dry and if we can get the washing done again.

Curiously we notice a New South Wales oddity. For the first time, we have to pay to use the camp barbecue. It's only a dollar, but it throws us. It seems a cheek, but I am also imagining the nightmare ahead of always having to keep change for every site. If you had been travelling the other way round to us, as I am sure most people do, I guess you would think it was payday when you got to Queensland and all the barbies are free. Molly has joined me at the cook area tonight for the usual dinner with added broccoli thrown in - guilt, I think, at the total lack of variety in our diet.

Before we can cook though, we have to get the change from reception and it is here that I got to the bottom of the zero stars rating in the Big 4 book. There seems to be some politics at play.

The owners of the Ballina Lakeside Holiday Park have pulled out of Big 4 and are switching their allegiances to another, known as Top Tourist Parks, yet because of something to do with print deadlines, still find themselves in our Big 4 book, though without a classification.

I am not sure if it is a punishment for leaving that it has no stars next to it, for surely, if it is in the book you would want to promote it, wouldn't you? Something doesn't add up, and it occurs to me that this is the first time that anyone has spoken disparagingly of the Big 4 organisation. But then, that *would* occur to me as that is all we know, of course. The receptionist seems to be expressing some sort of disappointment with the whole Big 4 thing and offers us the Yellow Top Tourist Parks guide. It is clear that there have been issues.

Nat suggests that we don't always have to stay on the Big 4, but even though, for me, there is no defined brand in that all sites are vastly different, there is some sort of element of comfort in the brochure and the map which is guiding us across Australia and I am happy to stick with it. It is also a much easier book to navigate than the Top Tourist Parks guide. I am fascinated to know what Ballina's beef is with Big 4. It has, I suppose, given us another option.

With the cloud clearing and a Gladstone type sky forming, we realise that the deluge of the last twenty four hours is passing and tomorrow will be a beautiful day. It is great that you can go to bed knowing with total certainty what the weather will bring. We decide to make the twenty kilometre trip down the coast to the legend that is Byron Bay.

Day Twenty-Four

Byron Bay is one of those places that I have heard a lot about but I am not sure why. I convince myself in the end that it is where *Home and Away* was set, or based on. I don't know if this is true, of course, but it is now a fact in *my* mind. I am also thinking hippies and wacky-backy.

We're up early and drive the coast, regretting instantly that we had only decided to come here by accident. If it hadn't been for the downpour at Surfers Paradise, we would have stayed on the Gold Coast even longer and just driven straight past Byron Bay. A bonus therefore, by default.

We also regret that we didn't abandon the van and stay in Byron last night, but that is the major downside of travelling with your house on your back. It is like being a snail, only quicker.

We park high up – there's little choice – just past a tiny, almost miniscule, 'box'. It turns out to be the primary school!

The path down to the beach is the stuff of adventures. In fact all beaches should by law have paths through woodland from which you emerge to see golden sands. There's no point just seeing a beach, you have to physically discover it, to appreciate it.

This really is surf country. Forget Surfers Paradise. This is paradise for surfers. All ages from toddlers to pensioners are riding the waves. Nat is bemoaning that she didn't get a wetsuit in Noosa. She'll never use it again anyway, but for a moment she is lost in the Byron Bay culture. She is also trying to tell me that if we just climb up to this lighthouse to our right we will be at the most eastern point of Australia.

It is one of those ascents that looks five minutes away but will probably take two hours, and I am not sufficiently fussed to knock off that particular tourist achievement. So what if we are at the eastern most point of the country? What does that mean? If you're Captain Cook, it might be interesting, but it doesn't do anything for me. I am not that kind of tourist. So, you make all that effort to get there, say you've done it, and then you climb back down again. I would rather just recall that Byron Bay has a very nice feel to it indeed.

Could you live here? Probably not. It strikes me as the kind of place that you pass through and leave with happy memories. Growing up in that primary school, I wonder how many kids have stared out the window and thought that there must be a life beyond here. Indeed there is kids, follow me, because we are on our way in that direction.

After our two hour stay at the Bay, Nat tells me as she always does about half an hour after we have left, that she would have liked to have stayed there longer, had some lunch or something, and that I am always rushing her. She does have a brain and a mouth but infuriates me that she is the classic after the horse has bolted woman. Or are they all like that?

It is too late to turn back now though, not that we are sure where we are going. Coffs Harbour looks favourite, and a reasonable size on the map. It sounds cute enough. Why not?

We hit the radio, for only about the third time. Sure, we've tried but we've hardly picked up anything apart from news of the Pope and I so want to be away from the medium. We're listening to a station on 104.7 and they are broadcasting The Grafton Cup, whatever that is.

They are doing a phone-in on what are the best things about horse-racing. I think this is possibly the dullest thing that I have ever heard so we turn it off again.

I glance in the mirror, and note that Sam has his 'I Love Wally' t-shirt on. My goodness me – The Great Barrier Reef seems ages ago, in time, in culture and in landscape.

We pass through a town called Maclean. It has a picture of a kilt and a bagpipe, and dubs itself 'The Scottish Town In Australia.' That is all it says. As though it were a selling point but leaving so many questions.

I mean, we are not even near anywhere here. Miles from Brisbane, miles from Sydney, and seemingly the only man who left his mark here was a German called Johann Schaefer. So, not Scottish at all then.

And in that fine example lies one of the conundrums of Australia – that every town, no matter how small, boasts its heritage in some sort of museum, yet, when pushed, its heritage is minimal, built on an overblown legend, or in this case, a total mystery. I can only assume, and applaud, that part of the great Aussie pride and culture comes from government funding making sure that everybody is on the map. Apart from the Aboriginals, of course.

I am further amused at the Grafton service station. Nat confirms that this is the best food in the world. It is to die for. Here, of all places.

Yes – we are on the road to Sydney, and a way back to Brisbane, but we *are* in the middle of nowhere. Yes – truckies and a few weirdoes like us pull up, but who has that amount of self-belief that they can build the best damn service station and food in the world all the way out here? If it is that good, park an hour out of Sydney.

Yet – it *is* amazing – and I think we could learn from that, as perhaps we can from Maclean, that if you take pride in the small details, and treat business the same whether you are catering for one or one thousand, then the world will be a better place.

Either way, Grafton has significance for us. Coming towards us, and to our amusement, is a convoy of Mauis. There are seven of them, and in that moment we realise that not only are we going the wrong way to everyone else, but that even with Sydney, Melbourne, and Adelaide still ahead, in many ways we have left civilisation, and what I mean by that of course, are the bits in between the cities, or nothing, as I refer to them.

We haven't seen a Maui in ages, and I think this sighting of seven underlines to us how much we miss the Irish and took them for granted. Something changed at Brisbane too. I saw it in a yuppie by the pool unable to remove himself from his mobile and wrecking everyone's holiday by doing business while his kids splashed at everyone, out of control. The city folk were coming.

There could be mass-murderers in those Mauis, but they are one of us, so we wave at them all. Then Nat reminds me of the guy we met in Cairns who told us about relocations and had gone into Maui to see if they had any. These are people who drive vans like ours back from one end of the country to another. They get an allowance, fuel, and insurance, and have a certain number of days to get the van back. The seven in convoy were either very good friends, or were relocating. Right after they pass, a massive truck hurtles our way and flashes his lights, toots his horn, and beams his redneck smile at Nat – presumably because she is driving and not me.

I am not amused, though obviously she is loving the attention. So, it is Grafton where she acquired her new nickname. This is the significance. I was now on holiday with the trucker fucker.

We're not sure where to pitch up for the night but we have plenty of options. Now, the Big 4 book has two Coffs Harbour sites, so we try the first at Emerald Beach. Again, it appears to be in the middle of a street, and there is a charge for looking around. Sod that, we just wander in anyway. It is described as '...beachfront indulgence, with amazing beach walks...spoil yourself with first-class dining at one of the local restaurants....the beautiful Coffs coast...blah blah..'

Sounds great hey?

Well, I wandered around and assumed that I must have the wrong site. Oh yes, there is a cute little bit at the back where it cuts through to the beaches, but I found it too gravelly again, and low on green grass, nor could I see these amazing local restaurants. Within five minutes, we were off again, heading now into Coffs.

I consult the Tourist Parks book that we picked up at Ballina, and as I find the four and a half star Park Beach Holiday Park on Ocean Parade, I am already glad that Trucker Fucker has just in that instant driven past it. I consult one of our Australia guide books, as I can't believe that this is the esteemed Coffs Harbour, so warmly are they all talking it up. It looks to me like a scummy end of Southport.

We drive the length of Ocean Parade, and then back again, and by now, TF and I both know instinctively when we don't fancy it and so Coffs Harbour comes and goes in a split too.

Once you dismiss one town, you have to look at the light again. We simply now have no choice but to stop at the next Big 4, whether we want to or not. The sat-nav says that we will arrive just before dark falls. We had naturally assumed that we would stay at Coffs, and would have plenty of time but now have placed ourselves under extra pressure by trying to race on to another site, and the kids have had enough of the drive too. I know it has been a long one because *Shrek* is getting its third play of the day in the back, and for the third time the surround sound has just belted out this enormous horn from the soundtrack that I am convinced is a roadtrain coming our way, and for third time today I have panicked Nat into swerving the Maui.

So, what is there to know in advance about Nambucca Heads? It is an afterthought in the guidebooks. It doesn't count. It's a no-go, an insignificance. Who would want to stop there? I can tell you now, even though this book of course is no travel guide, the Big 4 site at Nambucca Heads is the best-kept secret of camping your way down the coast of Australia. Miss Coffs

Harbour every single time, and stop here. This is what camping and campervanning always intended you to discover.

Like most of these places, there is a bit of hell involved in getting there, namely the world's greatest hill, which is fine on descent, but already Nat and I have no idea how we will climb it to get out of town tomorrow. I exaggerate not a jot. This is steep.

Scary and great fun going down but your only hope for going back up is the belief that you can't have been the first Maui to attempt it.

At the base of this mountain of a road, is a cute little campsite. Nowadays, all campsites have all the mod-cons and that campfire, twig-based campsite mentality, like in ye olden days, is rare to find. For that reason alone, get yourself to Nambucca. It is such a simple site, but so wonderful, and with such a kind welcoming owner.

I salute you Mr Watson. You win our award for just being lovely. On check-in he talks with such pride about how he had done the place up. We knew that his life savings had gone into it, and that everyone on his campsite was now his family. Yet, what he leaves us to discover is why this campsite is brilliant, and proves that your star rating can be determined by many different things. This is rated at four but I give it five, and pound for pound, I name this the best one night stop in Australia.

The key is what lies behind the trees that give the campsite its forest-like quality, and that surround its perimeter. In the trees, are several paths. Where do they take you? To the most gorgeous, deserted beach just ten metres the other side, that nobody saw coming. There wasn't even a hint of it. I found happiness today and its name is Nambucca. Genuinely, I am nearly crying at how perfect, how dreamlike, at how this ticks the 'this is what it's all about' factor. The reality is that you can define tourist star quality only when you just sit there and stare. Nambucca Heads is the ultimate sit and stare. You can take in the beauty, you can be alone with your thoughts, you can try romance, you can cook on the beach, and you can watch your kids running up and down, writing in the sand. Star quality is not a Taj Mahal or an Eiffel Tower, it is how a Taj or an Eiffel make you feel. Well, I feel great. Tonight I have fallen in love with Nambucca Heads.

Day Twenty-Five

Last night took its usual turn of events. Food, alcohol, music, drunken texts, Nat's daily moan about the towels still being damp from the morning, followed by the nightly call home to Nanny and Grandad.

I definitely rang or texted Harty, Stonesy, Findlay, Lisa and PC World. Now, I know that these people don't mean much to you, but they represent the very dynamic of the drunk texter. People I love (Harty and Stonesy.) People I feel bad that I haven't been in touch with (Findlay – twice recovered from cancer and then decided to run around the world.) People I know who are in the country (Lisa, an ex radio co-host and about to visit her sister in Sydney) and people that I need (PC World – my laptop is buggered.)

I remember vaguely Molly pointing out that the movie *Finding Nemo* is a lie because it makes out that the Great Barrier Reef is near Sydney. God, even I know that now. And I remember what Nat was moaning about – that these vans could only have been designed by a man because the travel plug doesn't fit in the socket, whereas if a woman had designed it, the contents of the van would have included an outdoor patio heater.

Having left very little time to make food plans, and some of the restaurants in town looked awesome, we went lazy and ordered a pizza. It wasn't the best, and we are all feeling a bit delicate over it this morning. I have a sore throat too which I know has come from alcohol.

We've been here at Nambucca too small a time. I can't leave without insisting that we have a bacon butty on the beach, and head down through to the tracks to take one last look at the beach. It is as good as it looked last night. Calm, beautiful and mine. It captures the very essence of the limitless ocean. You don't stand here without wondering what on earth lies beyond the horizon. I wonder, will I ever see Nambucca Heads again?

From here on, it is all about Sydney. We probably have two days travel before we get there. It's definitely time to do some miles, and to start thinking about the safe.

We ring Maui to tell them that we are coming and I speak to a guy called Sam who is very helpful and says that I need to speak to Frank, who will be in on Sunday. I said that we will probably be in Sydney tomorrow, but Sam says Sunday will be best and Frank will be around. Frank evidently is God.

I'm driving today – something of a rarity. Nat is in cracking form. We've been at it like rabbits too in a very casual manner. It is this that leads me to believe that she is a stress-head who can't handle the heat of the road. We've driven most of the way so far without a care in the world, no real regard for researching the local law of the land – like speed limits.

Suddenly New South Wales has a big speed cameras thing going on. They were so casual in Queensland, that I am very much of the mind that I will go at my own speed thank you very much.

Having just about taken 'Mount Nambucca,' with the aid of a massive run-up to get up the hill like a jumbo on the runway, our next significant town is Kempsey. I pause here for a moment to remark that one shop, in particular catches my eye. It is called Kempsey Firearms and Camping.

I so want to stop and observe its clientele for the day. You either go in for one or the other, don't you, and who wanders in with a shopping list of firearms? I feel that I have no choice but to stop the van, exit swiftly amongst the traffic, and proceed to order four patio heaters, and an AK-47.

We're having such a laugh in the van. Nat, I know, feels superior, by being my passenger. I play my trump card, when I see a road sign marked 'U Turn Bay'

'Funny, that's inland, isn't it?' I offer.

'Mm, that's odd.'

She consults the map, with a really studious, confused look. A minute later still nothing from the queen of map-reading, the silence interrupted only by me wetting myself laughing.

'U turn bay – perhaps for turning round?'

It's one nil to me. We have got so used to every place name being so literal, that she took it thus. She has yet to question why there is a Bald Knob in New South Wales, however. Little does she know there was also one in Queensland. You don't like to ask, do you?

I am on a roll here, imitating her driving, playing the role of the dippy blonde Trucker Fucker, screaming at an imaginary me for my lack of directions, effing and blinding at the sat-nav for its silence when you most need it, demanding diet coke as I drive as she does this all the time.

This is payback, and I refuse to let her drive to make amends. I inform her bluntly that she has lost her seat of power at the wheel, and that I am now in charge. By a mile, it is the funniest journey so far – what this trip was meant to be.

We're heading to Port Stephens, bypassing Port Macquarie, where there is also a Big 4. Oddly, Port Stephens isn't in the index at the back of our main map, and of the three sites available, all are listed as being in the Port Stephens region, which seems to cover a heck of a long way round the coast. I am sure we have picked the wrong one to stop at.

You know sometimes that you just sense that you are driving way out of your way. We weren't just hugging the coastline, we were almost in the water, and the fact that we were heading to the Big 4 Soldiers Point Holiday Park, at Soldiers Point on Soldiers Point Road should give anybody with a vague sense of geography or history the nod and the wink that we were clearly on the way to some lookout point from days gone by, where a garrison stood right on the tip of the coast, looking out yonder the horizon. This said to me, cold and wind, and a journey which we didn't need to make to a town that might not be as important as it once was.

The brochure built it up, of course, promising sand dunes, and a beach three hundred metres away. This happens to be true, though there end the attractions. The site is functional, and right next to a bowling club!

Crazy, OCD Sam is delighted, however, that he seems to have all free twelve playstations to himself.

It *is* cold – I was right, and the bay *is* cute, but that is it for this time of year. There are some obscene mansions being built, which clearly is a good sign that this is the place to be. They back onto the beach, and must be a dream when the sun is out. Today though, Port Stephens is closed for winter.

Indeed I am the only knob at the barbecue, and the irony of me cooking up summer food in my mankiest big winter jumper is not lost on me. I have taken to shoving bacon on the barbecue to vary the taste. To save time in the morning, I am also cooking a load of the stuff the night before so we can eat on the run in the morning. It works a treat.

I am absolutely whacked though, after my first proper *proper* drive nearly three weeks into Oz. I pass out drunk on the booze, the food, and the miles at around 8.30pm, after yet more 'life' texts with Harty.

We have both been forming a millionaire's exit plan from our current monotonies on the back of beer mats every time that we go to the pub. We simply have to regain control of our lives. I am hoping this trip and this book are my starting point. I am not sure why every evening now ends with text tennis. I *am* having the time of my life, but I miss a couple, and only a couple, of truly great friends, and I guess I want to share it with them. Less importantly, I also shag Nat senseless.

Day Twenty-Six

Today's entry should be called the road to Sydney. We're going to get up at the crack and go for it. Except we awake at 8.42 in a panic. I am first up, and the woman that was in my bed last night is unrecognisable this morning. So I sent her packing and told Nat she could come back after all. Boom Boom!

No – we've been at it like when we just met, when after about two weeks, Nat accidentally left her phone connected to her mum in Liverpool, while I was explaining to her why she had to move in with me. 1996 was certainly a long time ago, and I was a much kinder person.

She has flipped this morning because at eighteen minutes to nine, she doesn't think we can be off our pitch by ten. Women, eh?

We make it with four minutes to spare. As though all the pitches were really going to get snapped up today in a wintry Port Stephens.

Do you see how right I was to make those bacon butties last night? I point out to Nat that she had called me a knob last night for being so organised but today I am Bob Geldof in a famine.

As is the norm on our overnight stops, we tend to depart with the words 'well, that was Port Stephens.' I am sufficiently trained now in how this country works that I reckon it is a safe bet to assume that Stephens was probably Lord Stephens, and a buddy of Captain Cook. There is also a port. On reflection, I would have gone with Port Stephens too.

Now, yesterday afternoon, when we were definitely heading out of the way to make base for the night, it didn't really occur to us that it is when you retrace your steps that you realise what a time irritation that becomes, and as we head towards Sydney we could not have picked a worse day to arrive. The Pope is in town.

But first work calls, and I don't mind as I know that I am being smart. I haven't come all this way not to don my work hat for a tiny moment. I simply have to get a photo of the sign for Newcastle. My work brain tells me that I will need this for newspaper columns on my return, for marketing the book locally, hey just for fun.

We now have the ridiculously naff scenario of me slowing down on the Pacific Highway just so we can pull up for the photo of the road sign for Newcastle. You can't think of these things after the event, can you? We decline to take the turning for the 'Northeast' and from here it is still 169ks to Sydney. But why are there so many places on this stretch that have borrowed their names from where I work? How come? The northeast hasn't traditionally travelled so I find this staggering. Unless there were a lot of cons from there. That, I could believe. Stockton, Wallsend, Seaham, Gosforth, Scarborough... they're all here.

Either way I can't believe we're in touching distance of the great Sydney.

We're filled with such tremendous anticipation. Sydney is clearly one of the most photographed cities in the world. You feel like you know it before you are there. I am sure that you never forget the first time that you see the Bridge.

I always used to advise people wanting to see Venice to get the train in from Padua, where I lived briefly in 1991. Because you need to arrive.

Don't fly straight to Venice. It is all in the wonder of seeing it unravel before your eyes, approaching it. I feel sure the Bridge is the same.

There's much to admire on the approach too, notably the

spectacular views across the Hawkesbury River at Mooney Mooney, at Peats Ridge too, and before that about ninety minutes out, the absolute rollercoaster of a hill at Wyong. The Maui wasn't built for Wyong but like so many of these approaches and as with Nambucca before, there is only one way in, and we can't be the first.

The sat-nav says we are heading for a 12.25 arrival, but as we all know, it has been wrong before. From way out, we keep seeing signs about the Bridge being closed because of the Pope's visit. Stupidly, as people always do in these situations, we still drive in the vague direction of it.

We have decided to head to Maui first, rather than the campsite or Sydney itself. Let's sort this safe thing out before anything else. I figure it can't be difficult to find the Maui as most of them are obviously just across from the airports for people who want to pick up their transport after landing, yet somehow Nat manages to improvise a diversion and sends us, first onto a toll road, then in totally the wrong direction. In so doing, and in totally unsatisfactory circumstances we see the Bridge for the first time.

We're just past Bobbin Head, off Victoria Road but it is way over to the left, and we have no way of getting near it. I tell myself it looks fantastic then I tell myself that it is only a bridge. I am certain of one thing. People in Newcastle upon Tyne talk about the iconic image of the Tyne Bridge, as if it is all about everything that it symbolises rather than the beauty of the bridge per se. Well, it is clear from this far out that the Tyne Bridge is a load of old rubbish compared to this masterpiece.

I hate to break it to the people of Newcastle – yours is crap in comparison. It doesn't mean that I don't love the Tyne Bridge, but when you have two of the same to compare, and yours comes off worst, yours automatically becomes rubbish.

We're heading towards Epping – nowhere near where we should be. We are so lost, it's unbelievable. It is time to place our umpteenth phone call to Maui, who tell us simply to head to Mascot.

Nat, by chance and miracle, having casually ignored two automatic tollbooths that she is planning to distance herself from on the grounds of ignorance, spectacularly navigates us in the direction of Mascot only to think that the job is done and loses interest and send us on some coastal road out of town way past the airport. We are lost again.

Doubly frustrating, we can see the Qantas planes parallel to us so we must be near. In the process we have gone under the water through the tunnel and emerged at the feet of the Sydney Opera House, which like the Bridge, I do not want to see for the first time in this manner.

I am so frustrated with the navigation that I am starting to do illegal turns just to try and get back on track. The sat-nav has totally ceased to function. Even that has given up on our driving. Finally at half three we arrive at Maui.

It is always the way that when you think you have pots of time in this van, you get robbed of it. Three hours ago we were ten minutes from the city centre. By late afternoon, we have been round the houses and have just two hours light left.

The Maui depot is not easy to find – that much is true. Yet we couldn't have made a worse stab at finding it, and when we finally pull up, we don't know how lucky we are. The world famous Frank, whom we had been told to come and see tomorrow, is just about to leave and hadn't been in tomorrow after all, nor was he going to be in for the next ten days. While we're waiting, we get accosted by some neurotic woman who seems to have brought her Britz van in because the seatbelts are strangling her kids. Get a grip, woman. Some people will complain about anything.

As it happens, we have had the same problem, but it is not worth wasting half a day trying to find the depot on the same day that the Pope turns up just to get it fixed.

Sam and Frank are very helpful. Frank is too helpful, in fact, insisting on making good everything whether it needed it or not. In the process he wrecks our awning, leaving it half hanging off. Sam sorts us out a new DVD player, but still leaves us crippled with no option of getting past episode one of any box set DVD, and believe me this is important on these road trips. There is not a DVD remote in the depot that can help us. Frank looks at my toilet in disgust, not because we are vile as a family, but because he is now educating me on its use for the first time telling me stuff that the guys in Cairns just never even mentioned.

In fact, his depot has hundreds of everything, making the Cairns branch look like a PO Box – that being the solitary reason I pose for a snap next to twenty abandoned safes.

He calls the guys in Cairns cowboys, and tells me that he is the company. I dread to think what the Darwin Maui is like.

We are lucky that we came today, he reminds us. It is his sister's birthday tomorrow. (He is an Italian immigrant so you can only imagine what a party that will be, plus the Pope is in town so they are probably going for it.) I protest that Sam had told me to come tomorrow, and he replies,

'I know.'

And then there's the safe. Oh yes the safe. I have no idea why I worried for a week. It is all over in two minutes. It turns out that the cowboys in Cairns hadn't popped the batteries into the inside of the safe so it was never going to work anyway. This is very bad, in that it has the ability to shaft many people, but very good too in that it blows Nat out of the water with her 'get the code wrong once and you're buggered' theory.

Frank has a master key that saves the day, and gives us his spare master key, should we have trouble again. I dread to think how they keep track of all these parts floating around the country. He's clearly counting on me to be honest when we get to Adelaide and hand the whole thing back.

Anyway we're fixed and we have totally wasted the day. Our first glimpse of Sydney is unsatisfactory. We spent it in the depot at Maui. My advice to anybody thinking of replicating our trip is that if you have a problem, and nobody else can help you, call Maui in Sydney and ask for Frank. He is the A-Team.

On departure, Sam – that's Maui Sam– gives us an excellent print out of how to get to Narrabeen which is where our campsite is for the next few nights. Of course, by the first corner, some two hundred metres from the depot, we have already gone the wrong way.

On the way out of town, all we can see are that the streets are lined with God's disciples, in their vast numbers, all making their way into town to see the Pope. I can't help but wonder what kind of safety record the Sydney Harbour Bridge has. I mean, one errant bomb on today of all days and we're all done for, and the way that this trip is panning out, I knew that we would get caught up in it.

Before we can even contemplate checking in, I insist on the obligatory stop at Woolies. This is a disaster. Just some five kilometres or so from our site, it is the tightest car park yet, and Nat can't get in or out. I am the only one amused at the forty car tailback that she has created, just so I could buy some prawns to make a surf'n'turf.

Finally, finally, finally, as night falls at gone 5pm we arrive at the Big 4 Sydney Lakeside Holiday Park in North Narrabeen, about 24k out of town. It has been an exhausting day, but even though we have done so much already, surely this is where the adventure begins.

We're all stiff, tired and hungry. We just want to pitch up, cook and eat, so Nat goes to check in. And then nothing, she doesn't re-appear.

Well, the office is only fifteen metres away, and you just keep thinking that she'll be out in a second surely, but still nothing. It turns out that the God squad are on our site, some three hundred Italian pilgrims in a big tent all wanting to see Pope Benedict in Sydney. All, that is except the chief priest, who has just collapsed in reception, and been given mouth to mouth in front of Nat. I can only think that this string of bad luck has to catch up with us at some point, and maybe that the Lord is not as talented as his publicist has made out over the years. I mean imagine flying one of your top men round the world only to strike him half dead.

Bad luck seems to be about half a day behind us as we race across Australia. Perhaps somebody just pointed out to Father Whatever the stupidity of travelling this far to see the Pope in Sydney when they all live in Italy anyway and you can see him every Sunday at the Vatican.

When we finally are in and at our pitch, an odd thing happens. Both Nat and I notice that the same run down vehicle parked up next to us at Nambucca with a 'For Sale' sign in the back is parked up next to us here. What are the chances of that? Well, judging by the way that we kept running into the Irish, not very slim. Except these do look like some kind of fruitcakes who would star in some sort of killer in the outback movie.

Nat is fuming because Frank has now broken the awning that didn't really need fixing, and in our rush to get away, we omitted to change our power plug with the bent pins, meaning that keeping electricity on is all about balancing the cable very gently at a certain angle into its power flap – possibly for the whole night.

One good thing about Nat is that a rage is normally followed by an absurdity which leads to outrageous laughter. Her practical brain is focussing her mind on changing the sat-nav from a woman who was nowhere to be seen as we perished in downtown Sydney into a bloke that sounds like a Nazi.

Instantly, she is happier, feeling dominated, and then she remembers that we have four day old washing rotting in the van. Such is life on the road.

It has been a long day by the time we get to write this. I know that she takes out all of her frustrations at the end of each night by spilling the beans in print for her version of the book. I can't help but predict out loud what she is writing.

'T says there will be no sex tonight as he let me down over the awning,' I mock.

'There better had be, it's all your good at,' she replies.

God, I hope not. I can't keep this marathon love-fest up, and we have lots to do in Sydney tomorrow. First stop is Trailfinders. And could the Pope please leave and quick.

Day Twenty-Seven

It was a bad night. A cold night. We have a duvet crisis. We are in winter, of course, and simply the duvets aren't enough to go round. We're going to struggle all the way to Adelaide if the night-time temperatures are this low. Plus, the awning is worse than ever, almost hanging off. We've left the van unlocked all night and those odd Germans adjacent to us seem to be caravan hoppers. Thank goodness they didn't knock.

I've also broken the harsh news to Nat last night that we don't have to do everything together.

This is because we normally watch Michael Palin DVDs together on holiday, every holiday. Last night she was writing and I put one in our new machine without waiting. She took it badly, but you will suffocate one another in a campervan, if you don't do your own thing.

This morning I have to retrace my steps. I was running back from the cook area at dusk – about half a mile away – when I smashed the bottle of wine that I had taken over to get pissed to while I cooked up. In the dark I had tried to clear the glass from the road, but I knew that half of it must still be there. Terrible, I know, that people walk around campsites barefoot and of course, drive their massive vehicles around it, and I just left it there.

There is a bit of that in camping. It ranges from the very honest to the 'I can get away with anything.'

Today we head into Sydney proper. We take the bus all the

way in from right outside the campsite. It takes about an hour and we have no idea where to get off. The Pope is still very much in town, and frankly I wish he would just bugger off.

We cross the Harbour Bridge in the bus and probably should alight at the end of it but instead carry on all the way into town to the end of the line. Then, of course, we walk all the way back. The first part of the day is wasted, in a mission to find Trailfinders. We're going to book Ayers Rock.

It takes us about two hours to find. It is almost impossible to locate, and then we go away to think about the extortionate prices for an hour or two, and gutted, never return.

It is cloudy today in Sydney, perhaps not the best day or view or climate to be eating our sandwiches at the feet of the Opera House. The pigeons flee with my butty. Nat sheds pathetic tears of joy just to be here. She wants to go on a backstage tour, and I am more than happy for her to disappear for a couple of hours. Frankly, I think it looks better as an photo image rather than in the flesh. The Bridge though, is magnificent, and confirms that the Tyne Bridge a laughable inadequacy by comparison.

I suppose that when you arrive at these two icons, your own thoughts take over. It is all about what *you* feel in this environment. I can't shake one thought from my head, and it is this. The last, and totally worst, series of the TV show *Cold Feet*.

It had been brilliant but went to pot from the moment that John Thompson began the final series sitting on a boat just behind the Opera House. I loved this show, and it accompanied so much of our lives from moving to Durham, having Molly, moving from Durham, being sued, having Sam, nearly splitting up blah blah blah.

It was the ultimate watch to accompany our generation, but I suspected that the Australia scenes in the final series had as much to do with the fact that I heard that the writer Mike Bullen had moved there. Either way I thought a great show had faded and that's what I thought of now. Still loved it, of course.

We lunch in style at a cracking little bistro at Circular Quay – the hub for all the commuter ferries. I feast on a spinach and cheese crepe. It leaves me knackered and washed out. I am always sluggish after a lunchtime feast, and still nearly a month on the road, I can't shake off fifteen years of 4am starts.

I imagine what a delight it must be to arrive here every morning, then walk on into the city for work but then I recall Steve whom we met on the underground back on June 24th, who had been returning to England for a week for a wedding but now works in communications for Telstra in Sydney, who said to us that he walks past Circular Quay and the Opera House everyday and thinks nothing of it.

Perhaps we are better off living in miserable England. After all, if you can't be spoilt by this beauty because it has become your norm, what are the chances of anything spoiling you in life?

Fatigued, and slightly in awe, we decide that our master plan has to be to see Sydney from the air. We head to the really badly-advertised Skytower. Surely this is the best place to start yet we find it by accident. It is just merged into skyscrapers and office blocks yet clearly has the best views of the city. It is definitely a case of don't look down. In fact you can look up if you don a harness and are prepared to pay to climb up outside the tower and walk the skyline for the best views in the world. Now, why would you want to do that?

Much better is to settle in the observatory area and hog a telescope, and unlike Britain once you have paid to enter the Skytower, you won't be fleeced for more money to get the telescope to work, a trait which is very Australian and very un-British. You never get taxed twice here.

So, in a circular motion we spend an hour gazing at the skyline, continually spinning to the degree that initially we think that we have seen these views before but then we realise how a revolving tower works. I focus on the legendary SCG – the Sydney Cricket Ground, and again it is my thoughts rather than the ground itself which move me. I look forward fifteen years from now. I dream in fact, of Sam walking out to batter the Aussies all around the park at the New Year's test match. You see, I am at that age when I realise that my sporting ambitions were just wildcards, pipedreams, so I start living them though my offspring. Which Dad hasn't done that? He's not a bad little player either, but I can tell you now, nothing, absolutely nothing, would make me happier. I could die there and then to see him hit the winning runs in the Sydney test and remember this moment when I looked high across this fabulous city and set the dream in motion.

Still spinning with these thoughts, I have no enthusiasm for posing for the obligatory photo that they like you to buy on your way out. God, if we had bought everyone of these at every junction so far, Ayers Rock wouldn't have even been considered because we would be that broke. Easily done though.

We take the ferry back to Manly as night falls, and I read some promotional bumf on Sydney, discovering that I could have had 15% off the Skytower, if I had only read it on the way in.

Manly Wharf fascinates me when we alight. What a great way to commute, and not just a decrepit terminal for the ferries that you would find at a bus terminus in England. This has restaurants and bars that you would actually eat and drink at!

All in all it is a good hour from Circular Quay back to Narrabeen by ferry and then bus, which of course, pulls up just as the ferry docks. Everything is clockwork, not that we know which bus we are on, nor where to get off.

Our first day in Sydney is brief but enlightening. We know that we need to get there earlier tomorrow if only to escape the God squad at the campsite. Marquees are up everywhere, food is steaming en masse. I hear the musicality of the language, and see men of the cloth mincing about with bibles. Yes, the Italians are everywhere.

Day Twenty-Eight

We get the bus *and* ferry into Sydney and it is already noon by the time that we get there. This is not good. Sam, however is loving the bus. We rarely travel with the common people of public transport at home so this is a relative novelty for him!

I, however, am in a bad mood. Ayers Rock has blown it for me. It is going to cost us something like two grand (sterling) to fly there, stay there one night, and fly back, and that is unjustified in anyone's book. I know that I have let Nat down, who really sold her car before we came, so that issues like this wouldn't become...issues. I feel that my usual holiday tightness has returned and that I have failed her, but then, she must see that she is a bad person for expecting to blow two grand for a round trip to see an orange rock.

I'm cross with the pressure Nat silently puts on me; that I put on myself; with the bloody Rock; and with Qantas for holding the monopoly and screwing everyone senseless. I can't shake it off.

We pick up the ferry at Manly and the waters are choppy into Sydney. I tell Nat, that as commutes go, this *is* great but another day of half an hour of bus, and another half an hour of ferry under the world's most famous bridge and just like Steve said, the novelty will wear off.

This trip is wrecked by the Yanks, who are almost exclusively the most vile tourists on the planet, at the very least for their volume. They are making such a fuss and noise trying to take pictures of the Bridge and Opera House that nobody can get a look in. It's always the same. This simply reminds me of one thing – that the photos that I carry in my head will always be better than anything that I can take with my thumb over the edge of it. My photos are that bad and I am not into digital touching-up. What is the point of cheating eh? If you can't touch somebody up properly, why go digital.

Today I confirm my Venice theory. That it is always better to arrive into a city, rather than just land *in* it. It is winter and cold, but the magic is just about holding.

Without any sense of plan or planning, we decide to get off the ferry. And hop on a ferry. To Watson's Bay. I had definitely read about Watson's Bay before we left and I can't really remember why.

Well, firstly you must simply take a little trip around the beautiful inlays of Sydney. I think this is underrated, and too much is written about the Bridge and the Opera House, especially when you consider what a minority sport opera actually is.

Far better to travel the extended harbour and alight at the various wonderful stops in the bay, and see how the real people live... or at least, the real rich people.

There will always be something unbeatable about docking and seeing a guy on a boat throwing a rope to a local guy who happens to turn up at the same time every day, and as a favour, ties you up to the side with a spectacular knot that you could never make yourself. At every little dock, you will always find beautiful stone steps down into the water, and hundreds of moored boats, never really doing much. It says to me one thing: the TV show *Howard's Way*.

But, anybody disembarking at Watson's Bay will always tell you the same thing. It is the incredible smell of Doyles that greets you when you dock. And they are no new kid on the block either, serving up fish and chips and much more since 1885 which is incredible if you consider the relative youth of Australia.

Now, here's the thing, Nat hates fish. Absolutely despises it. Indeed nothing gives me more pleasure on holiday than ordering a full-on poisson in the Old Town of Nice and spending a good fifteen minutes removing the eye. Yet, even she is drawn to the allure of Doyles. What a bummer for her, that in my usual Hitleresque discipline I had ordered, before we set off, the daily making of butties to save money.

So instead we take a bus to Bondi.

Ah yes, the world famous Bondi Beach, that we had heard so much about. It just proves that an image can sell a place, a fragrance, a person, an anything if you like. We take a rather innocuous bus ride through some quiet coastal residential areas – nothing special, neither slummy – and then suddenly we're at Bondi, and like so many people arriving at so many tourist locations around the world, we uttered the ultimate tourist words.

'Oh, is this it?'

But then we are not eighteen anymore and nor are we on a gap year. Plus it is July.

I thought it looked like Eastbourne or Torquay, and indeed there's not much wrong with that. Yet, I fail to see what the magnetic pull is. Sure, it is a lovely semi-circular cove, and a cracking parade of cute little shops, bars, and youth hostels, but this is not the world's greatest beach. Let me assure you *that* is at Dickenson Bay in Antigua.

I don't care if it is Christmas Day and some gorgeous blonde from Qantas is sucking you off in thirty degree heat, this is just an average bit of sand, punching above its weight, and promoted anecdotally to be something that it isn't. I can see through it straight away.

Clearly it is the most fun place on earth for gap year students from the UK to spend one Christmas of their life, and blown away by the surrealism of it, combined with their first real taste of freedom, they create the legend, and intensify it through the giddiness that Christmas Day alcohol brings, and through the tricks that the memory and nostalgia provide. Sounds cynical, and harsh? Tough, this is a wise man speaking. Nat, of course, loved it.

I interviewed Kylie Minogue in June 2000 and I always remember her saying to me that at New Year 'everyone would just head up to Dono's house at Bondi.' Jason Donovan obviously.

From that moment, iconic has always been the sole adjective in mind. Still – enough about what I feel about Kylie and Jason.

I guess I had these deluding images of a series of gorgeous beaches in my head. Why? The clue is in the title. It says Bondi Beach, not beaches. I had sold myself a dummy.

The youthful setting is invoking feelings of regret too though. Probably, by the time I went to university, I had travelled more than anyone I knew of my age or older. Who else could say that they had lived in the jungles of Columbia at the age of seventeen?

Yet, I hadn't done Oz, and it hadn't occurred to me to do so, possibly because of the responsibility and desire to rebuild my life with my Dad in South America. Yet when you look at the ridiculously cheap backpacker accommodation, you can't help but feel that you didn't do that gap year right, and oh to not be a grumpy old man, and oh to be a teenager with no mortgage, no baggage, and just to be – If I can use the verb – bumming it.

Bondi Beach therefore, if you are reading this, probably serves as a checklist for your life. Where are you up to, and what do you feel when you are here? If it is slipping away, then you will have written just what I did when you write *your* book. If you don't get where I am coming from, you are probably twenty, and got laid last night. Congratulations. I hate you.

Of course, Nat says I cut short our stay in Bondi all too quickly. I'm holding her back. She's too young, and I am too tired.

Yet already the day slips away, not helped by the fact that the bus that we take back to Circular Quay stops forever, as there is no driver. This is London-type efficiency and comes as an all-round shock to us. I guess we are glimpsing the reality of real life within the holiday, of hanging out with the real people in Sydney

– the kind of stuff that you discover when you move here, having had an amazing gap year shagging at Bondi.

It is a wake-up call, and with it Nat and I slip into boring, relationship-type, mumbly conversation. From nowhere she produces this gem.

'Well, at least, being away this long means I haven't had to get my highlights done.'

This is swiftly followed by the depressing, 'three weeks Thursday and we'll be home.'

Where has this come from? Is it the staring out of an immobile bus that produces this, or is it that Sydney is the perceived pinnacle and it is all downhill from here? Maybe it is the recognition that this is an amazing trip and any return home can only be negative in comparison. Or maybe it just came out and means nothing.

I put it down to the fact that for a moment we got caught up in how the real people live, and that means we started thinking about the ferry back tonight, which means that our lives are controlled by time which is the one quality that we came here to both forget and rediscover, if you get me. And there from the subconscious, it slipped out, as the forces were dragging Nat back to reality. It is indeed a wake-up call, and a thoroughly depressing one.

On our return, I am most unimpressed. The pilgrims are there, and they have taken most of the camp facilities. It is therefore miles to the cook area, and I am gone for ages, only to find upon my return to our pitch that Nat has done no salad, no jacket potatoes, no nothing. Sam is gibbering away and she has passed out knackered. It must have been the extra effort of having had two decent thoughts in the same day.

Still, as I point out to my dear wife, the van hasn't killed us, which was definitely the fear of all our friends and family. They thought we would kill each other. Nat puts this down to me sleeping while she was driving. Oh the cutting one is back.

Then it is my turn to pass out to Michael Palin. I have now watched the same episode of him in Mauritania three times, and not yet once have I seen the end. We appear to have sex again in the night, which amuses me greatly. Nat says that there is no way that this is going in the book. Her mum will read it. I place my arm tenderly on her shoulder and tell her from the bottom of my heart.

'It's ok love. I think your mum has had sex before.'

Day Twenty-Nine

We awake to no water. Our hose doesn't work, because the nozzle on the end of the hose is different for New South Wales. As I have repeatedly said throughout, this is a country that functions! Clearly I was ill-advised to comment until I had visited more than two states.

There's a Brummie guy on reception who moved here for a better life and had promised that he would come and fix it last night, but alas he didn't show, though oddly, when I return from the communal shower, it is fixed and Nat is claiming it to be her work.

Unfortunately for her, Molly and Sam have been bought somewhat cheaply and are now singing 'Mummy and the hose-man sitting in a tree, k-i-s-s-i-n-g.' First the truckers, now the maintenance staff, I don't know.

I take my revenge. It is time to clean the portaloo. Unfortunately I choose the wrong dump area at the toilets, and chose to flush three days worth of piss and blue chemical down the disabled toilet. Ha – take that flirty from Birmingham. Think again before tampering with my beautiful wife, about whom I have never said a harsh word.

I'm still bitter about the Rock today. I tell Nat, that even though we are not writing a tourist book, but a tale of a family trying to sort their lives out through the vehicle of Australia, no book of Oz can surely be complete without the trip to Uluru. I don't call it that, of course, though she keeps telling me that I will be arrested for racism if I keep calling it Ayers Rock.

She has now turned it back on me which makes me feel doubly guilty, insisting that we mustn't go, that it is no big deal, and that she doesn't want me shouting about it all autumn as I moan about paying it off. This is a classic Nat technique.

That said, on this cold autumn day, that feels like a crisp September back to school morning at home and finds me wearing two t-shirts but cold at eighteen degrees, she has woken up this morning a changed woman.

Her plan is all over the shop. Out of the blue, she suddenly suggests that we fly Nanny and Grandad out for two weeks to see if they like it, with a view to joining us should we emigrate. These are bold words, as I technically am the one with nothing to keep me back home whereas she has everything.

I already feel guilty though at the thought. John, Lynne, Jenny, Jim and Ben, Helen and Mike – they are everything. My mind is made up that living somewhere out here is a very, very good thing, but I would never ask, for the seven reasons just cited. Nat is storming full steam ahead, convinced that Helen and Mike wouldn't be bothered about moving for a year or so, and Jenny and Jim would jump at it with little Ben. Well, that is that sorted then.

I do have a contact, Phil Dowse, who hails out of Adelaide, and once very kindly said that I was one of the top five breakfast shows on the radio in the world. Clearly, I have a green light to ring him when we get home, or indeed more sensibly into Adelaide, to sound him out about whether I could get work, though even that defies the point to me, that I don't need to earn as much money living out here, and therefore can lose some of the pressures of my life, principally that of being on the air.

Hell, you can get the paperwork done if you are a pastry chef or a hairdresser by all accounts. Australia apparently needs hairdressers. Extraordinary, I know.

I sense that this conversation, albeit brief, is now something that is part of our lives. It is up and running. It is live. It will be revisited.

Today, though, back to practicalities. I ring Maui to say that we will be returning. The awning certainly will not make it to Adelaide. Remember, this is an awning that was just about fine – not great but fine – until Frank got his hands on it. This will be our tenth contact in person or by phone with Maui. That's one every two and a half days. I would say it is going well, wouldn't you?

Oddly, I have also found that Sydney is ten hours time difference from home. We've been here a couple of days and just worked it out. Oh to be free of the man-made clock every day and just live by the light of the sun.

Today we get the bus all the way in. Nat thinks it is quicker. This is bullshit, but I let her have her way.

We get off at 'Commuter Church,' which curiously offers speed-learning sessions in Russian. Now, I am a linguist and I can tell you that you can't learn any language, especially that one, on the fly. Nice idea, though. Sam is more interested in playing the traffic lights game. In Sydney they make a gun-like noise counting down while you cross. Sam is determined not to get shot, which he won't of course.

We just amble and mingle for a while and that is how you get a feel and a passion for a place rather than ticking your list of monuments like a bingo card. As we head once again towards the water, and I think that you inevitably do in Sydney, it is obvious that the trip has had an effect on him. He's convinced that there are sharks in the water by the Opera House. He's developing conspiracy theories all over the place. Who knows, there might be?

There are some travel kiosks at Circular Quay and I start asking about Ayers Rock again. We're in trouble though, as it seems that you can't fly there direct from anywhere other than Sydney, and we have to push on towards Melbourne, so it looks like that we have blown our chance to go from here, once and for all. It has been eating me.

Yet, I can see Nat is excited that I have picked it up again. She was clearly lying when she said earlier today, and the night before, and the day before, that she didn't want to go and it would be irresponsible of us to do so. I don't like to tell her, especially as I am not earning while we are away, that the American Express bill for the trip so far came in last night at £1700, and I have no obvious way of paying it. These are the kind of worries that I constantly keep from her. I shall have to keep this one too.

Driving to the Rock is simply not an option at this stage in the trip and has never been on our radar. I am getting the feeling that our time in Sydney is up too. I think that I can gauge this today by the fact that shopping and a small amount of history are on the cards. It sounds like a last day thing, doesn't it, to cram in a few things and do a 'spot of shopping.'

First port of call – forgive the pun– is the maritime museum. They do these things so well here, and I am overcome with a sense that I should have been a historian rather than a modern-day social commentator, which in effect is what I do on the radio. But then I think what is the point of being a historian?

We never really learn from our pasts – look at how Australia tiptoes around itself to some sort of Aboriginal recognition - and I look at my sister Bev, to whom I was once very close, and I know that she has hidden her life away from the real world by immersing herself in academia, and that essentially is what historians do.

There is no great skill in listing facts and dates, perhaps some in analysing them, and you can really draw any conclusions that you like because the passing of time means that nobody can really argue and therefore you can shape your work accordingly. It is a bit of a farce, a sub-layer of intellectualism, and much as I fancy it as a lifestyle choice, I am glad that I didn't go down that road, even though I am widely derided amongst my friends, family, and people that have taught me over the years for the radio path that I did take. It is – in everybody's eyes– not a proper job.

Hey, I have to be sharp, funny and analytical every day and every three minutes when a song ends, not two hundred years after the event.

But I have a begrudging respect and increasing curiosity for Captain James Cook. I know already that I will be regularly googling him and hunting him down on the National Geographic/Biography/History channels when I return and learn more. His is an incredible story and told here at the Maritime Museum.

I just cannot imagine, how in a world of so little knowledge, he seemed to have it all, coupled with the fact that he discovered 'Australia' by accident really after getting grounded at the Great Barrier Reef, and being forced to come ashore or face destruction. I am unclear though why he called it New Holland, unless my gaps in knowledge will tell me that he discovered the land of the clogs too and considered this to be the latest equivalent, which it so clearly isn't in any way, shape or form.

Normally when faced with maritime museums and the like, I breeze round, rarely reading, yet I am taking in every detail. I am most amused by the note that his chef was a John Thompson. Was there more symbolism in the previously described *Cold Feet* episodes filmed here than I had given the writer credit for? Er, no don't be stupid – but a nice touch though.

There's also a chance to join a replica Cook trip. You know how it works – dress up like them, eat like them, sail a ship like them. I see people like this on the news on bank holidays at home, heading off for battle re-enactments and I just think they are the strangest people alive, and by any stretch of the imagination, more likely to be soccer thugs or paedos in their *real life* than any other section of society.

Nat is having similar deep and historical thoughts and is equally impressed. I can see it in her body language.

'We're off to buy some Ugg boots,' she announces.

I choose this moment to phone my Dad in Peru. It has been

tricky keeping in touch – the time zones are no good. Ultimately I am all that he has, and I want to look after him. It also takes my mind off my disgust at Nat indoctrinating young Moll into fashion, whilst trying to persuade me that she had done me a favour in getting a £100 off the price at home! Meanwhile Sam and I spot the best thing ever, just down the shopping centre. There's a cute little shop selling traditional English sweets that you just don't get any more or indeed are hard to find like Old English Highland Toffee and the old red packets of Toffee, or Sherbert Fountains and Double Deckers. They are all here, and I get talking to the owner, who, it transpires, has franchised the shop across Australia, which interests me greatly as I know that one way to get a visa is to get a franchise and then create jobs for Aussies. I part with a hard-earned tenner for stuff that I would never buy at home but may have once as a kid, and no, the irony is not lost on me of buying British stuff that I had forgotten about which has been imported from home to Australia, only for me to buy it when I wouldn't buy it at home, just for me to then take it back. Complicated I know.

After, we take the monorail.

Trust me, this is just a gimmick that serves no real purpose, though strangely you can see right up close into offices and boardrooms, which is highly entertaining as it skims a rectangular route above the city that normal people would simply walk. When we get off we begin a mammoth climb in search of Bills restaurant. My good friend Chris Lees had told us all about Bill, even bought us a cookbook of his. What a heterosexual thing to do.

Nat is no fan of eating on anything other than a functional basis but it is her who insists that we head in Bill's direction. This is a fruitless task. We have the address but just make no progress whatsoever. We've gone miles up the street and don't seem to be ticking off the street numbers at all. I reckon we are about two hours away on foot when I call a halt, only for us to retrace our steps, now on empty stomachs.

Consequently, as the restaurants are finishing for lunch, we virtually have no choice but to dine at a place called Baja close to the water's edge. Despite my reluctance to eat there, I feast on excellent barramundi. It leaves me sleepy and I recognise that our hours in Sydney are fading too.

Oddly it is time for us to do somebody a good deed after all the mini-disasters that we have had. As we take one last look at the Opera House, Sam finds four tickets for *Don Giovanni* on Friday belonging to a Mrs Caroline Rendt. They are lying in the street and blowing against the wind. This is quite normal. He is constantly finding things in the same way that it is rare for me to do a good turn. At home I would have laughed and left them but I feel I owe this country something, as it has already had a lasting impact on my world. I chase these tickets like an Olympian determined to get them at any cost, which we do after five comedy minutes, returning to them to security at the Opera House. The poor woman must have been gutted to have lost them, if indeed she knew that she had. My opinions on opera confirm in my mind that the intellectual thing to do was to let them go, yet the moral thing to do was to let her make the choice of sitting though such dross.

I hope one day Caroline somehow reads this book, and learns that it was us who found them. Either way, I feel magnificent at the free and helpful spirit that I am. Can I keep it up on my return to England? Almost definitely not.

Was this divine intervention? No – that was to come next. In one of the most uncomfortable moments of our lives, Nat is accosted by half a dozen Italians around Circular Quay, each claiming that they have had bad experiences in their life and they can tell that she has too and that they can show her the way as they have seen Jesus Christ in their life and do we have time to stop and chat. They have seen it in her face and they just know that they can help. Do we have five minutes?

Oh for fuck's sake, fuck off. And I can say that in Italian too if you like. This is the thing with religious obsessives. They just go too far.

In this very instant two strange things happen. An aircraft flies overhead and brilliantly spells out 'grazie' in the sky. Then Sam makes a run for the toilet, and in a rare moment of bowel leakage unseen since he was three, dumps his load just by our departing ferry. It was clear to me. It was a sign that it was all shit.

It's time to go. There's a rush on for the 4pm ferry. Unbelievably, and I just can't imagine this happening in any other country in the world, there are dolphins in the water on the way back to Manly. The captain of the boat, which is – please remember – a commuter tool, makes a detour so that everybody can appreciate their beauty. Can you imagine somebody on the Heathrow Express doing that? Not that there are dolphins to be seen, at Heathrow, of course.

I have left many cities in the world from Bogotá to Kansas City, and every time that you depart, you ask yourself whether you will be back. I know we will be. It is almost dramatic to leave by commuter ferry, so that you turn and wave to the Bridge like the closing scene in a movie.

Molly is gutted that she hasn't been allowed to climb it. It is a big ask, even for grown-ups, though it makes me laugh intensely that back in Newcastle upon Tyne they get into a right panic if one fruitcake or suicide wannabe attempts to climb the comparatively pathetic Tyne Bridge yet here they charge you for the privilege and positively encourage you to do it. If one thought symbolises the gulf in can-do culture, then this is it.

Back at the campsite, I re-assess privately the whole Ayers Rock thing. Nat is counting the days down to our return with a heavy heart. She also gives me a hug, which I don't think she has ever done. I think we both feel that now that we have done Sydney, it is almost the end of an era....in the context of this trip. What Melbourne will bring, we can only wonder. I am more anxious to see it than Sydney and I don't know why. Maybe it's *Neighbours*!

At least there will be no God squad there. Tonight they are singing beautiful, idyllic songs, all as one. They are so young too, and I know that at least one of them will look back at this indoctrination trip and be disgusted with all of the false dawns that they were sold.

I hate that thought for their sake, and I know that they mean well, but for me religion en masse is a very silly thing. Surely it is a private thing. Neither am I a fan of singing songs about Jesus and dressing them up as pop. I have only once in my life appreciated religious music and that was a fantastic gospel choir that I heard singing in Antigua – and they were all stoned.

I take my teaching tonight from Palin, watching last night's episode, only to drop off in the same place again. I just can't shake this monkey off my back.

Tomorrow there will be more deja-vu. We have to head to Maui again.

Day Thirty

There is no sign of Frank at Maui, and this time I find the depot without a problem. Our Italian Stallion (of yesteryear's generation) is off for ten days or so. How lucky were we to actually catch him on the day that we did, which if you remember was actually the wrong day? Isn't that typical on this trip that we only get things right when we got them wrong?

Liz meets us instead. She moved from Glasgow thirty-two years ago to give her kids a better life. I keep hearing this and I can see it all around me. She hasn't lost her Glasgow twang, and oddly if you think that it is a long way to go for a better life, well, that is the point. You really do have to travel to the other side of the world, but once you're here, you never do get that 'I miss home/I wonder what is happening at home' syndrome. I have barely thought about it to be honest. It is the closest that I have ever come in my life to living for today.

We're in and out of Maui in record time – forty-five minutes. This, compared to our expectations, is like a Lewis Hamilton eight second pit stop. We get a new power lead which was bent, they fix the awning that they broke, and crucially I manage to steal an extra four duvets knowing that colder nights are clearly ahead. All in all, I call that a good trip to Maui, and hopefully our last until Adelaide. Liz does leave me with a word of warning. The toll people will catch up with Nat eventually. So far in Sydney, we've definitely escaped four.

Well, toll people, you will have to chase us all the way back to England now.

We're quickly out of Sydney. It takes no time at all. This is normal for Australian cities – they are in fact just big towns. Our plan is Pambula Beach, though we're flexible and not entirely sure. Before you come to Australia, people will always tell you that you can just drive and park up where you want. It is a little bit like that, though not as clear-cut as people's holiday anecdotes sell it to you. Today however, out of Sydney we really have no choice but to attack the open road.

I think it may be this vast expanse ahead of us that leads to my moment of weakness. I tell Nat, and I don't know where it came from, to 'just get on the phone to Phillipa at Trailfinders and book Ayers Rock.'

I don't want to know how much it is going to cost us. Let's just get it done. The book is no book without the Rock, and the trip is no trip without it either. We then spend the next half an hour arguing about the fact that I will throw it back in Nat's face in the autumn when we can't afford Christmas. I cut her dead. There will be no Christmas – this is our gift. Finally, she caves in and remembers that she was the one who wanted to go, and breaks the news to us that to fly from Melbourne it will now cost us an extra £600. I hit the roof, but only inside my soul.

'That's great, I'm so happy, but I thought you couldn't fly direct from Melbourne.'

I fake my reaction.

'You can on Mondays and Fridays apparently,' my wife Judith Chalmers replied.

'Great, so how are we getting back?'

I thought this was a legitimate question, being stranded, not really amongst my plans.

'We're going via Alice Springs,' she said.

I didn't really know what this meant to be honest. Alice Springs is clearly – everybody knows – just about five minutes out of the Rock, so it should be fine, though I was starting to think that we were making some sort of pilgrimage of our own – sod the Italians – to something that might be the Southern Hemisphere equivalent of Stonehenge, an odd collection of stones and boulders, impossible to reach by public transport in the Wiltshire countryside and with no genuine tourist value unless you are a freaky druid.

Either way, Ayers Rock was put to bed. We were heading there in five days time. Now, having said that you can just be laidback and turn up wherever you want and just cruise the open road, this obviously presents a couple of small dilemmas in that we now have to find an airport and abandon a van or put it into storage. There is no way that we could drive this thing under all those low barriers at airports and park it in underground car parks. This temporarily gets placed into a mental compartment 'things to sort when we get to Melbourne,' just behind the *Neighbours* tour in its priority.

Now that she is happy having bankrupt me over some rock, Nat proceeds to give me her anthropological view on New South Wales.

'It's like Wales without the sheep.'

God, I can't wait to read her version of this book.

Today is a day for place names. We hit Meroo (Aboriginal for lightning) and that leaves me on my guard as surely they wouldn't have called it that if it hadn't been a problem. I can't quite get my head round if there is any truth behind Flying Fox Creek; Fairy Meadow just sounds gay, and ahead lay Merry Beach and Potato Point. Cracking stuff – do you get this anywhere else in the world?

Nat is making noises that she wants to stay at a place called Pebbly Beach, as she has read that there are kangaroos on your site, and that they have been known to bodysurf when there is nobody around. I tell her that is bullshit with the sole purpose of enticing us to stop there. After all, if they bodysurf when nobody is around, who has seen this to confirm it?

The problem is that there are four Big 4 sites around

Bateman's Bay so how on earth are we to know one from the other? They are all near water – it is a bay you see.

Price is never a problem as it really is peanuts to camp for the night but which one do you pick? This causes a domestic. I am driving so when she reads out the descriptions to me, I am not really in a position to make a judgement call, so what does she do? With about an hour's estimated driving before Bateman's Bay, she insists that I am tired and that it is her turn to drive. This is totally a power moment, engineered cunningly to let me pick the site for the night, and therefore allowing me to take the blame when I pick badly. I can see her game a mile off, though am powerless to prevent her from getting her way.

In the end we pick the site with the jumping pillow to give the kids something fun to do while we do chores.

The drive into the Bateman Bay area is very pleasant, well worth it in fact, and the site is a beauty when we arrive at 4pm. There is no jumping pillow, however, which the girl on reception explains to us was put in the brochure by Big 4 and is not coming until August. Bit naughty that, and bargaining power for the kids who get an hour's karting out of us instead.

Oddly the woman who was complaining about being strangled by seatbelts at Maui in Sydney is on this site. This is only the third time that this has happened to us. The Irish, some strange wife-swapping Germans at both Nambucca and Sydney, and now neurotic strangulation nag-face.

Amazingly, she doesn't realise the van has heating. Nat learns this after she was moaning about how cold it is in the night. My God, if Nat hadn't showed her how to do it, she would be probably dead by the time we get to Adelaide.

Our pitch is tremendous, just thirty metres down to the water's edge to not spot the bodysurfers. It is a good pick though, even if we are here for just a night, but what a night.

At 4.30 in the late afternoon Brett and Anita start chatting to us. Then Kenny and Pat join us. Either we are some sort of oddball tourist attraction or this is how most nights begin for them. We are still busy washing and drying but they are cracking the beers open. I think this is the oddest night on tour so far.

Anita is a Maori who came over sixteen years ago and hasn't gone back. God knows where Brett is from. They have a lad called Jacob. They also have a printer in their tent. My goodness, hasn't camping come a long way. They have been on the road for four months after taking redundancy from some other campsite where they worked, and have a job interview next week but no suit to wear at the interview! Jacob gets schoolwork emailed to him, though seems to be on his bike rather than at his desk. They are just about on the fringes of society, in their late thirties at a guess. She is frank-talking, aggression in her face. He couldn't give a shit about anything, drinking himself silly into an early grave.

Then there's Ken who has no teeth, is probably in his sixties and has once caught a shark and has the pictures to prove it. Every time he speaks I find it annoying. Pat, however, is much more interesting, and is related to Captain Cook.

I weigh this up for a while, and conclude that probably so is half of Australia.

These are the kind of old people for whom camping is made, and believe me they have everything that you would have in your home in their van, and they clearly do this early all-night drinking thing every night and these two families clearly do it with each other every night because until we came along there was nothing else to do, but now we are entertaining them with our range of English accent, David Boon stories, and my classic 'I shared a bed with Kylie' gem. (I did by the way, but it was just for a photo.)

We're all hammered quickly, but it is too crazy for me, so I retire briefly with some excuse to check on something fictional in the van, and proceed to ring my *best* best mate Crossy, who is off to Beijing tomorrow to cover the Olympics for *The Mirror* newspaper, and is very used to me only ringing him when I am pissed. You may recall that he has had a little girl called Daisy on the same day as my birthday, July 5th. We are such good mates that he planned it thus. Did he heck? I tell him that I will definitely see him soon. This of course, as much as I mean it, is a downright lie, and we both know it.

When I return to Captain's Cook's van next door, Nat is being carried back to our van having fallen on their table and broken it, with red wine all over her Terri Irwin clothes that she had wasted good money on at Australia Zoo. When I enquire of the state of the table, she summons up a great effort and tells me that it was a collapsible table, and was not her fault. Clearly.

Day Thirty-One

I awake at five in the morning and Nat is snoring like a pig. It had been a beautiful sundown and I leave the van to witness an even better sunrise. I am determined to attack the day, frying up bacon and eggs on the barbie while a big surf rages behind me. This is the life – unless you are Nat, for whom I have to piece together the details.

This is common on the road, I am sure. A long drive, fresh air, a whiff of booze, and you are out of control very quickly. Today, we promise the kids just a short trip to Pambula Beach, which Brett tells us on our departure is a crackerjack of a site. He promises us log fires in a beautiful upstairs lounge, and he guarantees us kangas on our pitch. Yeah, right. You can take the piss out of us when we are gone, but not to our face. Just say goodbye, and be done with it.

We may have had a cracking laugh last night that nobody can remember, but the morning after you are reminded that, even if you can exchange hotmail addresses and all that, we're all just passing through each others' lives.

As we have a relatively small distance to cover today, and we really have time on our hands, Nat decides that we will take the tourist route. Isn't it all the tourist route?

Suddenly we are off the beaten track and a coastal route right by the water's edge, which is going nowhere fast. The time on the sat-nav doubles, much to the annoyance of Molly and Sam, who are banking on a swim today at the heated pool. Swimming has been thin on the ground since Cairns. It is of course winter here, so you can forget your outdoor pools.

But we won't make it at all if she continues like this, as beautiful as places like Mogo are, just some ten kilometres south of Bateman's Bay.

There's a Big 4 at Narooma but it looks shoddy, a Townsville if you like, and right at the end of its street is an enormous turn and climb that is almost too much for the van. There is surely going to be an impassable route on this journey at some point. This is our third immense climb. One day our luck will run out.

We're in trouble either way though because we dared to program the sat-nav for Pambula and then chose to ignore it and whilst some of these gizmos can read you inside out, this one has the IQ of Karen Matthews, taking particular delight in taking us in reach of a very scary forest fire (our first) at Central Tilba, and then having the sodding cheek to take us to Mystery Bay, which frankly remains a mystery, for its lack of....mystery.

Finally at 2pm with some sixty-eight kilometres to our destination, Nat flips when I say that I really had expected to be there by now, insisting that I bloody well drive then, even though neither of us has a clue where we are.

When we get there... well blow me away, Brett was right, though we don't see them at first.

We have virtually the campsite to ourselves bar a pensioner's birthday booze-up going well into the afternoon, and Graham who tries to gatecrash a game of cricket between Sam and I, on the basis that he was once a schools cricket coach. (He is about seventy now, and has the air of one of those schoolmasters who used sport to have his wicked way with young boys so consequently when he offers to drive us around the area we politely decline.)

Then we start to see poo droppings, and wonder where they have come from. Away to our left there are literally hundreds of them just minding their own business as though they too have booked in for the night, as though reception has taken their credit card details, and as though I might run into them at the cook-up later.

In fact there are more kangaroos than people on this site. Better than that though, this site is almost Nambucca upgraded without the forestry that made the beach there such a dramatic discovery. Just ahead, less than a hundred metres away, is a ridge marking the top of the sand dunes, and over the other side is the ocean. Isn't this perfect?

The sun is out, the campsite is deserted, the beach is metres away and our only company are kangaroos.

In fact the site's owners haven't seen kids for weeks, so I physically have to ask them to put the jumping pillow up and the jacuzzi in the pool on for the kids. They list kids' activities too in the daily programme at reception but really, it is all too much to ask them to break them from their out-of-season slumber, so instead I resort to what camping is all about. I take out a chair, and one for my feet, with a glass of wine, and do fuck all. Literally for the rest of the day.

Night falls and Harty texts me from Newcastle to tell me that two of the boys from the Great North Run office are out in Melbourne organising this year's inaugural Great Australia Run if I want to meet them for a drink. Yes, I can see Nat allowing me to interrupt our Ayers Rock trip for that.

Then, a rare glimpse of work, as I ring my producer 'Dogsbody' to find out our quarterly audience ratings which are published today. We have gone down again, but it is fine as we plan to start again when I get back from Oz and blame my replacement Brian Moore for everything!

I am past caring anyway. I only do it for the money and the fun that we produce for ourselves within the show. There are so many factors in getting good or bad ratings that you can't worry about it anymore. Everything that 'Dogs' tells me about the place in my absence confirms that it is business as usual – in other words stuff that would make me cross. I am also aware that because Dogs is a professional and a great mate, he is not telling me the half of it!

I don't give him the chance anyway, cutting short the conversation with the words, 'I've got to go, there's a kangaroo at my door.'

And indeed there was.

Day Thirty-Two

I think the kangas come out at night, sensing safety in the dark. I wasn't expecting them at breakfast however. It is a beautiful but cold, crisp morning, the kind that can only start with an immense fry up on the barbecue, just twenty metres from the van. I can see and hear the sea too just over the dunes. It is perfect again. But then I have a problem.

I have company that I wasn't expecting. Despite Nat shouting to me from inside the locked van, from where the kids and her are peering, that kangas are vegetarians and not to worry, I simply cannot make it back to the van because the roo is chasing me and my bacon butty.

I literally drive myself dizzy, spinning and turning trying to make it back to the van, but there is no way back. I am not scared at this point, just frustrated and losing my balance. Nat and the kids don't bother to help, but instead grab the camera and begin filming me versus the kanga. I mentally note not to bother to cook breakfast again.

No amount of wit or brawn will get me past. Am I in his territory or does he really fancy the bacon? I have no idea what to do to get back to the van. If I run, he'll run faster. If I try and beat him with chess-like cagey manoeuvres, he repeats my every move. I try not to make eye contact, but I am at my wits end, just going round and round, even further now from the van than I was at the cook area. After ten minutes of being unable to pass, I am exhausted and dizzy.

Suddenly I am given a lifesaver. The campsite maintenance guy turns up to empty the bins, shouting mockingly.

'You got a problem mate?'

I ask what is the best way to get rid of a kanga that wants your breakfast, and he just laughs shouting back to tell it to shoo. So I do and in a second, it is gone.

I walk back calm but disorientated to the van where Nat and the kids are falling over themselves. They don't deserve their butty at this rate, especially when it turns out that the kanga has been in the van and there is roo poo everywhere. I can honestly say that in my entire life no day has begun like this.

Unfortunately we can't stick around today though, and as beautiful as Pambula Beach is, we have to crank the miles again, and with no fixed destination either other than that we have to get as close to Melbourne as possible. The problem ahead seems to be that the Big 4 sites come early so we may be faced with a dash in the dark later or a punt into the unknown territory of a non-Big 4 site.

We also need to ring ahead to Melbourne as we really fancy going to see the musical *Wicked* if we can get tickets. More importantly can we get ourselves on the *Neighbours* tour?

I am sceptical too whether we can get all the way to Adelaide in one piece as the lead on the awning is twisted again. Heaven please, we don't need another trip to Maui. Apparently too, Melbourne is about to host the Melbourne Film Festival. Please don't let this be another Pope.

Almost immediately that we leave Pambula I want to go back – some sites are there to crash the night at, others you need a week for, and even though there is nothing per se to do at Pambula it definitely falls into the latter category.

Within minutes we pass by the Eden Big 4 campsite. It is so touch and go which one to pick when there are two sites so close together, and how lucky were we to pick the one with the kangas. I guess that if we had been driving the conventional route from Adelaide to Cairns, rather than Cairns to Adelaide, then we would have hit Eden and not Pambula by the nature of having arrived there first, and we would probably be spending today at Eden's killer whale museum, which for a gentle bit of scarcely populated coastline probably gives you an insight into a more sinister past.

If we had come that way round we would have also panicked because from Eden you head straight into a vast national park. If this therefore had been at the end of the day and you were trying to radar in on either Pambula or Eden, you would also be convinced that you were lost and never going to make it, so vast and never-ending is the sensation that you get when you drive through a national park.

It is also icy on the roads this morning and it is a hazard. Such is the camouflage of the forestry that the sun cannot beat down and it is genuinely dangerous taking these sharp bends twisting and turning on a one lane highway through this woodland jungle. Ice was the last thing I expected in *our* summer in Australia.

And this is how we enter the state of Victoria, at what has to be one of the world's most innocuous border crossings.

What was the process way back when that determined that somebody just drew a line in the middle of the rainforest and said everything north of here is New South Wales and everything south is Victoria. There is a bit of a fanfare at the border, with lots of magnificent signs proclaiming Victoria's magnificent facilities blah blah blah as though just round the corner from here we were about to end the woodland and hit civilisation, as though the party were just around the next bend.

You expect things to change when you cross a border, particularly after the showboating at the crossing, but no, you just carry on driving into more and more forestry, making the random location of the border more bizarre.

Victoria's opening moments from this angle are not impressive. This is a problem for us too, as we are really low on fuel, and I mean really low. Everybody has this panic at some point on the road in Australia but today is our turn because we simply do not know when this national park will end. Sure, it might say so many miles on the sat-nav but that is not an A to B mile, that is a zigzagging mile, where the phrase 'as the crow files' couldn't be further from the truth.

The sat-nav indicates that there is diesel at a little place called Genoa, but even though we drive studiously through, there doesn't seem to be. I am now counting every mile and have already written off returning to look again at Genoa on the basis that I cannot afford to waste fuel in search of it.

By the time we pull up to dump the waste, I calculate that we have no more than thirty minutes driving left before we have had it. Nat is convinced that emptying out the waste will make the van lighter and therefore we need less fuel. I think she is splitting hairs, and believe me, when you are driving and convinced that you are about to splutter to a great halt, the person next to you could tell the funniest joke in the world and it wouldn't alter your very dark mood.

Trust me, you're driving in silence.

The next reasonable sized place on the map is Cann River right at the end of the Alfred National Park. We convince ourselves that there has to be fuel here as the next place of reasonable size after that is Oborst and we are not going to make it that far. I don't recall seeing any fuel near Pambula or Eden, so my advice to anybody taking this route is to be full to the max before doing so.

This clearly is old news to regular travellers of this route because, lo and behold, when we finally emerge at Cann River, there are three or four petrol stations. Evidently, this is a giveaway that you absolutely must fill up here, and the world and his wife are doing just that. I have to wait twenty minutes for a pump behind just about the coolest guy that I have ever met who is one of these truckies who is always on the road and loads up with 1800 litres, and advises me that there is a transport strike coming on Tuesday so I would do well to keep full. We chat for twenty minutes and become lifelong buddies, and then he is gone. It was ever thus. We had literally ten kilometres left in the tank.

Just over the road lies the Cann Valley Motel. I can't think who would ever stay there. If you have your house with you as we do, then you drive and park up. If you were staying at Cann River, well, why *would* you stay there? There is absolutely nothing here except the petrol stations and the motel. It clearly has the hallmark of 'last town before nothing' about it, as though this town grew up out of necessity only to fuel travellers through the park. Perhaps, if you were coming in the opposite direction to us, it was Victoria's last effort, a token stop before New South Wales.

I do spy across the street a solitary road sign of enormous significance – and it is not often when you are in such backwaters like this that you have a choice of where to go. The sign is pointing in the direction of Canberra.

Ah yes, Canberra the forgotten capital. How we forget, always assuming it is Sydney. You sort of feel obliged to pay a visit, but anybody who has ever been there always says not to bother with Canberra.

I am curious though. Can there be any other country in the world where you simply never visit the capital? Possibly America and Washington DC but even that is not on the same level in anonymity as Canberra. By nature, you normally fly into capitals when you land overseas, but Canberra, no never. I don't even think you can fly direct from the UK.

They have to have got that a bit wrong somehow. I have never seen it even marketed, never read an article about it, and couldn't name a sportsman from there. I can't recall seeing it on the news ever.

We choose not to follow that road! In truth we hadn't even

considered it before now, and this time we consider it for all of five seconds. We push on towards Lakes Entrance, but Nat is ill – or hungover – so there is silence in the van. I manage to pick up the radio for a bit. There has been another hit and run in Townsville. My goodness, that place is not good news. I am starting to think that we risked everything by even stopping there, the amount of nonsense that we have heard since we left.

Lakes Entrance is exactly that. Another classic Aussie title. Entrance to lakes, obviously. We park up opposite the Big 4 Waters Edge Holiday Park. It looks cute enough but something is telling me to push on. I get no response from anyone in the back. Molly is not feeling well either. The problem is that we are unsure what lies ahead, so I cheekily nip in to the Big 4 site, and pick up leaflets for a couple of sites further on. Not far down the Princes Highway is Bairnsdale, but frankly, we have come to be suspicious of anything now that is located on the Princes Highway. You wouldn't sleep by the M25 would you? Plus, the site really doesn't look up to much at all. After Bairnsdale though, we are on our own, into unknown territory. Not a Big 4 in sight.

I tell Nat that I want to make Inverloch. It looks a cracker of a site, sticking out on the map, and the sat-nav says we will be there by 5.15, which is probably the last of the light, and probably means nearer 6.15. Plus it is a C road.

It is this that wakes Nat from her slumber, and if she hadn't we would probably have gone all the way there and never made it. I have been driving all day, talking to myself, so I just look for the next destination and ignore the years of research and planning that people have put into writing the atlas, on the basis that my gut feeling must be wiser!

Nat however, is coming at it with fresh eyes, and rightly points out that Inverness in Scotland is easier to get to on this occasion than Inverloch itself. I am genuinely gutted, though she is right. The Big 4 book says Inverloch is just ninety minutes from Melbourne, and you can cruise for seals or stake out the famous

Philip Island Penguin Parade. It is right on the coast too. The reality is that we would park up late and leave early, and not p-p-pick up a penguin.

So we are staring into the abyss and have no choice but to consult the rival Top Tourist book. The next town is Sale, and we waste about twenty minutes trying to find the Sale Motor Village campsite, as it turns out that such a tiny town has two Macmillan Streets and we are in the wrong one.

Goodness the name hardly does it any favours. I mean you could have called it Sale's Sunshine Paradise or something more exciting. That would have been a lie of course, as we discover when finally the receptionist talks us in to the site, only for us to take one look at it, hang up, and drive away at speed. It just fell into that category of sites that we knew that we just didn't fancy.

We simply have to find something in the next town, a place called Traralgon. We will take whatever is left and despite the actual town just down the road being quite cute, the Park Lane Tourist Park is the end of the earth in our eyes.

If I asked you if you would like to be the only campervan on an almost pitch-black campsite that lay in between the main highway to Melbourne and an airstrip, would you drop what you were doing and beg me to take you there right now? Er no.

This may be why it is thirteen pounds a night. There are a couple of residents on site, and the resident factor always makes me nervous. I don't think it is unfair to assume that if you choose to *live* on a campsite, then either you love the campsite thing or you are on the run, you have no income, or you have no friends.

I don't think you find normal people taking up a residency in these places unless circumstances have driven them to it. It is spooky and scary to say the least.

I'm astounded that the owners even considered buying the land as a viable business opportunity unless the highway and the airstrip came later. The noise isn't crushing, though the concept is. I mean, do you fancy a bed on the runway at Heathrow tonight?

On the way to the games room, we spy a pathetic little white tent pegged to the ground. We do have company after all, but surely it is too cold to camp. Inside the games room, we find Chris all alone and settle down on the sofa to watch the first TV show that we have seen in five weeks. It is the American imported show *So You Think You Can Dance* and it looks shit.

I can only assume that Chris is watching it to pass the time and not because he is a dance aficionado, which obviously you wouldn't be anyway if you were watching this trash.

Finally, as everyone does in this situation, he tells us his life story.

He is twenty-four, spent a year working as a chef in Tetbury in Gloucestershire, and is currently undergoing divorce proceedings. I know Tetbury well. It is Prince Charles country – and we used to live a few miles away. A lovely part of the world.

What a contrast for him now as he camps out in a cold field for a week between a highway and an airstrip as he seeks to gain unpaid work experience in the mining industry down the road. Here is a young man, in every sense, at a crossroads in his life.

For the record, his tent blew away last night too. We can only wonder what kind of night we have in store as we drink everything in sight on what for us, is the campsite from hell. We are genuinely scared.

Day Thirty-Three

We awake. We're alive.

God, if I needed a location for one of those backpacker murder movies, I have just found the campsite. Of course, it looks fine in the morning in daylight, but if I ever sleep between a motorway and an airstrip again, then I have a made a terrible mistake.

I'm hungover and Nat is being superior. Days that start with a hangover on this trip normally start with McDonald's, and after leaving way much later than we had planned, to the degree that Nat says she doesn't have time for a shower, we soon spot the Golden Arches at Moe on the road to Melbourne.

It is not the food that is noteworthy however, it is the fact that on the TV in the corner, the news networks are flashing up the breaking news that a Qantas plane has just returned to Melbourne after the fuselage was ripped out somewhere near Manila.

Of course, we are due to fly Qantas, and out of Melbourne, to Ayers Rock this Monday. This always happens to us on holiday. We seem to miss plane incidents by days on every single trip. Nat deems this alarm significant however, as Qantas are well-known for having an excellent safety record.

Driving into Melbourne is a completely different ball game to Sydney. Firstly, the Pope hasn't shown up. Secondly, there is the small matter of the trams. Thirdly, Melbourne seems to have more of a structure to it like of those grid-like American cities. Sydney seems to have evolved more casually, and of course, the water in Sydney makes a massive difference in a way that the Yarra River here doesn't even contemplate.

The weather has turned too. In fact it is totally grey and miserable and I am wise enough and worldly enough for a spot of weather not to cloud my impression of a place but unfortunately as I spy to my left the one thing that I really want to see – the Melbourne Cricket Ground – I am feeling totally unimpressed with the place. I think I had been looking forward to coming here more than Sydney, possibly only because of Kylie and Jason, but it feels like rainy Manchester, though of course, it is nothing like it. I am hugely disappointed on first impression.

We narrowly avert a Horne disaster when following the unusually well behaved sat-nav, and believe me there would be no return from this error. Nat is proceeding merrily along when I just shout 'stop' like a driving instructor practising the emergency stop. She goes nuts but she hasn't seen it. Ahead is a sign saying 'Bridge Height 3.3.' We are 3.4.

I only know this because helpfully there is a sticker near the driver's mirror. This has obviously been a problem in the past or Maui wouldn't have put the thing there. Clearly somebody has driven back into a depot with their roof still in a low-level bridge. It sounds like just the kind of thing that we would do.

Nat, in her stubbornness is not having it, citing a bus coming our way that must be bigger than us. I tell her straight that I do not care what kind of hold-up she causes, she is reversing on this main road and we are going back the way we came. This takes approximately ten minutes and is very, very embarrassing. Slightly less though than ringing Maui for a new roof.

We had just been drifting towards disaster – she hadn't even considered that it might be a problem. The practicality of not having a roof on the van and then getting a replacement on the off chance that the Melbourne Maui had one ready to go suggest to me that we were probably about a hundred metres – or if you like within an inch – of the whole trip grinding to a halt. We would simply have had no choice but to abandon the metaphorical ship.

When we are moving again, the sat-nav is back to its old tricks still telling us to go the way of the low-level bridge, and Nat expects me to have the new route already in front of her. I point out that this is a city, and in every city there are several ways to go, and ours will become apparent if we keep driving north.

I struggle to fathom though, how we will find a campsite in amongst all this, particularly as we follow the tramline out of the city past a very bohemian San Francisco type quarter, to the point where the tramline ends and we are still going. You just can't picture a campsite in a city suburb. Yet there are four Big 4 sites in and around Melbourne but within one minute of arriving, I know that we have picked the wrong one.

We have opted for the Big 4 Holiday Park on Elizabeth Street in Coburg, principally because it has five stars, but also as it claims to be just nine kilometres out of the city. Well, it doesn't feel right driving out to it. It feels very out of the way, and is, located right at the bottom of a very long road, backing onto a very noisy sawmill or quarry or something. I would suggest too that they retrace the nine kilometre thing because it took us at least half an hour. Though, that could just be us of course.

In reception are all sorts of awards for tourism though strangely the fat girl behind the desk is very unfriendly. I hate to break it to the owners of this site, but you are not five star. In my book I would say closer to two.

The first pitch that we are given is 3A, and we can't get into it as the van next to us has taken up too much room. The second pitch is waterlogged. We both want to leave at this point but can't face the thought of trying to find another site in Melbourne today.

We plonk ourselves in a third pitch right at the rear of the site near the playground, nowhere near to other campers. I march off to reception to tell them and they respond by getting out all their maps and umming and ahhing to see if we can actually have this pitch. Who are they kidding? They have fifty empty places out there and they aren't going to fill them in the next few days, I can tell you.

Add to this the fact that only one dryer is working in the laundry room, and there only seem to be two barbecues on the site, and I begin to ask myself if the five stars were self-awarded. It is also one of the more expensive sites that we have stayed at. I can only assume that being an alleged nine kilometres out of Melbourne gets you five stars here whereas the excellent children's play areas and Disney-type magic of the Coconut Beach Resort in Cairns win you them in Queensland. Clearly there is no set of set rules in the allocation of stars. I can't hate this site more, and I urge Big 4 to look again.

The rain is pouring down. I take refuge with the kids in the TV room, and something very strange happens. I have always hated Aussie Rules football. It could be because I don't understand it, or it could be the jerseys that they wear end at their shoulders. Perhaps it is simply that I don't respect a game that is only played by one country, or maybe it is the fact that when you have two perfectly decent games like rugby and football, why would you try and mix the two?

That, I assume, is probably double the extent of your knowledge too. Suddenly I am watching Collingwood play at the MCG and I cannot tear myself away, and I still don't understand a game that I am becoming addicted to. That sentence alone exposing either my boredom, or the stupidity of my viewing.

I am surprised to see that they are playing at the Melbourne Cricket Ground. I thought that was hallowed turf, though clearly it makes sense to build a stadium and try and use it more than the Boxing Day test match. Spontaneously, I ring the MCG to arrange a tour but I just get an automated message which sounds superbly promising. Basically, unless it is a match day or you are a big party, just turn up at the ground and the tour shall be yours. Tomorrow Sam and I will be walking out for an imaginary bat to whip the Aussies around the park. I can't wait. It is as close as I will ever get to the real thing.

But first we need a meal, a proper meal. When you have lived the barbie diet, there comes a day every so often when you need something else. Your body rejects you otherwise. So, even though Nat has been slaving over the washing machines for hours, I urge her to cook some pasta. Ok, it's an order. This, of course, goes down very well. How slaving had she been? Well, the kids have blown at least thirty pounds, not dollars, some thirty pounds in the games room.

However, it is the call to the kitchen that throws a surprise twist. It is here that we meet the Irish.

No, not *the* Irish – we calculate that they must be back home now. These are the *new* Irish. Donal and Becky are love's young dream, and have a pathetic looking tent just outside the kitchen area. They have come into the kitchen to keep warm and because there is clearly nothing to do in their tent if they are not shagging.

They don't speak for a good twenty minutes, instead just play cards, which is the ultimate sign of boredom. When finally they do open their mouths and reveal their origin, it dawns on me how much we miss the real Irish, and how we haven't had any real 'friends' or contact bar the night at Bateman Bay where Nat broke the table.

With these thoughts, I reflect that though there is still much to do from Ayers Rock to the *Neighbours* tour, to wine-tasting and Auntie Celia, we are entering another chapter on our journey. Like it or not, it is today that I begin to think that we are heading home soon.

It was only hearing Donal speak that made me think like this. They didn't seem to be having the best of times or doing anything in particular. They were on some sort of world tour thing with a bit of Thailand and New Zealand, including four months working in Brisbane, but they couldn't go anywhere right now or in the near future because they were waiting to hear from Ireland if their tax had come through. Presumably some sort of rebate.

They are so young. I try and recognise myself in their adventure. It is not easy. I feel for them a touch, and contemplate offering them the van to kip in, while we go to Ayers Rock. Such is the spirit of Australia that we have inherited, and so good is it to be chatting again to people that you just casually meet, that I think nothing of the consequences of handing over the keys to two strangers whom we have only just met.

Nat wisely pulls me to my senses. I can't help thinking though, that they will probably split up after this trip of a lifetime.

It is a long time to be with someone when so young, and when they return home, well it is the return to normality that can kill you as you spend your whole life living in the past, reminiscing about the big trip. And then you split up. And then you fall for someone else, and that person wants to know why you go on about that big trip you had with someone else so much, and when are you two going to do a big trip, and that trip will always be special to you, therefore always linked in your mind to an ex. You will never be allowed to go to Australia with a new flame. So, Donal, good luck mate, you had better be in love.

Day Thirty-Four

As nights go, that was a shocker. Sam had growing pains. Nat climbed up to the kids' beds in the middle of the night and the three of them cuddled up together. Meanwhile rain bashed the van roof all night long, and with us parked right up against the perimeter fence behind which lies a massive drop, I had the recurring nightmare that there was a mudslide and gently the handbrake came off, sending us flying backwards to our deaths.

It was therefore with some relief that a text with the cricket score from my mate Martin Speight awoke me at 8am.

There's a tip for you by the way – always turn the mobile off before bedtime as people at home think nothing of sending you texts while you are asleep, and they know that you are too.

The rain doesn't lay off – there's another massive downpour. It doesn't stop me cooking up cheesy bacon and eggs on the barbeque. Clearly my one night aversion to the grill was over. The feast goes down a treat, and nearly at the expense of the campsite too. I have done my best on this trip to avoid cleaning up after cooking. Today, I figure it is pretty obvious who has been using the barbecue. I am the only one, so I can't hide my filth! However, in a bid to remove the mountains of grease and fat, I send a mini fireball into the sky. I am clearly living a charmed life.

We know that despite the weather, we can't sit around here all day, so just decide to grin and bear it. It is not warm. Far from it. On the way out, and on foot, the big girl at reception makes the necessary arrangements for storing our van while we go to the Rock. Unbelievably she is not sure if we can have our same pitch back when we return. Trust me, the site is close to empty, love. We also have to sign a contract to put the van into storage, one clause of which says that basically if any of these clauses turn out to be illegal, then forget the whole thing. What kind of a contract is that!

She also informs us that there are no buses on Sundays so we have to walk to get the tram, which takes us half an hour after Nat directs us the wrong way. There were only two ways to go, and she picked the wrong one. However, with the skies clearing though still cold, you do get an excellent view of the Melbourne skyline from the very end of the tramline, which is our stop.

I want to go to St. Kilda. It is a place about which I have heard a lot. I think Shane Warne played cricket there. I hear that the band from *Neighbours* does gigs there. Today the guide books suggest there are excellent markets. Nat, of course, doesn't fancy it, so we pick a random place to get off the tram then wander aimlessly before accidentally discovering the free tourist shuttle bus which tours Melbourne and is a thoroughly excellent thing.

You can get on or off pretty much wherever you like, and pick up the commentary where you left it, and did I mention that it is free? Can you imagine that at home?

I can't believe that such a thing would exist in London. I am sure that they charge you the earth. I've certainly been on such a thing in New York and parted handsomely with dollars.

It is as though they really want you to feel welcome and explore their city for genuine reasons rather than of commercial gain, understanding that if you get off at the MCG, you might take a tour, or if you get off at Flinders Street station, all the shops are right in front of you. They will take you round proudly for free knowing that you will spend wherever they drop you. Again, Australia doesn't make you pay twice. It trusts that you will pay at some point and I can only applaud.

The commentary too shows the wealth of experiences that

Melbourne has to offer. Perhaps they are making an extra effort to compensate for the lack of wow factor that most people perceive Sydney has, and there's obviously the weather too.

Our driver is not the first, nor will he be the last to tell us that Melbourne has four seasons in one day.

Maybe the weather is key here, and maybe it is a fantastic place to be in the summer but whilst there is lots to do, I so want to like Melbourne but just can't somehow. Perhaps there is so much to do on purpose, to give you something to do when the four seasons are making their mischief. In places I find it scruffy and bohemian, in others a mixture of Haight-Ashbury in San Francisco and Cologne if you happened to have ever been to either.

Nat insists that we have to get off at the MCG. Hey, it is not just the MCG at this stop incidentally. There are about three other magnificent arenas or stadia here. Every other developed country in the world seems to build better stadia than we do at home. There is no way anybody would dream of building another Wembley next to Wembley. Building one was traumatic enough.

My dream though, is in tatters. I can't believe what I see as we cross the walkway to the cricket ground. Hoards of fans are also making their way. I didn't think for one moment that there would be two games in two days and that we wouldn't be able to get in. I am absolutely gutted. I can just about peer in through a crack here or a crack there and I get to glimpse what looks an amazing sporting environment. Alone with my thoughts, I resolve that I will be back here just like at the Sydney cricket ground. To watch Sam open the batting for England four tours from now. Wow – that is not long at all. Sam is not impressed with me prescribing his life for him, but as we pose in front of some of Australia's greatest sporting icons, honoured in statue, I know that these photos will come to have great significance fifteen years from now. Assuming Nat hasn't got her finger on the lens. I'm sure the Daily Mail will buy them.

Nat can see that I am gutted and urges me to book a tour later in the week. There simply won't be enough time though. Instead I have a green light to book our trip to Ramsay Street. I think she was hoping to avoid it but clearly can't turn me down now! She had her reef, I get my soap. It will be on Thursday, though they may be filming.

This news is given to me by the girl on the phone as something of an apology. I think it is brilliant and my spirits are instantly raised.

I am in such a good mood and this is confirmed when I decide to treat everybody.... to an afternoon at....the Old Melbourne Gaol!

I have no idea why I thought this was a good idea. I think in a dark way, it sounded like fun, and indoor fun too.

The tour is eerie and the kids love it, despite some strong language on the audio commentaries. It begins with us all lining up outside the cell with Sergeant Schnitzer ordering us to call him sergeant at all times. Then we are thrown in the cell and the lights go out! It stinks of urine.

Nat is quick to point out that Sergeant Schnitzer is clearly an out-of-work actor. I am quick to point out that he appears to be very much in work and has locked us up.

How different has this trip become? A *Neighbours* tour and a trip to Ayers Rock loom, the Great Barrier Reef and Australia Zoo seem a lifetime ago, and now we're in prison, studying the legend of Ned Kelly, and it is indeed him, around whom much of this unusual tourist location is built.

Of Irish descent, Kelly was a bushranger who became an iconic figure in Australian history and folklore after several murderous brushes with authority. He was hanged in the Melbourne Gaol. Right here. Nice.

Striking though, are the many miscarriages of justice that are written about here which were subsequently overturned with the advent of DNA in the nineties. The most famous of these is the last man to be hanged in Australia, one Ronald Ryan, whose death is still being disputed to this day.

I fear one sly google when I get back could lead to a whole day on the laptop unravelling Australia's most famous most wanted, but how strange to think that crimes so tin-pot in their execution compared to today's troubles, and committed so very long ago, could be re-examined now through the development of science. Imagine turning to Ned Kelly over a century ago, and saying that his very presence left a DNA trace which would mean that long after he had gone people whom he never knew would discover things that they never wanted to, all because of his DNA. To anybody who has ever committed a crime and thought that they have got away with it, somebody nowadays will always solve it for you at some point. There ain't nowhere to hide buddy.

Particularly striking is the women's area, and some of the very real and revealing graffiti. This was still an active prison until 1994. That is very recent, and here we stand in the grounds, by the toilet, reading the protests, of some very, very bad people, some of whom presumably, are still inside somewhere else. For a second you are almost face to face with criminality.

Of course, in the souvenir shop on the way out there is all sorts of Ned Kelly tat to buy. I feel slightly intellectually challenged by the morality of trying to make money out of firstly a killer, but secondly a dead man. Killer or not, surely the Ned Kelly estate own the rights to his intellectual property?

A much better souvenir and a funnier memory to leave with is to get the kids to pose for one of those police mug-shots with their own police number. A bit like Hugh Grant after the Divine Brown affair but without the hooker. The kids love it and act out of their skin with their most miserable just-been-arrested faces.

On the tram back, it happens again. Strangers talk to Nat.

These aren't strangers like the woman by the pool at Port Douglas, or the Irish at Airlie Beach, or the engineering scientist at Noosa. These are stranger strangers as in stranger rhyming with danger like the Italians in Sydney.

I never like to talk to people on public transport. It is a volume thing. You can be heard by everyone, but this absolute nutter of a woman – probably twenty-five – just starts asking Nat loads of questions, and whatever Nat says, the fruitcake Sheila always replies with the words 'Oh ok,' and with an annoying inflection to boot.

The kids are sniggering. I want to get off. Nat endures it all. I mean she could have said 'I've just popped into Melbourne for an abortion, and got a good price for my two existing kids, and tonight I am going to set fire to some Aboriginals' and this girl would have still replied 'Oh ok.'

Molly says that she isn't even sure if it is man or a woman. I am just praying she gets off before our stop. Ducking in and out of the conversation, it is clear that we have seen more of Australia in a month than she has in a lifetime. In fact she has the dyke look of many of those pictured in the Melbourne Gaol.

And you know the funny thing? She only went into town to buy a cork notice-board. Ah ok.

Day Thirty-Five

Nat's mum rang last night. I went nuts. We are on a cheap rate on the mobile so, in effect, after a connection charge, we pay local rates. Nat's mum thinks she is helping us out by ringing us, when, of course, we pick up a massive tab if we answer abroad if somebody else makes the call.

I encourage Nat to ring every night now. I think she needs it. Sam – everybody agrees – seems to be ready for home.

This morning, I have no confidence that the taxi will arrive to take us to the airport. Nor do I feel particularly secure about leaving the van. I am sure that we wake everybody up with the reversing beeps going off as Nat backs into the storage area. I don't imagine for the life of me that everything will be in one piece, and indeed the van secure, when we return on Wednesday night. Today we're off to the Rock.

We make a good start. Nick's Taxis show up on time. It costs forty dollars to Melbourne airport, the last ten of which are spent crawling up the motorway exit into the lane where all the taxis offload. A very cunning trick indeed.

It is heaving though. I never imagined for one minute that Melbourne Airport would be so busy so early and there are all sorts of flights up on the board going to all sorts of places, some of which we have cruised through, others which we never would have imagined having an airport. It is a fascinating insight into just how badly connected Australia is unless you use the sky.

Of course, we are way too early but I take great pleasure in watching the sun rise against the backdrop of planes taking off. Who doesn't find that a magical thing in life, sitting there watching jets come and go with all these people that you have never met going to places you have never even heard of, all against the rising sun? Just think how your life could change if you actually talked to any of these people. You could be sitting metres away from love, opportunity or wealth, but you'll never know it.

I read a paper for the first time since we left. I read it in full as there is so much time to kill. It is full of Qantas analysis after the ripped fuselage incident. I always like to tempt fate like this.

I am not sure what my expectations of the next two days are. Firstly, nobody is calling it Uluru – it is Ayers Rock all the way. Secondly it is all incredibly barren looking from the sky. Nothing until the last five minutes.

Most importantly I will never ever forget Nat's first words, when she sees it for the first time from the air.

'That's it, there,' she analysed.

Except, it wasn't.

How, in a million years, amidst a sea of flat orange and nothing else, can you mistake something else for Ayers Rock? This is one of the funniest moments of my life. I just wish that she had said it louder.

From the sky, there is something wonderful about picking out the airstrip. It looks like the least likely airfield that I have ever seen, conjuring images that you had as a kid when you first heard about this thing called 'the flying doctor' where people would just land anywhere that was vaguely a strip in a bid to get medication to people. When we land, the airport itself has a gorgeous old-fashioned quality about it, as though every plane would have one of those old noisy propellers. Hours between flights rather than every minute, and just like the old days, we get to walk across the tarmac.

It is hot too, which is welcome. The first real warmth that we have had in fact since way before Sydney, almost since way before

219

Brisbane in fact. Was Brisbane on this trip? I can only remember today and yesterday now, to be honest.

Nat said that there would be snakes, dingoes and no roads here. This is a lie, as is the fact that Alice Springs is the gateway to Ayers Rock. It is about four hundred and fifty kilometres actually.

Within ten minutes of landing we are on a very comfortable road, orange admittedly, and pulling up at our resort, just off the Stuart Highway, and yes, *Neighbours* fans, the Lasseter Highway too.

The resort is circular. There are four hotels of varying standard and you just keep looping the loop on the free shuttle bus that goes round and round all day long and you get off wherever you want. Not even we could go wrong.

Our stop is the Outback Pioneer Hotel – sounds kind of country and western, hey? There's a bit of a giveaway when we arrive as the driver informs us that 'at this one you might want to leave your bags with the porter here.' This is not to show off the exemplary service at a five star establishment, this is to tell you that the room is not ready at what is a very expensive hotel, yet worse in quality than a Travelodge. Sure, it is cute and has a German bierkeller feel to it, but thank goodness that we have ordered a family room because this is backpacker territory. This is gap year student boulevard, not for thirty-somethings with two kids. This is the lowest of the low when it comes to Ayers Rock hotels, and believe me, the whole package with two nights accommodation has cost us two grand sterling.

You *can* just wander in and out of all the other hotels by taking the circular shuttle bus just like in Vegas but without the tack or the common people plucking witnesses off the street as they get married.

So, if you can just wander in and out and use their facilities, you might as well stay at the cheapest. There are literally four hotels in a circle either side of the main road and poor Jamie the bus driver drives everybody round hour after hour from dawn to dusk.

Who is he?

There is something odd about him. He has a bit of snivel and is clad in a scarf even though it is warm out there. At every stop he calls out the name of the hotel and couldn't sound more miserable in doing so to the degree that even the kids are copying him when he shouts 'Outback Pioneer' with the enthusiasm of a turkey a week before Christmas.

He does make you think though. This is a resort essentially built for the tourists, and the land is so flat with many of the buildings built into the ground, that you start to wonder where the locals live. There is no nearest town for them to commute in from, and what kind of life do they have? Jamie gives me the impression that he has been placed in society, as though he had done wrong in the past and had been given a new chance in the world but he had to start at the bottom and that bottom was at Yulara – the Ayers Rock resort. Who, in their right mind, would drive a bus round and round the same ten minute circle all day long unless they had been forced to, or perhaps, just maybe, unless they had grown up here, which doesn't look likely.

In my naivety I am surprised to see a supermarket. How daft is that? This trip has certainly exposed some very basic preconceptions within me, and I have travelled a lot. Of course, there would be a supermarket. Had I really been thinking that we were all going to be living off the land?

The sheer practicality of getting stuff into the resort is mind-blowing. I am curious to accompany any driver on the road to Alice Springs to see what is out there, though despite the fact that I can see a Maui like ours in the car park, I know that that would have been a journey too far for us in the van, this time at least, and it just has the words 'run out of diesel' written all over it. To think we thought Alice was just down the road!

We spend the afternoon at the Cultural Centre. This is not something that I would normally do. I am not the kind of person who can read every map or annotated diagram. I am more of a skimmer, but this place is fascinating on everything from the history of the Rock to Aboriginal land rights. We just gaze for a good hour or so.

It is also a very good shop – not a cheap, tacky shop where you can spend twenty dollars buying replicas of the Rock. In fact I don't see any of these – surely they have missed a trick!

Instead there is just a wealth of books, each one of them as good as the next though realistically you can only buy so many. I suspect too that many of these books are local books, not available outside of the resort. You can take your pick from recipes of the outback to the story of the woman who married an Aboriginal and then wrote it all down. We're here essentially to book a trip up to the feet of the Rock tomorrow. There are loads on offer, including the ridiculously pompous dinner under the stars, where you can have a champagne feast served up for you in the shadow of the Rock when night falls. It just doesn't seem in keeping with what it is all about. I mean, it is all very well handing it back to the locals, and it is clear that tourism is controlled in terms of the numbers coming in and in respect to the Aboriginals, but it just seems to be everything obnoxious and western to serve up gourmet meals underneath this iconic symbol.

That trip is clearly not for us, and with the kids, we have little option but to book a half day tour for tomorrow afternoon, even though Molly, budding geography geek, has begun lecturing *us* on the history and geology of the Rock.

On the bus back, I try a conversation with Jamie, but he is not really having it. He's friendlier to locals though and brilliantly the bus makes a detour to round the back of the resort and we get to see where the locals live when we have to drop off a teacher. Perhaps she is *the* teacher. Again, like many people she looks like she is passing through. I had heard that if you wanted to come out to Australia on a teacher or doctor visa that you had to do six months or a year in the outback or middle of nowhere. This must be this teacher's Siberian calling.

We also bear witness to the fire brigade show. With all its bells ringing, the fire engine comes tearing out of the fire station. I am the only one wise to this however, pointing out to Nat that there is absolutely no fire anywhere around the resort at this point and this is more a PR exercise, some sort of show-off self justification, just to let you know that taxpayers money is being well spent. God, that has to be even more boring than Jamie's job. You can only play so many games of cards, as the *new* Irish back in Melbourne will tell you.

I notice too that nobody, absolutely nobody, is calling it Uluru. It is very much Ayers Rock, through and through.

Around six in the evening, you sense the light fading and the heat coming off the land. Behind the Outback Pioneer is an excellent lookout point to see the sun go down on the Rock. Unfortunately it is not a secret and half the hotel gathers. We can see the coaches picking up too for dinner under the stars but this is better, and it is here and now that you learn the true meaning of the Rock. It is not that it is a geographical freak, or that it has some great dark meaning for the Aboriginal community, or that it is something absolutely beautiful to look at, it is an incredible place to visit because of the aura around it. It does feel special, almost spiritual. And I am a cynic.

I actually couldn't give a toss about it as a land mass or tourist attraction, but it does feel calm, healthy, wonderful, and positive just to be here. At the lookout point, waiting for the perfect angle and the perfect light, you just sit, stop and stare. That's what I mean about the aura. All that matters is what it does to you and how it makes you feel. It reels you in to contemplate your lot. Then in an instant, it just goes black, and everybody gets up and trots back for dinner. The spell is broken but it will be there again tomorrow and the night after that and the night after that.

In the evening, the Outback Pioneer comes alive. It clearly is the most sociable and fun of the four hotels. It really is like an old-fashioned back of beyond pub with country music live every night, and rows of tables for you to just plonk yourself down and join in with anyone and everyone. Sometimes, country music *is* acceptable. They are clearly making a packet too, even though wine is rationed to one bottle per person for fear of it ending up in Aboriginal hands. Some of their young like a drink apparently and consumption is regulated.

You would be wasting your time and money to stay here, but then book for dinner under the stars. They serve a barbecue dinner every night that looks fantastic. I fancy the Outback special with emus and kangaroos but I stubbornly discipline myself. I need to change my diet so opt for the salad but here's the thing – you have to cook your own dinner.

Now, obviously we have barbecued almost every night for the last month, so we are not averse, but now they are charging you full restaurant prices for the privilege of *you* cooking your own dinner. You hand over your cash, and they give you a plate of cold meat, and you cook up. I think this is a bit cheeky actually, but everybody is falling for it as row after row of barbecue is full with people keen to meet each other over dinner. They clearly haven't spent the last month barbecuing every night, and see it as a novelty rather than a con.

We're very tired anyway after the early start, so we retire early and it is musical beds again. Sam is in with me. He has developed a dingo obsession, gibbering on about them all the time. Any dog is a dingo. He is convinced that he is going to be eaten by a dingo. I think this is because somebody mentioned the Chamberlain family earlier in the day.

Day Thirty-Six

The Chamberlain family's story of course gripped Australia and the world. I remember it as a kid and I was only nine. Lindy Chamberlain convicted and then cleared of murder after claiming that a dingo had taken her daughter Azaria. The body was never found.

Of course, in 1980 there was no internet and no mass media. If you google 'Dingo Ayers Rock' today, you will be there for hours, the most fascinating postings concerning a twenty five year old girl who wandered into an Alice Springs police station relatively recently to claim that she was, in fact, after all these years, the dingo child. Of course, the internet can be a breeding ground for the deranged and even when it is honest and true, it doesn't give you all the answers. The last thread that I can find on this is a report that the Chamberlains (now separated) didn't want anything to do with this girl, including her offer of a DNA test.

Why, if this is a true-mour rather than a rumour, wouldn't they want to know, why wouldn't they just do what they can to dismiss it by allowing the test? Like Madeleine McCann, who can really know?

The internet makes one thing certain – that no stories like this will ever go away, and twenty five years from now, someone will walk into a Portuguese station too and claim to be Madeleine. It just never goes away.

And Sam awakes this morning still asking questions about dingoes, even though we have yet to see one, and despite the fact that since the Chamberlains there has only been one case of a dingo killing a human. We have either tormented him, or his imagination has been set to active.

We slept well though. We had been trying to stay up to watch Gordon Ramsay on the Andrew Denton show. Denton is one of the few Australian broadcasters that I have actually heard of so I am keen to watch his work. Instead, the last thing that Nat and I can remember watching is a show called *Farmer Wants A Bride*. Sounds classy, doesn't it?

After breakfast I text my mate Findlay Young. Fin came to Ayers Rock as part of his challenge to run twenty four half marathons in twenty four days in twenty four countries in 2006. I know this because I rang him to do a twenty minute podcast every day.

Findlay's was a wonderful achievement and I was proud to be part of it, but now I am here at the Rock, I can't help but chuckle to myself as I recall his words that they had cleared a path for him to do a half marathon around it. Somehow it doesn't seem right!

You probably have never heard of Fin, or his extraordinary run, and that was part of the problem. It is a magnificent story. Unfortunately the people doing his PR weren't good enough. You would have heard about it, you would think, if a man who had twice recovered from thyroid cancer ran around Ayers Rock, wouldn't you? You certainly know who Jayne Tomlinson was.

This morning we are back on the bus. Ever-present Jamie is driving. Of course he is. We ask him to take us to the camel tour, and in the most casual of timetabling, he promises to come and pick us up in about an hour or so! I think this is brilliant.

In a short two minute journey, you get an insight into how this community functions. Jamie slows up the bus to talk to a buddy of his. It appears there was some incident last night. A cyclist was hit. This is big news in Uluru. Jamie thinks the guy could be in trouble. And then he drives off! There's no need for a newspaper or a radio, just tell somebody and they will tell somebody else. Perhaps though, this is why the fire brigade were all singing and dancing.

At the camel tour, we get chatting to one of the staff. She is from New Zealand and left her partner in 2001 to go travelling. They're still together apparently! It is a different world out here. I imagine that she doesn't realise it is 2008, that the time just drifts when you're cleaning and riding camels in all year round sunshine. You wake up eventually and realise a decade has passed.

But why wouldn't you? It is so still out here, so peaceful. No cars, no media, no noise, no bad things – just peace. I am almost hypnotised just watching Molly and Sam trot off on a camel, staring beyond the horizon contemplating, wondering if I could chuck it all in and walk camels for a living.

I'm pretty sure that the answer is yes as long as you don't worry about having to go back to anything. If you come you have to come for good, but then surely you become Jamie, and that's no good either. At some point you surely have to leave and then you ask yourself about the seven years you spent walking camels when you didn't get on the property ladder and didn't pay into a pension. I conclude therefore, that life out here is wonderful, but it is not permanent reality.

I am curious to know more about those from the Aboriginal community who have done this in reverse. There comes a point, and it may be now, when this generation of Aboriginals turn their back on their forefathers and traditions, and see their future in the big world out there. The internet again makes all things possible. The alcohol restrictions, I sense, are an inkling of what is to come. There is a world beyond the Rock and they know it.

Nothing shouts this point louder than the tour that we have chosen this afternoon.

On the drive to the checkpoint before you enter the national park, Nat tells me that there are thirty-five deaths a year at the Rock. I do not know where she has got this from, but I make that about one every ten days. You are asked not to climb it, out of respect. I am sceptical.

At the visitors centre before we meet our guides, one thing looms large and sets my suspicion radar to maximum. I am reading a collection of extraordinary letters from all around the world from people in South Africa, Germany, England, all of whom claim to have got back home after a trip here and having climbed the Rock, or stolen a bit of it, have found that very, very bad things have happened to them. Their letters are rarely addressed to anybody specific and normally include the phrase '...please pass on my sincerest apologies to the Aboriginal community.' These are people who have convinced themselves that they have betrayed the spirituality of the Rock, and now, suffering ill fate, write to complete strangers with their entire life story.

I am fascinated but equally find it ridiculous. Your interpretation of these letters may be determined by your own personal religious beliefs, but I am stating on the record now that if something bad happens to me after writing this, then that's just bad luck. There is no way, all those thousands of miles away when I get home that the ghost of the Rock is shadowing my every move and waiting to pounce. If I skid on an icy Tyneside street at 5am this winter, it is because it was icy or I was driving badly, not because I dared to question the Rock.

Oh yes, the Aboriginal stories and histories are fascinating and plentiful, but it is this whole myth thing, this formidable perception of power over the weak-minded that leaves a lasting impression.

Then there's the tour itself, and I bring you back to my point about the merging of the Aboriginal world and the modern world. We are guided by our interpreter – one of *us* from the western world, if you like. Then there's Elsie in her wheelchair, who doesn't speak English or allow photos. Next to her and learning the ropes is her grand-daughter, at a guess. I am thinking – is this the same girl I saw renting a DVD in the supermarket yesterday?

Equally, as much as they may wish to educate you on Aboriginal life, they are not daft, fully branded in their blue polo shirts with the tour company logoed in the top left hand corner!

The tour is boring as hell, though the kids are really well behaved. It is strung out to eternity as Elsie puts her spin on the formation of the Rock, and everything is meticulously translated. It sounds like a fairytale to me. She is also telling stories that date back some forty thousand years in time which I think is brilliant as it blows the whole Christianity thing out of the water.

I am tempted to take a piece of the Rock just to quash all those nutters whose letters are posted back at the visitors centre. Nat reminds me about the strong quarantine rules across Australia so I promise not to, even though of course, the Rock by its sheer colour, automatically leaves so much of itself stained on your shoes, clothes and bags. You are destined to take the Rock with you – that's the point which the culture here has overlooked!

One of the problems with tours like this is that you can't get off them. Nor can you pick and choose who else has paid. Today we have two of the vilest, commonest, and most annoying couples that I have ever met. They are from Birmingham.

What is wrong with them? They are not funny and they think that they are. They are the worst of Brits abroad. They are rude. This clearly is their big life trip.

They are the first to start talking amongst themselves, in tandem with the guide, talking to other people in the group, even talking to Elsie, despite the fact she doesn't speak English.

Wait a minute, she is laughing at them. She *does* speak English. Ah, the myths are unravelling. Listen, I think a lot of what I have heard is nonsense, but at least I have the respect to listen to the woman and to behave as they asked. Maurice starts laying on innuendo, and tells Elsie that she wouldn't be out of place as a page three girl, whilst taking her photo uninvited.

They really are low class people, and once Elsie has had the imposition of her photo being taken, everybody in the group is forced to take her photo, as she joshes with us in English. What is going on? The myths unravel again. Then, the killer defining moment...Elsie hands out her business card.

Her *business* card? What, so you have got equipment out there beyond the Rock to print your business card, or have you been playing us all along? Our guide tells us that as we have now taken her photo, it is our duty to send the photo back to Elsie. Yeah, right. I am sure that only the very gullible and scared ever bother.

Here is my conclusion. This tour is a sham. The Aboriginal community would have been better off not even attempting to educate the rest of the world on their history and culture. I fear that they have undermined themselves. Clearly too, they are taking steps, very large ones, into what we know as the 'normal' world. I would be surprised if one hundred years from now, whilst the Rock will still be there barring a sandstorm or violence, you get decent odds on their community not being intact.

I have no problem with them being business-like. It just seems to conflict the rawness of everything else that they claim to be.

Just before sunset, we are driven to a viewing point for a glass of champagne and the chance to take a hundred photos, all of the same thing! Actually, this is an excellently organised bit of the trip. There is ample room and not a tailback in sight as coach after coach arrives, in plenty of time to catch the extraordinary light patterns that fall as the sun goes down. I think we are incredibly lucky. The weather isn't great and it looks like a thunderous storm is brewing. I can tell you now, that this is the shot that you want to take. This is Ayers Rock at is most dramatic and most moody.

Within a twenty minute segment, you can build your own portfolio of every shot and shade of the Rock, enough for your own calendar. You would perceive that at any other location in the world, you would have to stalk the land for months to get twelve different aspects. Such is the mood of the beast and the fickleness of the elements that here you can do all that in moments.

Unfortunately the shocking Brummies still linger. It becomes one of those scenarios where you have to ask a complete stranger to take a photo of your family in order to get the entire family in. One of the most amazing and poignant photos that you could have taken, and it is in the hands of people that you despise!

However, it is their parting words that make me sit up and take note. They break news to us of a Qantas strike. They are flying to Hong Kong as we are, on exactly the same day. We depart from Adelaide and pick up in Sydney. They got a call just a couple of weeks ago informing them that there was now no flight from Sydney and that they would be leaving from Melbourne.

Melbourne? No, this can't be true. Today's seed of paranoia is sewn. Were our travel plans about to be thrown into chaos?

Day Thirty-Seven

Last night was a disaster. We arrived back at the bierkeller bench area and Ray Malone was strutting his stuff again. He is the camp entertainer. Camp as in outdoor living rather than camp as in air steward, hairdresser, or anybody called Julian. And you know what? He is great – in a country music kind of way, bashing out Waltzing Matilda and the classic 'G'day, G'day How You Going.' It just sat right. It was naff but tuneful. It was very, very Australian. Later we found out he has a tumour and has probably not long to live.

No, he wasn't the reason that it was a disaster. Nat got talking to the government.

I let it pass last night but I am cross this morning. It cost us dinner. We were going to dine at the Bough House restaurant on site. I was nervous that there might not be anything for the kids but I certainly knew that there was a feast there for me. Molly, surprisingly was up for trying it and even threw a little wobbly when we were just making no progress about deciding when to eat, even though I warned her that camel, stir-fry croc and emu were all on the menu. I went and sniffed it out too. It looked wonderful. I knew that Nat would hate it but this is the biggest drawback of being on holiday with her. She thinks eating is gross. I think it is cultural and very, very essential.

Believe me if you can think of every animal in the world, they had it there with a sauce on it. This is a missed opportunity.

The kids and I were twiddling our thumbs, tummies rolling and all because I went to the bar only to return to find that three very unmatched individuals, one of whom was born in Leeds, were chatting to Nat like they were at a school reunion. I was deeply suspicious of the whole thing. They may not know it but if they are undercover they weren't very good at it.

Three adults, clearly not in a relationship with each other, not really drinking and certainly not touring but just here for the night. Why they tell us that they work for the government but don't reveal any more is baffling, and what they have come to learn or spy on is even more mystifying. If it is not a cover story, it is certainly only a portion of the truth. Tomorrow they drive back to Alice Springs. All very, very odd. I have quite a good understanding of 'intelligence' and these guys were bullshitting.

So that was the disaster. Nat, trying to uncover the undercover, left us all starving, but more importantly, culturally deprived. That camel starter looked awesome.

To top it all, she misses the alarm this morning, thinking we are still on Melbourne time. For some reason there is a half hour thing going on with the Northern Territory time-zone. I don't really understand the need to be oddball and do a half hour time difference but it throws us today.

We have to fly – literally – and I leave armed with books, one on Peter Falconio, another on recipes. I knew I couldn't resist. At the airport, it is the least complicated airport experience of my life, despite being singled out for a body search. It is so calm and so un-busy. Air travel should always be thus. We're starving though because we are late and take the unusual step of ordering a delicious beef pie for breakfast.

As we wait in departures, some twenty metres from our plane, I study the history of the airport and salute those people who got this thing off the ground. It is easy when you can see an airstrip to take it for granted, but dreaming it up out here from a sea of orange is just incredible stuff. If I have failed to paint sufficiently good pictures of what the land is like here, next time the French Open comes on from Roland Garros, that is the colour of the Northern Territory.

The pilot is clearly showboating at take-off, unnecessarily showing off and hamming up that pilot voice on the intercom. Nat wants to cry and is doing that childish 'say goodbye to the Rock' thing. The view from the sky is spectacular, better than on landing, and the take-off is so simple. Anybody who has ever been pushed back at Heathrow and has spent thirty minutes trying to depart needs to get to the Rock.

I can only imagine the conversation.

'Are we clear to take off, control tower?'

'What the fuck do you think?'

The next flight is about three hours away.

Ours is a twenty minute hop to Alice Springs – you remember some four hundred and fifty kilometres away by road – yet still time enough in the air to take off, serve a meal, clear up and land. This has to be a record and the best service in airline history. The food is decent too. I can only assume that it is law in Australia that if you fly, you feed. At home, health and safety would deny you this moment.

In Alice it is hot, and very laidback. It is a trouble-free airport, where clearly the same planes take off from the same gate every day without fail. No variations. Oddly though, we have a slight delay that gets passed off with a certain amount of internal disloyalty as not being the problem of the ground staff. Oh no we run a tight ship here, they seem to be implying. This delay is another airport's problem. They haven't heard the Qantas strike rumour by the way, but then it is the kind of place where news would break months after it has happened.

We have a small amount of time to kill so I read the local paper, full of tales of unrest in a town where clearly nothing goes on. There are loads of jobs too. We both agree that we would use up our entire holiday allocation, and mine is up to eight weeks now, to come here and do a mundane job, just to hang out.

There's a cracking little feature about a guy called Graham Hall who seems to be running some sort of flying business and doing very nicely. Our eyes are opened, as Nat is a half decent pilot. You see, our world is changing, our perception of what is needed to survive is different. Life as we used to know it is over. I see everybody back at work as small and insignificant, my own radio show too, an unimportant nonsense in the history of our lives. I have truly seen the cliché at play. Work to live, not live to work.

When we board I get stuck into my literature. Terri Irwin's book awaits and I read up on the Falconio case. The book that I have bought is written in a totally 'Joanne Lees had nothing to do with it' kind of way, which is nonsense really because anybody who followed that case, regardless of the outcome, must have at some point had doubts and suspicions. The court ultimately agreed that she was blameless, but that doesn't stop you having serious questions along the way.

I have become a tourist sucker and realised that I should not have bought this book. It devotes a chapter to Falconio, and barely touches the surface. Something journalistic within me however wants to track the Lees girl down. She must have a lot in her head. Her life, in short, must be ruined.

I feel devious, as though I would like to get chatting to her in her local, which, I understand, is in a small village in Yorkshire, and unpick those private, locked parts of her mind. She can't be too difficult to find, and I am clear in *my* mind, that she still has some story to tell, even if they did get the right guy. If you google the Falconio case, it just leaves you with more questions, particularly about the guy that she had a fling with in Sydney who seems to have escaped a media mauling, and let's not forget the supposed sightings of Falconio after his abduction. The outback clearly takes its secrets with it. When they do those TV shows entitled *Where Are They Know?* then perhaps they should challenge themselves a bit more and rather than concentrating on sportsmen who opened sports bars, they should try and find people like her. There is still so much to tell, even though she has written about it herself. It preoccupies me for the entire return journey.

Back in Melbourne, it doesn't feel good at all. It feels like the trip is over. It feels like windy Newcastle or rainy Manchester. It is a wake-up call. Qantas staff know nothing, by the way, of the strike.

We head back to the holiday park, depressed at what was a truly captivating – for its aura alone – whirlwind trip to the Rock. We are also miffed to get back to our campsite. We want to get the hell out of Melbourne as quickly as possible. We can't leave just yet though. All four of us have to go to the doctors.

Day Thirty-Eight

There was nothing to do last night, post the Rock, except to get pissed. I rang Stonesy, Damian and Harty. Apparently I signed off to Harty with the words 'I love you babes.' I must have been wasted.

It was also a big sex night. Apart from that I remember nothing.

The mornings are getting colder and colder and barbecuing breakfast is getting more and more ridiculous, but still, a good fry up is just what we need to get on our way for a very long day. Today is *Neighbours* day. And after that we're off to the theatre to see *Wicked*.

We are probably staying a day too long in Melbourne but I would have been absolutely gutted not to have gone to Ramsay Street, and *Wicked* is everybody else's compensation for my guilty pleasure.

On our way to the bus stop we see the Irish packing up. They're off to St. Kilda to crash with some friends for a bit. All they ever seem to do is sit in the camp kitchen and play cards. They don't seem to be having the time of their life. Oh bring back the original Irish please!

This is the first time that we have actually taken the bus all the way into town – good job too as it is only now that we realise what a dump where we have been staying actually is, out in the suburbs. Sure, it is a city, but Coburg is grim. Officially, this is my worst location on tour so far. Still, tomorrow, we're off again. Destination Adelaide. Vaguely.

At just before half one, we walk down from Flinders Street station to a little office on the corner, from where the *Neighbours* tour begins. There are two a day, and it is a very simple formula, nicely padded out to last three hours. It begins with a good drive of close to forty-five minutes in a very colourful minibus with 'Official Neighbours Tour' daubed all over it. A little bit embarrassing, if you happened to have been dragged along as I have done to my family.

On this drive, unsurprisingly, they play videos of the show. Brilliantly simple.

One of the videos is the first ever episode which, at a guess, hardly anybody has ever seen. I am sure the show was a fad in the UK, a bandwagon that people joined. In Australia it got pulled and changed network so the chances of anybody saying that they were there on day one must be minimal. I think that I joined it after about six months.

I am pretty certain that my earliest memory is of a character called Shane being interviewed in real life; perhaps on the TV show *Wogan*, explaining that he was leaving to join another show called *The Flying Doctors*. I also remember Madge had a brother called Max. Now this, you see, is going way back.

But this afternoon, as the first episode plays, the ghost of Townsville comes back to haunt us. Will we ever shake that monkey off our back? Jim Robinson – what a star he has become – is explaining that Scott (Jason Donovan, though not originally) has just called from Townsville and is having a ball. I laugh out loud in the bus and nobody else understands why. I can't possibly imagine what kind of ball he could have been having. This, for me, is an early factual inaccuracy!

There is nervous chatter amongst the bus, and groups from all ages – though mostly British – bring their own *Neighbours* memories to the party. There are two posh Geordie girls sitting in front of us, clearly here on Dad's money. They can't really understand the Scott and Charlene wedding sequence as we relive it on the video. They must have been about seven at the time. This proves one thing. That everybody *does* join the show at different stages in their life, and nobody can really remember why they stopped watching it.

For me, it probably came to an end in 1989 when I took a gap year, so in all I watched it for about two years in total, and as we arrive at Erinsborough High, I have to confess to everybody that I haven't seen it since, unless I happened to have turned on early for the evening news. This will explain why I do know that Paul Robinson is back in the show, and that I have heard of Toadfish, but little else. As for the plot – well, does it really matter anyway?

I don't really recall much happening at Erinsborough High after Scott, Charlene, Mike and Plain Jane Super-Brain. Possibly Todd and Phoebe too.

So at this stage on the tour, I am not particularly bothered either way. Still we all pile out for photos, at what is actually a language school for overseas students. How they film and teach is beyond me. Surely filming involves noise; studying requires silence.

The tour guide, by the way, is excellent and knows absolutely everything about the show. I don't catch her name though she did tell me that she was running for Melbourne City Council – was the *Neighbours* tour really her running ticket? Put me on the council as I have shown all these Brits around Melbourne!

Erinsborough, by the way, is an anagram of *Neighbours* with an extra o added. I have just learnt that, and am amazed that I have never heard it before.

After the school, we head out to the studios. It is pointed out to us that the front of the main building, whilst it might just look an administrative block of the TV network, has actually featured in many different scenes over the years, including acting as an airport terminal! We are shown the clip to support the theory, and as we park up alongside it, it is clear that the show is cleverly edited and very much on a budget using every drop of resource, sometimes time and time again!

The next bit is the really smart bit. We pull up at the back of the studios where there are a couple of permanent sets. Away to our left is Lassiter's but we can't get in there today. Behind us is Lou Carpenter's car workshop. In front we are left staring at a shop frontage with our backs to Lou's place. This is deliberate, because with a wonderful piece of comic timing that puts the fear of God into us all, Dr Karl Kennedy emerges through Lou's workshop, walking at speed and just bouncing in.

'Good afternoon everybody.'

Everyone is aghast, even super cool Nat next to me loses it for a moment. The Geordie girls are virtually orgasmic, but then I hear it doesn't take much.

I should point out that this is not a chance meeting but it is a guarantee of this tour that you get to meet a cast member, and even though Alan Fletcher has been playing this role since 1994, so long after I stopped watching, I recognise him instantly and seem to be able to recall half his plotlines. This must be the *Neighbours* effect. You don't actually remember ever watching it and you can drop in and out of it at any point and none of it matters. It just sleeps in your sub-conscious.

Clearly, no other TV show in the world has this relationship with its audience – and remember that these tours go every day, twice a day. Fletch, as he seems to be called, is relaxed, warm, fun, polished, and professional. He's an actor, don't forget.

I believe that the viewer-show relationship here does merit Karl Kennedy's overtime, but I also think he and the rest of them would be nothing without the BBC, so he should bloody well do it.

This is unfair of me. Today the show airs at 6.30 in the evening in Australia, and stands at eighteen in the ratings. That is pretty good, I can tell you. Clearly now the show has also moved to Channel Five in the UK, which I think will kill it, and I put this to Fletch. I think he spots a journalistic question and bats it back well, saying all the right things about getting an omnibus on Five, and great online content. This is a standard media answer, and he is well rehearsed. I remain sceptical however if the show will find a new generation of fans on Five and whilst it may still be going great guns down under, the area that may suffer is in all that extra work that its stars have acquired on UK shores over the last twenty years or so. There have been so many records, so many pantomimes and so many careers that I think *this* is the *Neighbours* effect and why there seems to be a UK loyalty. The show *may* survive but will actors have the career platform that they historically have had? After all some parts of the UK still struggle with a good picture for Channel 5 and I can't name any other shows on it apart from this and *Home And Away*.

Fletch, for example, tells us that he has panto in Aberdeen and a gig with his band at Liverpool University scheduled in his diary. I wouldn't imagine that he has this option anywhere else in the world. It is a good job too because when you have been Dr Karl Kennedy for fourteen years, what do you do next?

Whilst anything he says to me could be an act by nature of the fact that he is an actor, I am very confident that he lives and breathes the character, the part, and the show. He must love it if he is prepared to do a weekly trivia night or gig with his band at St. Kilda, where the only audience is ....fans of the show. And this by the way has been going on for years.

I think his significance in my world is this. Yes, I think it is great that you can wander round the set and shake his hand, nay even become a little star-struck, but like so many of our experiences so far, you have to place it in the context of your life. Nat is clutching the 'Twenty Years Of *Neighbours*' book, freshly signed by KK himself. I just wonder where the years went.

It is ridiculously shit to say so, and this is where I lose

credibility but the whole Kylie and Jason era was just a great escape from adolescence. In their world nothing seemed to happen, and everything that did was wonderful, and if there were ever a problem, it would always be solved in the next episode.

It was just perfect and fluffy and the exact opposite of our home-grown, miserable *EastEnders* which was launching at the time with a dead body in its first episode, setting the scene for years of dramatic misery. Here the stunning belief that two kids of our age were having such a ball and an idyllic existence while I was really hating school, studying, and life in general was something that never left you. The best bit of school was getting home for *Neighbours*. Fact.

So what does this teach you? That life is flying by bloody fast and you can't get any of it back. Karl Kennedy put me into context.

I make no secret of the fact that this is a dream come true to be here. Nat finally comes unstuck too. She has been playing it cool but she is now gushing at having got her book signed for her Mum. I feel smug because I told her to buy the book before the bus left so we could get it signed, rather than getting it on our return, when the moment would have gone. The kids couldn't be more bored.

It is time to move on, and I watch as Alan Fletcher leaves. I watch him all the way as far as the eye can see to see if he is on autopilot (acting) or genuine. A job is a job, and whenever I have always done a gig over the years, I always leave as quickly as I can. I am always on autopilot. I hate the whole thing, in fact.

I think he's genuine. I like him.

Next we're off to Ramsay Street. This is the big one. Our guide apologises for not being able to walk up it, as they *are* filming. I am glad. Nat is disappointed – and she's the actress! We can see Toadfish with two other stars plus about twenty crew or so, but there is virtually no security. The eighteenth most watched show in Australia doesn't care less if you are a tabloid journalist sniffing around or some crazed stalker fan. You can just stand there and watch. There is nothing really to stop you, even though they ask for quiet, from beeping your car horn as loud as you like during a take. Life goes on all around Pinoak Court, which is the real Ramsay Street that you and I know and love.

It is fascinating. The scene that we are watching involves a character, whose name I know not, running up outside one of those famous houses and taking a newspaper out of the mailbox outside the house. That's it. That's all that they are filming, but I learn so much.

The speed with which the umbrellas appear at the slightest drizzle, presumably to preserve continuity; the fleeces that the cast get to keep warm whilst waiting; the make-up lady constantly re-applying; the effort gone into wrapping up the local newspaper in plastic bags; the printing of the fictional paper in the first place; and the pillow.

The pillow? Yes, the pillow. The pillow is not picked up by the camera but it serves as a prop at ground level as to how far our character must run before stopping. That is his marker on the pavement. Who dreams all this stuff up, and how far in advance must they be working? The answer is that there are four producers working on different planning aspects well in advance.

But what about the real people that actually live in this street? Surely the novelty must wear off, and they must be tempted at some point to turn around and say '...er, sorry no more filming' but we are told that not only are these houses at a premium, there is also a massive waiting list to buy them, and that one of the conditions of sale is that you allow filming. It doesn't sound very enforceable to me.

One day this show probably will end, and I suspect then that the houses will be worthless or we will all be watching a show entitled *Meet The Real Neighbours!* The scene that we are seeing today will not be shown at home for six months. Doubtless, it will be cut or we will miss it.

I text Cliffey, one of my producers, to tell him where I am and what we are doing. I am delighted as he only got to meet Stephanie Mcintosh when he came out on the tour.

Stephanie who? Actually she was Jason Donovan's half-sister in real life, but that is by the by.

I think I am getting a little giddy here actually, insisting on a family pose by the portable Ramsay Street road sign! Sam needs a pee too, so we sneak round the back of the park that surrounds the set and urinate up Harold Bishop's back passage. I am glad that we did, at least for the innuendo that it allows me to include.

At the end of the tour, there's the drive back into the city with more *Neighbours* Greatest Hits playing. Technically we have driven for over an hour and watched videos of the show. We met a 'star' for twenty minutes, and watched a scene being retaken four or five times. But, you know what, it made my day. It was totally awesome to stand there and think of all those scenes that you watched from so far away at home, and all the individual journeys that we had all been on in the interim years, of how I had actually met both Kylie and Jason through work, and here I had been standing where it all began. It was wonderful in a really simple, naive kind of way. All good things must come to an end, though.

We have time to kill. Time for a nice meal before we head for the theatre. Except, we can't find anywhere to eat in Melbourne.

We must be doing something wrong here. We just can't find anywhere and instead opt for 'Amazing Asia' in a food mall. It is disgusting. Positively vile. A total waste of.....three quid.

We arrive at the Regent Theatre an hour early. It is a beautiful theatre, not that I care about these things. Nat would say that an hour before a show is just the right time to arrive. I tend to think it is about fifty nine minutes too long.

Opposite, I witness one of the best pieces of marketing that I have ever seen. *Wicked*, is the prequel to *The Wizard of Oz*. Across the road, they proclaim that 'Shane Warne The Musical Is

Coming – The Other Wizard Of Oz.' I love clever gimmicks like that. I can't believe, however, that a musical about a cricketer can be in the mainstream, even when the cricketer is as colourful as Warney.

Inside, Nat wishes to try the Ozmopolitan drink. It turns green when you press the light switch with it (!) and you get to keep the glass. I overrule on the grounds that this is the kind of gimmick that I *don't* approve of. Overpriced and tacky. Everyone in the bar seems to have one but theatre merchandise always annoys me – a tenner for a programme is an extravagance too far.

The show is a hit. Truly excellent. I had been worried that I might drop off or the kids might start whining but they are spellbound. I can't believe that this musical is not more widely talked about at home. It is stunning on so many counts – the score, the plot, the colour, the acting, and the cheeky little references to the actual *Wizard of Oz* – the whole show is incredible.

It achieves that great musical feat of leaving you with the sense that you know all the songs in the show, even though you had only heard *Defying Gravity* before the night began.

We're high up in the theatre, but the view is outstanding and the seats are spacious. British theatres, those that are still open, could learn a lot. In ten years time when we are all obese, it is theatres like this that will survive. In Britain, you will literally have to buy two seats to park your one bum.

I try to take a critical stance to engage Nat, feigning an interest, but she dismisses my two observations as nonsense. That the guy from *Australian Idol* nearly fluffed a line and that there was a blue light reflecting off a wardrobe that probably shouldn't have been there. I'm amazed in fact that more things don't routinely go wrong. For example, in a stunning conclusion to the first half leaving an entire audience breathless into the interval, the character Elpheba is flying around on the stage, clinging to ropes and hanging onto her broom and singing one of the hardest songs ever in *Defying Gravity*, some of which is in duet. And the performance is faultless. Professionals, I suppose.

I'm left with one thought, shared by millions of people the world over, no doubt. Why do some people arrive twenty minutes late? What can there possibly be gained by missing the first chunk of the story? That, alas, happens here too.

On the way back to the campsite, we take a cab. Our driver is the third in five days to have never heard of the campsite. This, a five star campsite, and winner of numerous awards, you recall.

I am more than ready to leave Melbourne as we hit the sack, sharing a read of the *Neighbours* book that we bought for Nat's Mum. We appear to have done that thing where you make sure you have good use of something before you pass it on as a present.

Unfortunately, there are tears at bedtime too. We have lost Kenny.

Day Thirty-Nine

We have a week left. That is all. Just a week in Oz. And we hear that it is thirty-four degrees in Hong Kong, which I am guessing is hell. We are both wary of the ever-increasing use of the phrase 'when we get back.' It seems a constant now.

Life has changed, and how so much. It seems there for the living for the first time. We can't change who we are or what we have done in the past, but going forward there is clearly so much more to getting up, being on the radio, being professionally sarcastic and falling asleep again. In fact, I am not even sure that I can still do it.

This morning we have to console Sam, who has left Kenny in the cab or the theatre. Kenny was a koala that we bought some way back at the stage where every stop meant a new animal. Sam had named him, after...well, our taxi driver in Singapore, of all things.

There is no comforting a small child when their overpriced souvenir animal has been cruelly taken away to koala heaven. I mean you can try and comfort him. You can say 'we'll get you another one,' or 'that will teach you for insisting on taking him everywhere.' But, ultimately you, the adult, will end up laughing, and he, the child, crying.

So we have this to contend with as we depart Melbourne. Again.

We seem to have been here an age, but actually we have hardly been here at all. Today, I am not sure where exactly we are heading, and we're genuinely frightened too.

It is the worst possible weather to be driving a campervan anywhere. It is wet, windy, and scary, and as we rattle on to Geelong, we literally take the left hand lane, then into the right in the motorway, officially out of control and being swept along by the gods. The road is very exposed. It is like nothing that I have driven on anywhere in the world. Hitting something seems the least of our worries.

I make Nat take a turn-off at Geelong. I tell her confidently that this is the place to stop. How do I know this? Well, in 2004, I was scheduled to do a week's outside broadcast with a guy called Tim Jibson. The destination – Melbourne and Geelong.

We never made it and I had a very large hand in getting it cancelled on intellectual grounds – it served no purpose to our listeners. The best thing about the cancellation was that I was working for a guy called Ande Macpherson at the time. I liked him but didn't rate him at all. We were all scheduled to fly out first class from Manchester in early January, but Ande, being a Kiwi, stored up some holiday and went early, so he could go home on the way. Unfortunately, for him he had to make his own way back though, as his cover in his absence, a chap named Giles Squire – whom I did very much rate – was calling the shots.

I enjoyed immensely seeing Ande's face when he walked back into the station after the OB got pulled, with him having been half way around the world. I am still unclear to this day, why he was even on the trip in the first place.

So listen, Geelong was sound. If Tim was doing a week's OB from there with us and several other stations, then there must be a week's worth of stuff to do there. WRONG! It was just a bad seaside town.

I definitely did the right thing getting that OB pulled, and this is why I fall out with half of the radio industry who cannot understand why I would not be interested in a free trip, first-class around the world to broadcast live in a warmer climate at a better time of day. Answer – because I am a professional. It serves very little purpose to my audience.

I can only apologise to Nat for the duff advice.

Looking ahead, the weather is dangerous, but we need to make some miles. There are plenty of Big 4s ahead, but it would be a waste not to push on. Portarlington is too close but also too out of the way. It is clearly a choice between Queenscliff and Anglesea.

At the next garage I ask the attendant which she recommends. She looks at me like an alien and doesn't have a clue what I am talking about. Clearly, we are back in that part of the country where people don't travel very far, though I would guess that if you work in a petrol station you are going to get asked questions like that every day.

Around noon we pull into the Big 4 site at Queenscliff. And pull straight out again. My campsite radar says no. We follow the road to water. The weather has cleared slightly and we're able to pull up in what is a very Victorian little town. There are around three thousand residents, mostly in the services, and the town had the dubious distinction of being part of the borough of Queenscliffe with an e. All very odd.

We're parked up next to a sign that claims that here are a hundred dolphins resident in the bay, yet we don't see any of them. One of our guide books also claims that you can see Melbourne from here, even though it is about a hundred kilometres away. Well, let me save you looking. You can't. I can see what I guess is Anglesea across the bay. It looks slightly brighter that way. That's the place to head.

As soon as we hit the road however, the weather turns again, now even worse than coming out of Melbourne. Today's paranoia is that the van will either blow over on the highway or in the night. We are literally taking a battering, and these vans are really very,

very fragile. They might look like you have your house on your back but you could flick them over with your little finger. May I remind you that they have also designed the beast with no rear windscreen wiper - a massive mistake if you consider the type of road that you get in Australia, dust being in large supplies.

As we pull up just a couple of miles outside the campsite, we see a sign that we had been perhaps subconsciously looking for since day one. Or perhaps we haven't but we only see it now because home is on our mind. It simply says 'Sunday Roast Served Here.' What a shame it is Friday.

We have only stopped to get Sam a new Kenny. That means, of course that Molly has to have something too. The new Kenny is called Kenny, and is joined by Wendy the Wombat. It is a different world, I guess. We also have to pay another trip to the pharmacy for you know what.

Our campsite is fine. I quite like it, in fact, but Nat is right. Your experience is so metered by the greeting that you get and they couldn't be warmer at the Big 4 Anglesea Holiday Park. As with many of the receptions though, you can get leaflets for all the other sites, and those for Queenscliff make it look a hell of a lot better than it was. Big 4 always present a glossy outlook, sometimes the truth is somewhat different.

I think the owners are surprised to see anybody heading this way at this time of year. Our real destination, of course, is The Great Ocean Road, and this is just a stop-off. I know that we chose this site because it has a heated indoor pool but clearly nobody has been in it for ages, and they warn us that it will take an hour to warm up, so out of season are we.

The kangas are back too, but these are a bit wilder than those at Pambula. Indeed the campsite owner tells us that she has had three bad car wrecks with £5000 worth of damage with roos coming down from the golf course. They are tagging them now, to see how far they come, and Nat is not impressed with this lot.

Oh how we take things for granted that we are now in a

position to dismiss one lot of kangaroos from the other. She also thinks that she is the next big thing in comedy when she tells the kids that the kangas have heard it on the roodio that the bacon butty man from Pambula is coming, something that she won't let rest to the degree that when I cook up, I have to close the kitchen doors after she pretends to be one scratching at the door. And a very good impression she does too.

Day Forty

Disaster.

The kids dropped off last night watching a DVD from the camp shop. They chose *Santa Clause The Movie*. This is a choice based on the lack of DVD variety on the trip rather than a seasonal one.

And then disaster struck. Firstly, there was a knock at the door late at night and we froze. Literally didn't move. We knew that there was almost nobody on our site and the experience on tour so far had been that when lights go out on Aussie campsites, they stay out. Was this finally about to be our scene in our own murdered-in-the-outback movie? No, it was the owner asking us if we had seen the kangas.

Bloody hell, I could have died. I genuinely opened the door with a kitchen knife behind my back. Had I seen the kangas indeed? Is the Pope catholic?

No, but listen – disaster. I have woken up this morning with red wine everywhere and I mean everywhere. On the duvet, on the floor, on my clothes, dripping through the duvet onto the framework, and worst of all, on my notes for this book. Pages literally stuck together, and Alistair Campbell's diaries and Terri Irwin's excellent autobiography both ruined. Consequently, all of what I have written so far is bullshit. I had to make it all up. No, I am joking, of course. But we do have a problem.

I had fallen asleep with the box of Stanley on top of me on the bed, so drunk and cross was I.

Sam had passed out, as he puts it, 'flicking his widge.' Nat, consequently, gave me her view of men, and I quote, 'a dick is a dick.' I countered somewhat crudely with 'a vag is a vag then.' And it all got a bit silly and exploded into a full-on row about why I wouldn't have the snip ages ago after her umpteenth visit to the chemist yesterday. Nat just couldn't understand that she was only my current wife and the next one might want more. What is wrong with that?

The whole campsite would have heard our eruption, had there been anyone on it, and therein lies one of the great problems with living in the van. You're public all the time.

Our first task this morning after Sam was told that he was now sleeping with me, was to somehow get this van liveable again.

It's sunny though – always the calm after the storm, and today is all about The Great Ocean Road. I remember sitting in Trailfinders in Manchester when Paul Steele, our consultant, was booking the trip. He just casually dropped it in...

'So, you'll do the Great Ocean Road. Wow. That's brilliant.'

Nat and I had looked at each other. We hadn't even heard of it.

We had to get there first though, and the sat-nav Nazi was doing everything possible to direct us off the Princes Highway – that same bloody road. We're ignoring it. It is clear that we have to hug the coast for as long as possible but that isn't easy. We're on another one of those cliff-top roads – think *The Italian Job* at the end – every twist and turn almost too much for the campervan, every drop petrifying, every climb a dread, every descent down the other side way too out of control. And all the time waves, ferocious waves, are lashing the shoreline.

It would be a terrible way to go.

We stop for lunch in Apollo Bay under the most incredible rainbow that I have ever seen, colours brighter than...well, a rainbow. Certainly a lasting memory of Australia will be the knowledge that the weather at home is pathetic, and no extreme that catches out the whinging British public (two inches of snow) is anything near an extreme. I mean, we're heading towards the Murray River in South Australia where they haven't seen rain for seven years. And they get by. Fact: we don't have weather in the UK. We're amateurs.

Nat, incidentally, is fancying cheese. I tell her, without a shadow of a doubt, that she is pregnant. I, however am fattening up for different reasons, eating two of the world's greatest meat pies.

I know Apollo Bay from somewhere. It is lying dormant in my mind. I had seen a show on BBC2 called *The Ten Pound Poms* some time back. I caught it by accident on a Saturday evening when I just didn't fancy the reality television dross on the other side. It was the most moving tale of several of those British families who had paid a tenner to seek their fortune in Australia. Some made it and some didn't; some returned and some stayed. Nat's Auntie Celia was a Ten Pound Pom.

One of the guys featured in this show had settled here in Apollo Bay, and he really made it big. He spotted the potential of the place long before it became the holiday place it is today. In fact he built half of it, and as a result is now an Australian citizen and absolutely loaded. Any one of these houses could be his work. I salute him. To have made that journey and to have made so much of it, against a backdrop of general ignorance of what lay ahead, is a very brilliant outcome. I am proud of the guy and I have never even met him, nor do I recall his name.

He did the right thing too. It is a beautiful little spot, and definitely the best place on this stretch of coast to stop, as though we have instinct now of where to pull over, because after this, you're full steam ahead back into a national park. You can't actually follow the coast right round. You have to cut inland through the park. I am wondering why. Perhaps Blanket Bay holds some dark secrets.

We keep spying signs for the Otway Tree Top Cafe, which is the kids' idea of an afternoon's worth of fun.

Molly *was* supposed to be keeping a scrapbook - she's still up to Port Douglas so far, and had intended to keep up her blog with her best pal Robyn but it lasted for all of a week!

Home is being mentioned even more and more today too, not because we crave it like you do at the end of most trips, but just because the days are getting ticked off, and there are four air tickets with our names on them scheduled for next Friday. I have, for the record, had the same jumper on for the last six weeks, and it stinks by the way.

We have to take a left before the tree cafe, and I am not sure that we really have the time today. At Yuulong we find ourselves on ....Horne's Road. This is quite an achievement. There are so few roads, and even less road names. To find one, named in our honour, is warmly high-fived all round the van. Every family has little things that make only themselves laugh. This is ours.

Now here's the problem with this entire stretch of road. There's nothing. We have, of course, encountered this before. This whole route is only about the Twelve Apostles. That is the sole reason that the road is there, so *you* can get to twelve strange rock formations sitting in the sea. At one point we think that we must have missed them. First Ayers Rock, now this. Only we could be unsure if we had missed a major landmark, but no they are well-signed for the retarded amongst us, and just like everything else in Australia, they are done perfectly.

After miles of nothing but twisty road, up on our right is a massive parking area, with helipads next door for the aerial view, and then an underground walkway that takes you back safely under the road to a viewing platform with the Twelve Apostles right in front of you. You need this protection too as the wind and sea-spray are intense. Most people will have photos like ours – turning slightly away to protect yourself from the sea. Just to paint the picture fully, you are up high above the ocean, not technically actually near these time-eroded deities of the sea, but the waves and wind are that strong that the spray is going to hit you, even at fifty metres away.

It is a wonderful sight. Well worth the stop, but essentially just tall rock formations abandoned by a previous generation's climate change presumably, left by the chance of nature to congregate in a form that now gives us a tourist trap, and there are many other examples across Australia of rocks just all arranging themselves into a beautiful landform – Ayers Rock being the obvious example. It is not just the way that they form, it is also the colour, the beautiful stone so rich and photogenic. Stonehenge is amateur by comparison.

There are many people here too – strange as we haven't seen a soul on the road. Most, I am sure, are heading back the way that we have come. We also see our first Maui for some time – very comforting.

Like all these places however, after fifteen minutes somebody will be first to dive in with 'well, that's that then...shall we make a move,' so we head to a place called Warrnambool.

There is a Big 4 site here but we dismiss it as a possibility as soon as we enter the town. It looks like a Rockhampton, plus we don't actually see any Big 4 sign, and signs on this trip are one of the great learning curves.

In every town that we enter, there is always one that makes me laugh. Today we hit the jackpot. There are two. Firstly a permanent erection (stop sniggering) proclaiming that this is the finish line of the Melbourne cycle race. A couple of thoughts here. Firstly, do you want to be cycling that road twisting and turning into Apollo Bay or risk getting blown off (stop sniggering again) as you pass the Twelve Apostles. Secondly, would it not be better to finish in front of a big crowd in Melbourne?

Even better than this is the temporary sign – the national cat championships are on. Wow. You can see at this point how hard it was not to stop, other than for diesel.

I insist on filling up, and as I do it occurs to me that we haven't seen fuel since Apollo Bay. This was a potential Cann River disaster.

On we press to Port Fairy. This is a cute little site, on a main road, but the town is tiny. If Warrnambool was Rockhampton, then this is Gladstone. We can have any pitch that we like, it is that quiet. There has been some flooding here too but it is a cracking one-night campsite with jumping pillows and go karts for the kids, heated indoor pool, great mini golf, DVDs to rent *and* not very busy. The lady behind our pitch is transporting a white china horse to Adelaide and rates it even higher than we do, saying it is an amazing site, but she is not the Big 4 expert that we are now. This is common amongst many Aussies that we have met, which may explain how the Melbourne site got five stars. They all seem to think the most petite of sites with minimal facilities are world-beaters. There is nothing wrong with Port Fairy, but Cairns it ain't.

We get chatting to the guys in reception too and reflect with them on the varying quality of Big 4 sites up and down the country. They, of course, hardly know any of the others other than from the leaflets in their reception. I advise them that the propaganda does a very good job of bigging up average sites, and that, on countless occasions, we have found many sites that bear only a little resemblance to the brochure.

They will regret our presence for sure, as one thing that *their* entry in the brochure does promise is a free pancake breakfast on Sundays, and Molly Horne is looking forward to it. My guess is that, as we are out of season, they wouldn't be cooking up in the morning if we hadn't showed up!

Nat wants to go into Port Fairy tomorrow – whatever that means. I am confident that we will leave as usual at 10.01 and just hit the road.

South Australia looms, and a curious time difference of half an hour. I don't get it. The guys in reception also give us the nod about the quarantine laws when you cross the border. They take this very seriously. I do not, given the amount of grape and orange rock that are resident in the van.

I also have one eye on Qantas. I think that, after so long on the road, and the experience with the Brummies, it would be wise to reconfirm our flights. I am sure that I haven't done this up to this point as I am delaying the inevitability of facing up to home. Nat has a standard line for moments like this, and I have heard various equivalents on every holiday that we have ever been on. She tells me to think of it as a fourteen day holiday with ten days left.

I don't want to go home. Fact.

Day Forty-One

Molly loved the pancake breakfast. There were five people at it and three were from our family! I'm sure that it is mega busy in the summer but that is a tremendous effort to get up and cook pancakes for free for people in the middle of winter especially when they already have food in their van. Still, a nice touch before we head off to the town of Port Fairy.

Which we then we leave. That took a minute.

We pull up literally about a mile from the site and gaze out to sea towards Griffiths Island, but there is only so long that you can stand there and go '...wow Sam, look at the surf.'

I am driving today. It is a sleepy Sunday and the world around reflects this. Mount Gambier is our aim, but we soon pass that.

I wouldn't say that our guide book was telling a pack of lies here, but it definitely makes the Blue Lake Holiday Park sound more beautiful than it is. I take particular offence at the line '...in the heart of the lakes and volcanic area, Blue Lake offers comfort and convenience amongst beautiful surrounds.'

If I were writing this I would have said.

'This is a one-horse town, at the top of which and only after a steep climb, is a big lake. On the right hand side just after it is a campsite that looks like it is laid out like barracks. Don't stay more than a night.'

We didn't stay an hour. The site looks to have good facilities, but when the brochure boasts about great hiking, I just don't see it. We tread back along the road to the lake itself, and what is so special about it, I hear you cry? Well, it is formed out of one of Australia's youngest volcanoes, but has the unique characteristic of changing colour to a turquoise blue in November, and then changing back in March, which is no good, of course if you happen to be here in August. There are caves too and limestone, some thirty million years old, and the Australians, just like at the Twelve Apostles, really take care of their little heritage, thinking of things that we just would not bother with at home. Again (because the road is tight and bendy and unsafe for pedestrians) they think nothing of constructing an underpass for you to cross the road safely and view the lake.

I don't understand how you can make a day of it, though. In fact I am struggling to make five minutes. Much more interesting is the lady who we meet on our return to the van, who is parked up next to us, her truck loaded with booze in massive plastic containers. She is the neighbour of an Adelaide winemaker and on the way to a show for a week. She is literally laced up with grog. I'm fascinated that she has to go such a long way to sell her wares, and that she will be on the road for a whole week. Seems slightly old-fashioned to me. There's this thing called the internet now, you know. We promise to call in when we visit the Barossa Valley. A minute later we have already forgotten her name and Nat confesses that she thought it was called the Jurassic Valley! Odd for someone who drinks so much.

On the way out of town we fulfil a subconscious dirty little pleasure. We visit a Red Rooster. These are essentially chicken takeaways.

As we pull in, Nat informs me that she knows that I have been dying to visit one of these since I read that the Alice Springs branch was key in the Peter Falconio case, and I confess it is true. I am curious to step into the place. In fact I am obsessed to the degree that I actually go back on myself to stop there. I want to know what the appeal is. Sickly, I tell Nat that I am going to order the Falconio special. Curiously, inside is some Harold Bishop type character ordering a massive takeaway for his church congregation with two enormous gravy boats and it is all going in the back of his car with the help of two young assistants. It looks a bit strange if you get my drift.

As for the food, I have concluded my soggy seeded chicken roll by the next crossroads, whereas Nat positively devours every bit of bone on hers, exposing talents with her mouth that I didn't know that she had. I decide to rename The Trucker Fucker, my Little Red Rooster.

So dead is the day and so quiet the route that the highlight of the trip is stopping for fuel at Millicent. There's a delay in the garage and Nat seems gone for ages. It turns out – get this– that the cashier has never done diesel before!

We're so bored waiting that we decide that it's practical joke time. When Nat goes to pay we are at the pump to the left on her exit. By the time she comes out we have hidden the van behind the shop bit of the garage and set the camera to roll, waiting for her double-take to stop her dead in her tracks. This is how dull the journey between places has become.

It reflects too our state of mind, limping to a climax in Adelaide after the trip that we have been on. We've been away so long by British standards (though not for Aussies) and the sites and sights have come thick and fast, to the degree that I have to spend at least five minutes every day scratching my head to remember the name of the previous place. We hardly even bother now for hygiene so at home are we on the road. We wash every day but my brown baggy jumper is into week seven and was last seen rolling around in roo poo on the van floor. Equally, every night that I barbecue, my jeans that have replaced my shorts at night due to the weather, also double up as a nice grease rag. It seems clear that tonight is also our last night in the middle of nowhere as surely we will reach Adelaide tomorrow. We are saying goodbye to the sticks.

We choose Robe as our destination and pursue a coastal route that defies the dominatrix that is the sat-nav. It goes nuts when we reject the established Princes Highway, perhaps fearing that we haven't yet seen enough of it, instead choosing to tank it on the B101 through Rendlesham, Beachport and Bray Junction, all the time hugging a deserted road running parallel to water but void of inhabitants. When the sat-nav finally realises that we are going our own way, we are delighted to give it its comeuppance for weeks of abuse, watching it backtrack from our original estimate of a 3.50 arrival time when 2.30 looks more likely. It calculates that we will take four hours to race sixty kilometres. Hey, I'm driving, you know, not Nat.

On route we cross the border just before Yahl. As borders go....well, it's a sign and by the side of it is a big bucket marked quarantine. There is hardly anywhere to pull over and we're not sure what to do. You are supposed to dump everything – all the fruit and veg that you are carrying. This road clearly is not busy because that bucket would need to be emptied every five minutes, but there is nobody around anyway, so we take a typical British decision....to put a bit in. A token gesture of a potato and some strawberries. I laugh at our effort and their enforcement of it, and by the time that you read this, South Australia will be wiped out by the fruit fly that we brought in. Will it heck.

I am not disrespectful of what they need to run their country but the food in our van is staying in our van until it makes its last journey to our stomachs. That's it. Furthermore, just like entering Victoria from New South Wales, there are a barrage of signs promising so much ahead and then, nothing.

When we check in at Robe, the sea emergency radio is blasting out behind the front desk. I am intrigued. We don't really have communications like this at home – this whole concept of flying doctors, schools radio and a community listening on a frequency for anyone in distress seem frankly, dated, but therein lies their quaint beauty. Archaic or not, do they have alternatives in this enormous land of beastly temperament? It is ten times worse than Skegness in the winter, the weather terrible, waves battering the shore a few hundred metres from the site. I am sure again that we will blow over in the night, yet I can see that Robe itself is a cute little holiday home village. It is obviously one of those weather pockets that just catch the elements that everybody else misses because there was no hint of this gale force turbo until we turned left into the town.

The site itself is fine, with just one permanent resident (in fact it is us and them) but let's be honest about why we are here. We are killing time, resting up before the final push to Adelaide, the route to which I take advice on, as there looks like some tricky impassable water ahead on the map. We can't come all this way to not be able to get past. Well, obviously, *we* could!

It is classic understated Australia counsel.

'Go to Kingston and take the coast but make sure you stop at Policeman's Point.'

I enquired if that was *the* place to stop.

'Oh yeah,' says Pam, 'there's a shop and a toilet opposite.'

Well, that's a done deal then.

I have a lot of questions about this conversation. Was I the first to ask it (unlikely) and if so, how many people had she similarly sent on this groundbreaking expedition? Had she been there herself (possibly on a daytrip) or was this word of mouth? What's in the shop? (I predict – next to nothing.) Is there actually a copper there? (Doubt it.) Most importantly, was this really the summit of a travelling Australian's expectations? (That would be harsh as most are in London.)

I mentioned earlier that they thought even the most basic of campsites were amazing, now this lady is talking up Policeman's Point like it's the Grand Canyon. It is therefore, entirely plausible to understand so much about Aussie character from a statement like this. They *don't* expect much because they came from little, and they all at some point make that life trip round the country at which point they remember that out of the cities you might as well be in the third world. It goes some way to explaining the mangoes by the side of the road, and the fact that they call towns cities, even when they are hamlets, and at each of these, they all have some sort of heritage museum, even if they have nothing to show. It strikes me as modest and humble, proud too, grateful for small mercies yet taking nothing for granted. Much as I can only mock a sightseeing tour that includes a point where there may or may not have once been a policeman, what it reveals about you and this land is vastly significant.

As I am departing, Pam offers me the Big 4 book. I assure her that I have ten of them in the van. Just then an Irish woman and a bloke from Salisbury appear and enquire of the forecast. They only have a tent. Idiots!

Five minutes later, I don't see them and assume that they have seen sense and left. Then I catch them warming up in their car. It is too cold to get out. Nat wants to go into town, so I make an excuse that we should warn them that that we have hogged the communal washer, though they themselves look like they have never washed in their life. I don't really mean to be so kind advising that the laundry is busy. I really just want to talk to them, anybody in fact, and like *the* Irish before them, the lady...she can talk.

They are heading to Melbourne on a working year and tell us horrendous stories of travelling down the middle, of theft and drunken Aboriginals. We'll shelve that trip for another book then. We are there for forty minutes just nattering, exchanging stories, and tips like experts, when I realise how poisonous this process can be.

You see. They are dreaming of Melbourne, and I told them that we didn't like it. And they are planning on spending a year there. They'll be worrying about that all the way along the Prince's Highway now, but that is what happens on adventures like this. It is all anecdotal and, so chilled by the atmosphere in this country and so relieved to see someone in a place like Robe that you just chat, and in one errant sentence, you can precondition the next phase of their life.

It is nonsense of course. How many times have you been on a website like Tripadvisor and read a review, only to say stuff like '…well that's not the Venice I know.'

You see individual experiences do not make a pattern. They shouldn't have listened to a bloody word that I was saying, especially as I am prepared to reconsider that Melbourne in the summer may be a better place.

The highlight of our trip to Robe is our visit to the liquor store. This is a daily habit, following our rules that you stock up while you can, except when I load the stuff up in the van, I realise that I have miscalculated and that our nights remaining to cartons left ratio is out of sync and unless we drink like a fish between now and next Friday we'll be leaving half of it behind. I suppose I could always give it a go.

Consequently I begin at the barbecue, but let me tell you this is the worst night in the history of the earth to be grilling up, worst than the hurricane that hit the UK in autumn 1987, worse than the tsunami of 2004, worse even than the Big Bang that supposedly started the universe.

I admit, I've cracked open those cartons and they are kicking in.

I exaggerate a tad, but picture this: This site is so badly lit, the wind and the waves are in torment, and there is nobody on the campsite. Murder anybody?

There is one solitary light hanging from a cable over the barbeque. It sways as I cook. It reminds me of the advert for *Carlsberg* when there's a phone ringing in a deserted office, and finally a man locates the room, enters, blows dust off the phone and clears the cobwebs, only to answer to find that it is a wrong number. When he departs, the sign on the door, untouched for years, simply reads 'Carlsberg Complaints Office.'

It is that quiet and eerie, that solitary and scary.

Then some weird Germans turn up in an Apollo and I wonder if this is it...if tonight I will perish at the hands of some mad Nazis in a place nobody knew I was. As the trail for the outback movie *Wolf Creek* says, '...how can they find you when they don't know that you are missing?'

The night is bitter. You can smell it too. Literally two hundred metres inland from the coast and the air smells of sea salt. Like at The Twelve Apostles but this time lasting all night.

I feel safer inside the van than out, which is probably daft because you would be trapped if faced with an intruder, whereas outside you could run or burn them on the barbecue. I can't wait to leave. I settle down for the night with my cartons of wine and the rescued wine-stained copy of Terri Irwin's book 'My Steve.' I need to find out more about my new hero.

Day Forty-Two

We awake this morning to a calm, clear morning, as though the skies needed to get it out of their system, as though someone would laugh at you if we told them that we had had the worst night on tour ever. Last night we had seen the national weather map on a TV near the indoor pool, and it said twenty-seven degrees for Cairns and fifteen for Adelaide. It made me incredibly nostalgic and I am still on the trip. This must mark the measure of the journey that we have been on, and I use the word journey in a literal sense and not in that awful reality television way. If I am pining for the trip and still in the country, time must be slipping away. I assume that the accumulation of experiences leaves me unrecognisable from the person that left the UK late June.

Nat and I just couldn't get to sleep last night with the gale raging that we had no choice but to go for the sex option again. This is probably now more times than in our entire marriage, and I warn her this morning, as we seem to have given up on the whole contraception thing, and the shocking 'was it consensual' visits for the morning after pill, that she is definitely pregnant. I just know these things. The current cheese on everything obsession, I explain, is mere confirmation. She won't even joke about it, saying that she can't take being pregnant again, that her bones are brittle and won't sustain another birth. I tell her that is bollocks.

It is a good way to ensure silence for an hour or so.

I would read some more Terri Irwin but after casually

dumping the waste on my pitch on the basis that everything is flooded anyway then a little more won't help, I find myself driving, which is a shame as I can't put her book down.

I have done a complete u-turn on the Irwin family. I love them like my own and can't see the criticisms that I had previously, nor understand the mimicry that I exuded on the air. They have so much more content and so much more value in my eyes than perceived role models such as the Beckhams. They are truly inspiring, as is their love story, destined to meet through animals after a chance visit from Terri to Australia Zoo, coupled with the almost telepathic relationship that they have with animals and each other. I won't spoil the rest, but read the bit about Bindi looking at the clock on the day Steve died. An incredible book and retrospectively, I feel honoured to have sat ten metres from them in what is effect their garden, and I thank them publicly for the impact that they have had on our lives and the icons that they have unknowingly become for my children who talk about crocs, koalas and Bindi every hour of the day now.

The road past Kingston is bumpy. Nat claims that my driving is making her sick but it is actually the road. Or morning sickness perhaps.

What do you expect when you are heading to places called Tilly Swamp? After an hour and a half of her moaning, I am ordered to pull over. I then witness the most comical throwing up that I have ever seen in the world. It's pathetic but I get the message. The red rooster wants to drive.

Policeman Point comes and goes. Oh, the temptation to stop was.....minimal, and I didn't see the shop or the toilet. Certainly no copper either. Suddenly, there's drama in the back of the van.

Everything goes flying as screws hit the floor. What on earth has happened? It's the television. It's falling off. We have to stop the van, but Nat can't and goes crashing into a dirt track, with just unstable mud flats flanking us on either side, and that from coming off a speed of 110 kph.

It has been attached to a bracket above the door but has swayed all the way from day one, so part of the job of whoever is not driving is to constantly get up and turn it back around for the kids to see, because they haven't watched the *Shrek* DVD everyday for the last forty!

Sometimes, you are up more than you are in your seat, but this time the bumps, the battering in Cooktown, me being too tall for the van and head-butting it, plus the general wear and tear have all taken their toll. There's lead on the floor. There's no way that either of us can drive without fearing that the TV will fall off for good, and the implication of that is that it will probably go crashing through what is a very flimsy door, meaning damaged television, damaged door, and no possibility of making Adelaide, and if we do, then no chance of locking the door at any point.

On the plus side, I don't think that we have had a disaster for a few days.

This is why every Maui should have a Swiss Army knife as an essential. Damn that has been useful. It is time to issue running repairs on the spot, with still a hundred and fifty kilometres to go to Adelaide.

I am left holding the door and the TV in the van while Nat drives off. We vow to stop again at a place known to us as Taliban, though the locals call it Tailem Bend. It is so big in its typeface on the map that it looks like the place to stay though in reality it boasts nothing except a cute little project called Old Town Tailem Bend, where they have constructed a 'how we used to live' like village. Just a shame they haven't bothered with the current town.

We pass Blind Creek, but honestly I didn't see it.

Lunch is in the car park of Monarto Zoo but we don't even bother with the animals. We are zoo-ed out, and after Australia Zoo, is there a point? Ahead and to our left we see ferocious hills, enormous obstacles to climb. This is the gateway to Adelaide.

Again the weather is ever-changing, though it is warmer. Nat patronises me by pointing out that there are hills and changeable weather so it is obviously wine-making conditions, like she knows anything about wine except how to bloody drink the stuff.

She doesn't know this yet but in my mind I am taking up wine-tasting upon my return. I won't of course, but it is the kind of thing that you tell yourself when you are miles from reality, when you have time to plan and time to dream. I would love to be in the wine business.

At present I remain merely at the consumer end.

But no, nothing would give me greater pleasure than to be in and around wine all day long, except for the fact that when you become a wine connoisseur, how on earth do you go down the Co-op and order a £3 bottle of wine?

It is going to get pricey and you're going to get snobby.

This wine-tasting pledge is right up there with two other things. I have always wanted a pinball machine – a legacy too of all the games rooms that the kids have been in since Cairns. Add to that all the clear nights that we had star-gazing. You forget that you just can't do that at home on a regular basis yet here every night you stop and stare. This is where the big plans and dreams begin. I tell myself that I have to study astronomy too.

In reality on August 18th I'll be back on the air and depressed to be so, posing the question to all those people who have been in those 'if I ever get out of here alive' situations, how many are true to their words and do fulfil their dreams? This trip will only be life-changing, if I do indeed break the cycle when I get back.

We approach Mount Lofty. I still laugh at the fair dinkum nature of the place names. It really is called Mount Lofty and it still makes me laugh. It is quite high up by the way!

No, it is positively monstrous. All the hills are.

They warn you to drive in low gear. Nat obliges, dropping her speed to a mere hundred. These aren't just hills like mountain roads in the Lake District. These are whoppers. They're catered for too, with crash lanes off the motorway. Yes, crash lanes. If you're going too fast and out of control, you just take your own lane. Nat and I look at each other with the same thought. Most people do Adelaide to Darwin (or bits of it at least). We are rare in doing the other way round. How on earth does the Maui climb these hills on the way *out* of Adelaide. Not only are they steep, they go on for miles too.

Then to our relief, we're low again, and the streets have a quality to them that I expected of Melbourne. Instantly I like it, but it is clear that people in Adelaide are sunken in a fortress with these invisible hills around it. It is almost like another country within the country. It is hard to describe why I take an immediate pleasure though. I think it is a snob thing. It just looks classier, perhaps like Richmond upon Thames in Surrey.

We ask our usual vacuous question as we sense that a campsite is near.

'What is your gut feeling?'

This, of course, is nonsense. None of us have been within a whiff of here before, but we are desperate for a great final campsite, and in the Adelaide region, there are three to pick from. Nat, though has her mind on other things. Adelaide is all about Auntie Celia.

'Any of these people could be my cousin. That could be my Auntie,' she muses.

I reply compassionately, pointing out her obvious error.

'I hope *he*'s not your Auntie.'

She's buzzing with excitement, removing the address of the campsite from the sat-nav, to replace it with Auntie Celia's, leaving me clueless as to where to go. I should point out, by the way, that she has never met Auntie Celia.

As I try and feel my way, by instinct, towards the campsite – ridiculous I know – I notice the extraordinary weather that this city has to offer, or maybe it is just today. Towards the city ferocious storms, towards the coast, and I assume the campsite, bright light and clear blue sky. I feel good, and happy chasing the clear blue sky, and when we pull up at the Big 4 Holiday Shores

Park on Military Road, I know that we are ending on a high.

It is a gorgeous site, spacious and with great facilities, all backing onto the beach. We book in for two nights, which is daft because I know that we are staying for four. The hesitation really is only over a possible trip to Kangaroo Island, which had been on our wish-list before we left Britain. With the sun roasting, it feels almost like we have come full circle from 'the crackerjack of a day' mentality of Cairns. It seems fitting that we park up here and that we stay put.

Crucially, we know (without identifying precisely where) that we are just down the road from Maui, and we can feel the airport just a few miles away. For that reason alone, this site is perfect.

I decide to take a hit on the cash. You see, Trailfinders had booked us in for the last night at a hotel, which was clearly now, the other side of town.

This site is where we need to be, and I am positively skipping for joy when I see another Maui checking in. It has been ages – nothing for weeks bar The Twelve Apostles. I vow to sniff them out.

After clearing out reception of all their leaflets with so much on offer locally, and some great discounts too, we park up at our last pitch. Descending from the van, Nat spontaneously hugs me. It is not like her at all. She shouts out loud.

'We did it.'

And we had.

What of those people in Cairns who told us it was some trek to do in five weeks? It is an emotional moment. And one of huge significance too. It really is all over.

I am relieved in a way in that I have never enjoyed driving the van, but I am very introspective too. I have two questions. I feel new, but will I feel old and battered again, when I return to work, and secondly, when will we do this again? This is what the wedding vows are about – thick and thin, better or worse. Or whatever it was. The trip has made us.

Slightly giddy with emotion, I continue on autopilot with the daily chores that coincide with every arrival and departure, heading straight for the drain at the back of the van, where I dump the waste. I shouldn't be doing this here, but this time I am not thinking rather than just being lazy and I flood the drainage, causing me to go into panic overdrive, spooning out the manky, flakey tissue from the drain. I begin to stink of urine, and am sent for a shower.

Afterwards, I still stink.

I hunt out the other guys in a Maui. Anyone who has ever been camping knows that a one minute conversation can soon last an hour, and they haven't even unpacked before I'm telling them the whole story from Darwin onwards. We compare Mauis too. What a strange thing to do. I have no interest in automobiles, but the Maui, the Apollo, the two berth, the four berth, the sixth berth...it has all become a conversation, the like of which I normally associate with chauvinists. Male generally.

Proving that nobody is from anywhere these days, and that the world is a small place, he is from New Zealand, and she is from Liverpool, reminding me that you can travel half way round the world and you are more likely to meet your neighbour than if you were putting the milk bottles out at home.

It must be the Liverpool vibe but it inspires Nat there and then to call Auntie Celia. They haven't spoken since Cairns, and she hasn't forgotten that we are coming. Imagine, if we had changed our plans and decided to give it a miss, and she had been hanging on for all these weeks after Nat's drunken call on the evening that we arrived. She has all our photos up, she tells us, and is very Scouse, but that could be emotion kicking in, or after being surrounded by Aussies for so long, it could be simply that you just turn more Scouse when talking to another.

With night falling, Nat rings home to report back to her Mum. She is also very emotional.

This, it seems, is the reason why they have never done

Australia – that thought that Lynney might be coming out to say goodbye to her sister – after all these years. I remind Nat that you have to confront your emotions and that I will have to make this same journey to my Dad in Peru. I think about that most days.

It has been a tearful end to a landmark day at the finale of the most important trip of our lives. I crank up the emotion by calling for a photo session – our first review in fact of all seven hundred that we have taken. I shove the iPod onto the most poignant tracks from the whole journey. We laugh and we cry. The end is very much coming.

We have one last text to send before lights out. A massive text to the entire world detailing our last hurrah, but really all that we want to do is piss everybody off. Nat has booked wine-tasting in the Barossa Valley! You can't *not* tell everybody that.

Day Forty-Three

We knew that the airport was close but not that close. The roar begins at 7am, making me think that I like this site, but I couldn't put up with that every night, as a stream of Qantas flights dominate the skies. I don't think that I can recall a country where one airline seems to be the only airline as much as in Australia.

It has not been a good night either. Poor Sam has growing pains again. He is ready for home.

In the spirit of camping and family love, I invite the whole family to come for a morning cuddle, snuggling under the duvet. Nat, however, piles in on me as I wince after Sam jumps on my bollocks. There is no woman in the world who understands that particular testicular winding feeling. If I haven't got her up the duff on this trip, it ain't going to happen now. I am officially out of action.

We then ridiculously waste the next thirty minutes holding the camera at a distance trying to take a photo of ourselves, including myself mocking Nat's fake vomit from the other day, which causes today's particular volcano to begin its eruption! She is not happy with that, I can tell you.

We're off into Adelaide today, to potter around and explore.

As ever, Nat is befriended by the resident nutter on the bus. He has no teeth, and is purring over his mobile phone. I am not relaxed at him talking to Molly and Sam. Physically he reminds me of Barry George, the man just cleared of the shooting of Jill Dando. Why do we – or Nat – attract these people? Am I one too – she married me after all.

We leave blue skies behind, like yesterday, and there is cloud ahead. The weather seems to have a structure, as does the city in its beautifully uncomplicated grid system. The rain that the cloud promised arrives, but it turns out to be a bonus, as retreating for shelter, we skulk out in the indoor market, itself exuding that rare quality of being both a tourist attraction and used by locals.

This is a good spot, and I totally recommend it. You wander, you sample, and you buy. And it is not tacky or crowded. Nat is keen to try everything. She is definitely pregnant or has some cheese gene. We prompt for the gorgeous Tilba Trilogy. Oddly after seeing so much of it as free samples, we get fleeced when we actually stop to buy some. It just happens to be the most expensive stall of all of them. Who hasn't had that happen to them? It is the luck of the tourist.

The cheese seems earmarked for dinner tonight, so we had better have a good fill-up for lunch, as the kids won't really do the cheese, but like Melbourne before, we are either really unlucky or ignorant as there doesn't seem to be anywhere to eat.

Then, after walking almost every street we discover a gem. If you are ever in Adelaide, please visit The Original Wood Oven, right at the end of the main street. I wouldn't have chosen to go there myself, preferring a fish restaurant, but remember I have in tow the least adventurous food family on the planet. The type who always order margherita pizza. Inside, I can't believe what I see.

Nat hates it when I talk about food, especially in terms of quantity. She thinks it is an illness. Even she is blown away by the mountains of food. The prices are small, the portions are enormous. Un-restaurant-like, miles away from fancy chefs who place a berry and a leaf on a pink steak and charge you the earth.

By examining everyone else's portions, the Chicken Souvlaki looks the best value at twenty-one dollars. Oh, for heaven's sake, just put this book down right now, fly to Adelaide and order it. I'll sound obese if I try to describe it.

I recognise that I copped out there in a literary sense and offered you no description of merit. I felt it vulgar to do so.

Nat does her usual trick of ordering two starters – a bruschetta and a minestrone soup. I just crave something different. As long it didn't say burgers and salad, anything would be fine, prompting in the end for chicken ripeno, whatever that is.

Now, having said what an amazing place this joint is, I swear that once again, we order the worst two things on the menu. The food is fine, without being spectacular, but part of the problem is that you spend your meal staring in a sick way, remarking at what other people are having, a bit like in *The Royle Family* sitcom, when they always ask if you've had your tea yet.

The puddings frankly are ridiculous too. I have no room for .....a pizza pudding???

It is a great place that didn't do us justice, and that is our fault not theirs.

Of course, half drunk and bloated from lunch, after my wife orders tons of wine, I have no appetite for shopping. I am alone in this opinion, however, whereas Nat seems to be of the attitude that we have only so much cash left for so little time, so therefore we have to spend it. On shit.

Just like the last day of every other holiday that we've been on, though interestingly, she remarks, that there can be no more Lanzarote holidays after this adventure.

Sam gets his fourth animal of the trip, first a koala then a dolphin that makes a noise. She is called Dave, he tells us.

Molly gets a t-shirt. Ben, our nephew gets a cuddly wombat. Molly's best friend Robyn now owns a koala bag, whether she wants it or not. Nat, a sucker for a brand, buys the entire stock of Rip Curl. Me? Oh I just get one of those Aussie beer-holder things.

My favourite shop, though, is called The Australian Geographical Company. I have never seen such a fun shop in all my life. This is the place to go for presents. It has everything from awesome telescopes to make your own volcano kits. I vow to order online on our return. I won't of course.

Laden with shopping that we can't possibly fit into our rucksacks, we attempt the bus back, though we have no idea of which bus to get. You can't just join a bus network in a foreign city, can you?

It is clear when we return that we must book in the extra two nights at the campsite and cancel our last night's hotel scheduled for when we have given the van back. We ring Trailfinders back in Manchester and speak to Paul Steele, who is amazed to hear from us and is pretty accurate in his assessment of where we are on our trip, despite us not knowing him from Adam. His service has been terrific, but he can't offer us a refund even though we ring three nights before we are due to check in, which is odd really because in the UK, unless you have booked a promotional rate, you can normally cancel on the day.

The hotel is called Breakfree On Hindley, and it is miles away, but we took it on *their* recommendation, and remember that they booked the Maui for us, and knew that we would need a night at the end in a hotel before a 5am airport departure.

It wasn't actually Paul that booked this chunk, as he wasn't in the office at the time, but I feel aggrieved because we have spent over £9,000 with the company, and took their advice, when clearly they haven't been to the hotel in question, and when there is perfectly good accommodation in the cabins on our site, just over the road from the airport. Of course, they don't know that we are writing a book and your opinion of them may now be formed, but I just think that it is very shoddy to quibble over £100, following *their* bad advice, when *you*, as a family, have spent £9000.

I won't let this rest. I shall be pursuing this on my return too, and this one is one that I actually will follow up.

Back at the van, the cheese is out and it is to die for. Naturally red wine flows as we play the highlights game, where we all talk about our best bits of the trip. To Nat's utter joy and disbelief, Sam cites the musical *Wicked* as his highlight and does so without a prompt. I have seen them grow so much before my eyes in the last few weeks, and as a parent you don't see that happening normally. You just wake up one day and they are ten and twenty, such is the rat race. Yes you can grade them at the end of school years, and chart their progress accordingly, but to watch them develop hour by hour is rare. This trip has allowed me to live life, and to the full each and every day; to understand and appreciate as we go, not always looking forward or fondly over my shoulder. For the first time in my life, I have been in the moment. It is special.

Molly and I potter off to the games room on the way to retrieve some lost money that has got jammed down the side. Suddenly, she shouts at the TV.

'Look, it's him.'

Karl Kennedy and *Neighbours* are on the telly behind us. This too, is a moment, as Moll admits that it looks like a good show, though she didn't like the tour. I can live with that, knowing that the seed is sown and when she returns on her gap year twenty years from now, she too will be hooked and also making the pilgrimage to Ramsay Street.

Do you see how this adventure has you at extremes? The ridiculous emotional content of Auntie Celia, Sam pulling a memory from nowhere, and of course, the end in sight, all coupled with such nonsense, but powerful nonsense as *Neighbours*.

We have one last job before sleep. Well, I do. I make bacon butties for the morning. Nat declares that it is now official. I am a food obsessive, ignoring the fact that she will want them tomorrow. I am just being practical. She is also moaning that she can't write any more of her book, as she is tired and cross that we have wasted the hotel room on Friday night but still have to pay for it. Still these are moderate complaints compared to the many that have left her lips these last two months.

Nat, darling, if you are reading, these are my three favourite moans of yours in the van:

1. The van rocks because of me.
2. There is no room in the bed because of me.
3. My snoring is because I am fat.

There. It is done. I have been waiting since Singapore to write that, and tonight I will prove that Nat snores too. I secretly set the camera up to film for the moment she drops off.

It happens sooner rather than later and I toast myself with a plastic cup of cheap Stanley wine.

I am careful not to get too pissed. After all, we have wine-tasting tomorrow!

Day Forty-Four

It is an early start. I am all for seeing the world, but in my time zone please. That was the problem with the Barrier Reef – too bloody long a day!

Becky picks us up and sets a friendly tone, confirming one of our lessons of being in the tourist game down under, that you would never find at home. Everybody in Australia is a proud guide. She is only meant to pick us up, like a taxi, but she is straight into action with the headset-cum-microphone set going straight on for the short hop into the city centre. I retain one piece of info and it is a good one, and suddenly it all makes sense.

The skyline, not that this will mean anything to you, reminds me of living in Bogotá in 1990. The Columbians were about to wreck it back then with endless construction but the rulers of Adelaide have seen sense and passed a magnificent rule that no building can surpass thirty-two stories in height, and I can tell you, coming from a crowded world, it makes your quality of life a million times better. It is a unique view, feels healthy, devoid of claustrophobia, and full of common sense. I think this is the main reason that I really like Adelaide. It has clarity. Plus you cannot not admire a government that thinks in this way.

The reason, by the way, is the visibility required at the airport.

My mind is on the wine though, even at this early hour, and again, I promise myself that this is day one of my wine-tasting education. Life is too short not to take it up. This is going to be one of the great days, assuming that I can remember it.

Just before we pull up across from the beautiful architecture of the old railway station (what stories lie within?) we pass 'The Cheesecake Shop,' a wonderfully unique Aussie franchise that we have passed before, though never seen anywhere else in the world. This really is a fine place.

And then Becky is gone, to be replaced by Ross, who continues in the same vein, making a lot of info go along way.

'There's a park up on the left,' was a slightly tame early offering. I can see it, after all, and it is a park, just like any other park.

He makes up for it, though, with an impromptu stop as we leave the city, having spotted a sole koala sleeping in the trees on the left of the roadside. How he spotted it, I will never know, unless it is his party trick that he always stops for, perhaps giving it a fiver for its co-operation before he drives off again. It is the first koala that we have seen out of captivity, so to speak, and frankly, who couldn't take it home?

His patter is good and natural, arming us on what is a drizzly day in its appearance though rain hasn't fallen, that some of these parts haven't seen water in seven years, others nine. The Murray River is in trouble, and Adelaide may be too.

Auntie Celia had told us on the phone that they say in these parts, that you have to go over the hills to make it. It is true. You felt it on the way in and we sense it heading out today. Adelaide is a metaphorical valley and a physical one too, a closed-shop world, where opportunity seems to lie beyond.

Our first stop, after a twisting, turning, almost mountainous route, past free-roaming kangaroos all the way, is The Toy Factory at Gumeracha. What a wonderful place, a fantasy for adults and children alike.

Outside is the world's biggest tree-house. Inside, a shop and a workshop. It is straight out of a children's book. You can almost picture an old man, up late by candlelight on Christmas Eve, hand-carving the toys with the elves, finishing just on the stroke of midnight. It is quiet and quaint, and they make everything.

And what pleasure you must get from working here, though I don't find them over-friendly, considering I am enquiring about shipping back to England a purchase of a considerable sum. Perhaps, I caught them on a bad day.

They've got dolls houses, train sets, abacuses, helicopters, toy boxes, ironing boards, tables, chairs, and toasters, puzzles, games, clocks and jigsaws, and my personal favourite – the subject of my enquiry for Nat this Christmas – the wine truck! A wine rack, with a truck at the front so that you can move it around your house to wherever you feel like staggering to. Brilliant.

I could find happiness here, high up in the hills, emus wandering around, seeing just a few people every day, checking the online orders, and carving the day away. Except I can't carve, of course, and your orders would break in the post!

Already I need a little doze as we head into Singleton. I think it is only the very tranquil surroundings that make me drowsy as I am not hungover, and I haven't yet tasted the grape for today. Perhaps I am going early, as I know what is to come.

I am surprised to learn of German infiltration here. I consider Australia's DNA to be wholly British, but I am way off the mark, as it transpires that the Germans first saw the potential of the wine, noted in a small tribute to one of its first winemakers, whose house still stands on the edge of what is nothing more than a small village. What is so unique about that? His house is a carved-out tree, and his family lived within it. Oh yeah, he had sixteen children too.

And I should have been more aware. Wolf Blass, after all, sounds German, doesn't it? I had never made the connection until the moment that we enter its premises, the big Wolf Blass statue with its famous logo, a photo opportunity all by itself.

I can't believe that I am here, after so many Blasses making up so much of my nightly routine! It's an education as well as the beginning of a bloody great piss-up. In my Co-op, I have a choice of one Wolf Blass. Here, I can buy a zillion, some of which don't even make it to the shelves. We are at something known as 'Cellar Door.'

This is new to us, and Nat doesn't understand it. She thinks it is flawed as a business plan. After all, you are going to drink your six free glasses and stagger off to the next one, and probably only purchase on the last stop when you are wasted and feeling guilty. I tell her that she will never forget Wolf Blass, if she can remember it, and that this is the beginning of a lifelong brand loyalty. She might get it for free now, but she will pay forever. From here, she will always choose Wolf Blass. That is why they have cellar door.

It is an impressive set up, by the way, juggling the three elements of daily production, testing for the connoisseur, plus becoming a tourist venue. It is also a different world. I love wine, but if I am honest, then I probably have not tasted more than ten different brands in my entire life. In the next few hours, I will have coiffed twenty-five. And yes, we do have the kids with us to get us home safely.

Outside the mighty Wolf Blass, is a classic picture of Australia. Here we have a fabulous international industry, globally known, located in a town of 'population seventy.'

I had heard Sir Ian Botham say a couple of years ago that you could find any tiny Australian town with an Olympic swimming pool because they had invested in, and believed in, sport so much. Here, this village of less than a hundred has its own floodlit football stadium. It is ridiculous. Ridiculously good.

But what's this? We stop for lunch at Nuriootpa. I have never witnessed anything as idealistic as this. We are eating at a community-owned restaurant in a community-owned hotel opposite a community-owned store with a community-owned bank nearby. The community own the community and all profits go back into the community. What a concept.

It just wouldn't work in England. It would be rife with in-fighting and angry militants running off to the *Daily Mail*, leaking nonsense and undermining your neighbour, but here the dream is alive and kicking. I am impressed, and I have no idea of what their motivation is for forming such a utopia. Presumably bad experiences have befallen this place in the past, and to unite was the only way to survive. I don't know. I am only guessing. I don't believe that everybody woke up on the same day and sang John Lennon's 'Imagine' and built the town thus. It must have been a reaction to something, surely some kind of fight-back. Nobody seems to know.

Naturally, we are not alone in Ross' bus. We are in a group and group scenario scares me, but luckily ours is sound, and lunch throws up even more wildcards. Two, in fact.

Joan is a Kiwi from Liverpool (again!) who is helping her husband round. He is suffering badly from a stroke, and you feel that this may be his last trip. She gives us the ultimate travel tip. They got half-price tickets on the legendary Alice Springs train, something which we will save for another trip, when we are older and have less energy to drive down the coast of Australia. How did this sixty year old woman manage this? They are members of the Youth Hostel Association.

Yes, that's what I said too.

Evidently there is no age limit. I guess that is the Aussie way. You are as young as the woman you feel.

Then we get chatting to curious Madga from Poland. She is a couch-surfer.

Yes, that's what *Nat* said too!

Now, I had read about couch-surfing a year or so back, so I knew what it was, but with two kids, and approaching forty, googling 'Adelaide – bed for the night,' is a part of our lives that has already passed us by.

It wouldn't exist, of course, without the internet, and its irony in that big bad world of cyberspace is that it relies totally on trust to work, and trust is not something that you would put in a list of online values. Total strangers from around the world chat to you on your PC and then tell you the key is under the mat. You turn up, crash on their couch for a night, a week, a life, and off you go. The only fee is that they will get a couch themselves somewhere along the line too. Its community-owned couches, if you like.

Nat is astounded. Nothing surprises me these days.

After lunch we're off to the cellar door at Vinecrest, a much smaller operation, but with a very personal touch. It is a family business and Lee is at the helm. My lunch is kicking in, and I'm feeling giddy. I'm asking lots of questions, much to Nat's embarrassment. My best is this.

'Would there be such a thing as a breakfast wine?'

Well, blow me away, there sure is. Oh my goodness, I simply have to become a wine-taster. It is heaven. I buy a bottle of it immediately. It is red and fizzy and I am now contemplating that all-day drinking finally has a beginning, middle and an end, not just a sprawling through the afternoon stumbling to a forgotten conclusion.

Nat is kicking me to say 'enough questions.' I remind her that Lee started it by describing one bottle as a 'late afternoon wine.' How specific can you be, Lee? What, about 4.30 to 4.45 just after the kids have got home? Something like that, or earlier, to help you through *Countdown*?

I want to ask about all the cheap boxes of Stanley wine that we have been guzzling – complicated stuff like... is the yellow box better than the red, but, with Nat turning away, I rephrase it so it comes out as a question about whether the cheap end of the market or the posh end of the market is the market to be in. The answer seems to be the cheaper end, though not if you want respect amongst your peers.

Lee tells me that it is a small community and they all sit around talking about wine. Sounds awful, hey? Imagine though if the winemakers really are friends having barbecues every week, and suddenly someone is holding it back that they have the next big thing in wine and they just can't say anything but they want to, especially the more that they drink. Oh, it must be agony. But an agony worth living with!

Lee claims that he only drinks about a bottle a day. I don't believe him for one moment, and if it is true, hand your gig over to me, because I can double it!

Next ...Mecca calls, and I didn't see it coming. We're in the middle of nowhere, just driving down a decent road but still a country lane all the same. There's a little dip in the road, not quite a valley, and then I see it, and I wasn't even looking for it.

Jacob's Creek. Welcome home.

It just didn't occur to me that it was here. I wasn't sure if it was a creek, and a true place at all, or just a brand name, but sure enough I'm pulled up right alongside it. It is great to make the connection, and means more to me than an Eiffel Tower or a Machu Picchu, and to find it by surprise is doubly pleasant. I text all my mates, knowing that they won't care, or reply. I feel great excitement that I have made the connection to every Friday night in my house. And a few other days too. Sod it, every night to be honest.

We're not scheduled to stop here, but I like this cheeky touch. We are on quite a basic tour, the kind that serves chicken nuggets for lunch and accommodates kids, but as on the way, there is no such thing as a definite tour. Ross takes us where he is meant to go and a little bit more. Inside you feel like you are getting a bonus, though I suspect that he has done this before, as though perhaps he knew that some mad family would write a book and include an anecdote of stumbling ignorantly by surprise upon Jacob's Creek when in fact it was always part of his plan!

We're actually on the way to Grant Burge, a man so homely that he lives next door to the cellar door. So what, you cry? OK, well, do you have a cricket lawn in your front garden with a bowling machine that fires balls at you all summer long? No. Well, apparently Grant does.

This is the landmark stop on the tour, because it's the second stop after lunch, and you have had a dozen glasses by now. However, Ross reminds us, comically, that this is an unstructured session.

Come again? Yes, apparently, the last two stops were structured, presumably where they shove their best-sellers your way. This is unstructured, and you can have anything. Bugger me, I'll try everything then.

Clearly, the structured is for those in the know, and the unstructured is for the boozers, who will just take anything. No, perhaps I have that the wrong way round. The structured is intended so that they don't waste really good wines on the uneducated public, and the unstructured is to try and flog really dear stuff to the man in the know. Either way, my structure is beginning to become unstructured.

I think I am done with the booze by this point, though we have one last stop to make at a curious little outlet called Kies run by a lady with an obsession for teapots. She has an agent in North Yorkshire who imports her wine and I just keep wondering how they ever struck up a relationship. Pissed, I presume.

By now, nobody is drinking. So, I offer to do the honours on their behalf, shouting at the top of my voice that 'two white portsh shoundsh fantastic.'

My goodness, I only allow myself port on Christmas Day, but why not? Glass in hand, I see this as an excellent opportunity to try and sell some CDs on the shop's behalf as I notice that they are flogging some sort of outback classic compilation and I spot our favourite track from the Outback Pioneer at Ayers Rock. Within moments, I have taught and am leading a chorus of the classic 'G'day, G'day, How You Goin?'

I won't print any more lyrics, in the knowledge that if you have made this trip yourself, you will have wanted to forget this tune, and if reading us has inspired you to mirror our journey, you will know now which bits to leave out!

We have one last stop on the way back to rush-hour Adelaide. Welcome to the Whispering Wall. This is a curious quirk of culture that is essentially a dam. Well, it *is* a dam, once the highest in Australia, but in their brilliance, with that make-the-best-of-everything attitude, they have turned it into a tourist attraction, and there is nothing else here.

It is a curved, arched construction, from the other side of which some one hundred metres away, you may utter any profanities that you so wish, only for Nat and the kids to pick it up loud and clear at the other side.

It was built in 1899 and supplies water to nearby Gawler, and is a shining example to anyone who thinks that all the exciting advances have come in the last twenty years. It is five minutes worth of fun, but good fun all the way, and it is supposed to be a dam! Can you imagine going to a reservoir in England and describing it as entertainment?

On our way back, Nat and I are both drowsy. Heaven knows what the kids made of this. Ross is still filling our minds with all things Adelaide. I retain only two items. Firstly, a dream come true. How beautiful, even at this time of year, is the Adelaide cricket ground and the park around it? Sam, you can play here too, son.

Secondly, I wake as Ross is describing Hindley Street as a 'den of iniquity.' Wait a minute, this is the place that Trailfinders have us booked in for on our last night, and it looks shocking. Suddenly, I am bolt upright and focussed. I shall definitely write to them and get my money back. We have spent thousands with them, and they are contesting a £100 or so, and they clearly haven't been here. No, I will park that until we get back. They are behaving unreasonably and with no inkling for customer care. I shall win on my return.

We are the last left in the van, saying goodbye to many people who have entered a great day in our life and then they are gone again, and that is the nature of touring that you share some of the finest moments with complete strangers.

As it teems down I advise Ross that it will be sunny at West Beach by the time that he drops us. He looks at me quizzically, but sure enough I am right. You learn quickly. Tomorrow, we have to meet a complete stranger again. And she is family. It is time to meet Auntie Celia.

Day Forty-Five

Today is a big day that gets off to a bad start. Some daft old woman in an Apollo, just across from our pitch, is putting out tins of tuna for a cat wandering around the site. What an idiot. It is not even leftover tuna. It's the whole tin, bought especially. This means that not only does the campsite stink, but that cat will stop there every day from now on, and then probably try every other van. It is ok to live in your own world love, but don't drag me in with your poor hygiene.

Now, how do we feel today?

Nervous is the answer. Nat has never met Auntie Celia, and her family back home in Liverpool haven't seen her since the early eighties. She lives alone after Uncle Eddie died and she has a son. I don't know much more other that she was a Ten Pound Pom, one of the many who came cheaply for a better life, and one of the few who stayed when many others went back.

Today, we fulfil our destiny.

How much more different would expectation of this be if we had done the trip the other way round, as we probably should have done, and as most people do. Is this moment more poignant for waiting for it? Probably.

If we had landed in Adelaide on day one, and got straight there, then we would be looking back fondly now. The wait creates emotion.

We pack up the van and drive right out of the campsite, along the coast to Glenelg. The town looks fantastic, and I nudge Nat that this would be the perfect place for our last night. We pass the cricket ground, and I can only dream of how exciting and how alive you would have felt to go to school here, play cricket every evening, and surf the beach at the weekend. I think this is a life to be dreamed of. I can only regret, as we head closer to Auntie Celia's, that we hadn't made this whole trip sooner in our lives, and I bemoan the whole lack of sport in my life, other than from the armchair. You can see why I live my dreams now through my boy's eyes.

Of course, we are stupidly early, hours early, so we take on some massive hills up and down to Hallet Cove, an inconsequential little town of twelve thousand people, with a beautiful beachfront and little else. It is deemed important ecologically, indeed part of a conservation park, and gives clues to an unlikely past that you need reminding could have ever been possible in these parts zillions of years ago – the glaciation of South Australia.

We potter, we wander, and we kill time. Then I just tell Nat we should go. After all these years, she is not going to complain that we are early. We type in Hallarthans Court and drive cautiously. It is almost as though this whole trip has been about this visit, though the reality is that is not the case at all.

Everyone knows that feeling when you are homing in on an address that you haven't visited for years or indeed ever before. You drive slower, you turn the radio down, you talk little, and suddenly you make that turn, take a deep breath, and utter the words 'this is it then.' Then you have that silence, when they can see you in the house, and you take an age to get out of the van, the built-up emotion and stress of arriving about to be released.

The street looks more like the *Neighbours* street than the actual one we visited in Melbourne. We have parked up at her corner plot. The van looks a monstrosity, parked on a street rather than a pitch. And then I hear her rather than see her, as, like Scousers do, the accent is automatically accentuated in their own company. She is Nanny in disguise!

Inside, well, it is just like being at any older relatives. We could indeed be at Nanny's in Liverpool, or my late Grandmother Bridie's in Surbiton. The routine seems similar. Sandwiches, cake, photos, stories, and the TV in the background. I am watching *Judge Judy* and incredibly *Ready Steady Cook!* My gut feeling? Auntie Celia has these on every day!

In many ways, it is both comforting and equally curious to watch the TV. We have literally seen, at most, five hours in two months, and I feel that I am discovering it for the first time, a sensation that for any Brit or American is almost unachievable in life. You should try it. It is fantastic, and you'll realise that you don't need it at all.

There's a picture of Nat and I on her fridge. It is our wedding day. There aren't many of these left in circulation, I can tell you. She shows me a picture of 'the twins' and I think that they look hot. Then I realise that they are blokes!

I have no idea who they are, in the same way that Celia had my picture on her fridge but didn't know my name. Still, at least we are next to Ronnie Corbett, who appears to have attended a golf lunch some years back with Celia and her golf buddies!

Yes, that's the point, isn't it? This is the true value of photos. Who cares for the view, what is the story behind the picture, and with that I go into interview mode, and I ask Auntie Celia to tell me about the Ten Pound Poms.

She has regret in her voice. Others that came with her have gone back. She knows that she should have returned after Uncle Eddie died, but she has a son and he is Australian. How much of your life *do* you give up, when your best years are behind you but when those that you love are very much building their own? I do not see why there can be any reason why we as a family cannot fly her back for her eightieth next year, but maybe she will have fear too after all these years.

She tells me movingly that the Australian government are still advertising for Brits to make the trip over but warns that her hairdresser – a much sought after trade for some reason – is going back after two years and has no work, and the feeling is that once you land, opportunities are very limited. Many still go back.

But surely, it is much easier now than it was then? She tells me that she didn't even know where she was going and came out of total naivety – hadn't even seen a map, and got off at Adelaide, only because it was the first stop. What a way to make the biggest decision of your life. Of course, for younger readers, please remember when I say 'got off,' I am talking about the ship, not the plane!

I try and relive the journey in my mind, imagine what it must have felt like, physically and mentally. How anyone with any depth and life experience and emotion actually went through with it in such undiscovered times compared to now, I can't begin to know. I have total respect for the step into the unknown that they made, and I can only assume that post-war Britain was not the promised land that their forefathers fought for.

I feel close. I feel responsible. I feel the helplessness of the situation at this stage of life. I think of my Dad, and I am determined to get all these people in the right places if they can't make the decision to travel themselves, and I'll start with those two who have a greater opportunity than most... Nat and I are giving each other knowing looks that we will force her parents to try Australia, even if we book it behind their backs.

Today is sobering. Not a wake-up call, but a real chance to give yourself a healthcheck and see your life again for what it really is. I am delighted that we made the effort, and when we are getting ready to leave she tells me that it is a council house, I am staggered because it is the best council house that I have ever seen. Picture Ramsay Street in your head, and take any of those houses as they all look the same. Imagine it is two bedroomed. That's what the state pays Auntie Celia to live in. On second thoughts, she can stay right where she is!

There are tears at goodbye. We're not sure why. Blood is thicker than water, I suppose, though she is not technically my blood. Has there ever been a case in your life where you met someone for two hours and then flooded the place when you left?

I feel our journey is complete, and this is its symbol. And it almost *is* over. We have the small task of sorting the van, and then we are done.

I say small task...

Day Forty-Six

Last night was....well, tricky to remember. You know how when you have had a big drama of a day and you have a drink and after just one you feel slaughtered because of the intensity of the day that you have had? Well, that was us to the power of ten.

A glance at my phone tells me that I rang my mate Chris Dinnis in Exeter. How strange is this? I have rung him three times since 1992. My phones have been increasing, the closer we get to home. I have a text too from Damian, thanking me for my message from Ayers Rock. I don't remember that one either. I think it is safe to say my Stanley Wine face is on.

All I can remember is that the drinking began as the deconstruction of the van got underway, during which an excited Nat was at the laundry, having run into a South African couple, who are so fed up with their homeland that they want to move to Brisbane. Nat is convinced that they are getting our van tomorrow.

Well, this is where I piled in, telling them firstly that Cairns was the place to be, and secondly would he like a tour of the Maui before he picks one up.

He tells me that they were at Maui yesterday and that there were none there. I feel duty bound to point out the errors, the tricks and the hazards of the van, most of which we might have had a hand in creating. I pointed out the hanging television, and the fact that the toilet jams, and that the awning is wonky and ended up passing him my checklist which, of course, I wouldn't be declaring to Maui, for fear of punishment. For me, it was a certainty that this was about to be their home, and I didn't really want to hand it over. By the time he left, I was half wasted, had told him the contents of this book, and by chance had discovered that he was born in Ferryhill but had left at three. Where is Ferryhill – just about eight miles from where Molly was born in Durham!

The world continues to gets smaller.

All of this means that Molly and I had got no further in sorting out the van than chucking out noodles, soup, ice pops, vegemite and olive oil. Olive oil, I hear you cry? Yes, olive oil. It is a barbecue culture in the van, but Nat still has to have her olive oil, and now I am chucking it out. Full.

So today, hungover, but with Nat declining my fry-up, we have to make sense of this mess and make some big decisions. Not everything is coming with us.

We drive, with the kids standing upright in the van holding all the loose stuff, via reception to our cabin for the night, romping over the sleeping policemen. It is called Beacon 5.

It is fine, and so much better an option than trekking back into the den of iniquity, as had been the plan. We're right at the top corner of the site, and have no company, which is great, because the clearout that is about to get underway is going to include some sneaky tricks and some choice language. I back the van into two spaces adjacent to our cabin.

I dump the bog for the last time, and not very well. I will certainly miss that! There are drains nearby, so I don't go to the dump point to shed the waste water. I just let it roll. Nobody is looking.

We chuck so much stuff – objects that we haven't seen since Cairns like fly spray that we had thought that we would need but had forgotten that we even had as they all, one by one, chose to find their own little corner in the nooks and crannies of the van. The bedding has to come out. There is mould on the backside of one of the mattresses, possibly sweating after I spilt the box of wine on it at Anglesea.

Nat is all up for washing these and cleaning every inch of the van. I tell her not to be so stupid. Does she not think that they are not going to clean it before handing it on to the South Africans? Of course, they are. Don't do their job for them!

We find our alarm clock, just in time actually, as we will need it in the morning. This hasn't been seen since Cooktown. Oh no, I forget, we didn't make Cooktown.

Leaflets from the Whitsunday Islands, Sam's shades gone since the Reef, Molly's shells battered all the way down from Hervey Bay, the Chitty DVD missing in action in Melbourne, orangey sand from Ayers Rock, and four unused boxes of Stanley.

All of this accumulates to nine bags to take home. Nine – we came with four!

Right, here's some advice. If you take four rucksacks as we did, you only need one pair of jeans and not three. That's the first thing.

Girls, you will hate this but only one pair of trainers will be all that you need. And to everybody, deliberately fill your rucksack to four-fifths tall, rather than jamming it tight with things hanging off the side. You will thank me for this, if you have an equivalent of Sam Horne with you, who has purchased every replica animal on sale in Australia, and he is not giving any of them up.

Instead it comes to me to abandon a very good read. Somewhere in Adelaide right now, somebody will end up reading my wine-stained copy of Alistair Campbell's book. Sorry, Alistair, you didn't make it. Likewise Nat bids a fond farewell to *Charming Man* by Marian Keyes. One is a great analysis, of course, of deep significance that should be on every bookshelf, and the other is Alistair's book. Looking back, what on earth was I thinking packing a five hundred page-plus hardback?!

Bit by bit, we pack a bag, and unpack it, squashing a few bits in here and there, and abandoning more stuff. How can I tell Sam that we can't take his cricket bat, or football? I try once and he bursts into tears. I send him and Molly on a compensatory final lap of honour at the karting so I can make some devious decisions behind their back.

Tucked away in a cabin in the corner of the site, suddenly we don't feel like we are on the trip anymore, let alone the campsite. After three hours and with some improvisation still to be done, we drive an empty and incredibly light van to Maui, on the impressively named Sir Donald Bradman Drive. The depot is tiny, smaller just than Cairns, and a dot on the landscape compared to Sydney. I dread to think what they have got at Broome.

In the car park sit some Maui jeeps. I can only imagine the adventures that they are heading for, perhaps Perth or Coober Pedy, or all the way down the middle to Alice, maybe Katherine or Darwin. To have all that ahead of them fills *us* with emptiness and despair that it is all ending before our eyes.

Chris takes excellent care of us inside, greeting us with the words 'we've been expecting you – you've been on quite a trip,' as if our tale of adventure *had* been the talk of the Maui intranet. He invites me to fill in a questionnaire which I have no interest in completing as I can't really do it justice, because you know what these things are like. They set the parameters with marks out of ten or vagaries like poor, very poor, not so poor, bloody poor, better, good, better than good etc etc, not really giving you the chance to express an opinion until you get a solitary space at the end to summarise what, presumably for most people, has been a long journey. Has anyone, for example, ever written in the 'Any Other Comments' section that they would like more space in the 'Any Other Comments' section?

Nat tells me to help the next generation of campers by demanding a rear-windscreen wiper. This is an excellent piece of advice. I ignore it and give up the questionnaire, signing off with the words, 'just buy the book!'

Meanwhile Chris is checking our vehicle, but barely bothers, much to my relief. I tell him that I can't do the survey justice, but he ought to know a few things. So, out of compassion for the South Africans, I tip him off about the television, the awning, the bog and leave a few things for him to discover. I also have a little moan about the safe and the amount of time that we wasted in Sydney, and I have to say at this point that his reaction disgusts me.

Within a second, he asks me what compensation I would like.

What? Come on Chris, make me fight for it. Get me ready for home, please! I am so taken aback that I turn it down.

This in itself represents how far we have come. I just wanted him to know a few things for the overall Maui experience – for his benefit. I don't do this at home. Also, I care a little for the next travellers. I make it clear to him that we have had the time of our lives. What would I have said at home?

'Yeah, it was alright, but this bit was crap,' which would, of course have been met with an unsatisfactory 'you'll have to take it up with head office,' leaving me disgruntled with the company and the holiday forever.

Chris can't do enough for me. He offers me compensation three times, and I turn it down thrice. I attempt to buy the kids two replica Maui campervans – how sad – and he gives me them for free. And when finally he asks if there is anything else that he could do for us, I just suggest that he could shout us a cab back to the campsite, as we have no transport now. Realistically, Maui could do worse than offer this as standard, as most are near airports, and most punters are in this position just before a flight back. Instead, for a ten dollar fare, he waves fifty dollars at me. He couldn't have been kinder, and racks me with more guilt.

Yes, Sydney and the safe, and the DVD, and the power cable, and the bog, and all the little things are irritations, but they are funny now and we wouldn't change it for the world. I don't have the heart to tell him that after six thousand kilometres, we only discovered this morning how to wash up with hot water!

We step out of the Maui office. I am almost tearful. Nat feels empty. I can read that. It is almost as though we are asking each other what we do with our lives now. I feel really in love with her in this moment, and believe me, we have been in and out of love over the years. By rights we shouldn't even be on this trip together the amount that we have hurt each other over the years.

She tells me that she would have gone nuts with me if I had pushed for compensation. I tell her that I would have been mad with me too. That's how far we have changed.

We take glum photos outside the vans in the car park. They represent this moment. In years to come, we may reflect that they were a little bit odd and staged.

'The fines, ' Nat suddenly shouts, 'they didn't charge us any fines.'

High-fives all round. We had been led to believe that any toll evasions in Sydney would end up with Maui in Adelaide and that we would have to pay them at the end of the trip. We appear to have got away with it. This briefly lifts the gloom.

In the cab back to the campsite, we are both feeling that the roof from our head has been removed. Physically we feel light, unarmed perhaps. I feel like I should be driving something, or carrying something. I feel naked, and am certainly not used to being down at the physical height level of a taxi. I feel like a huge weight has been removed from my shoulders yet none of this has been a burden.

The campsite holds no purpose for us now on this our last afternoon, so after dumping one cab, we immediately summon another, and decide that Glenelg beckons, and what an excellent choice this beautiful town is.

These are the suburbs of Adelaide just five minutes round the corner from our site, but essentially Glenelg is all about one street, through the middle of which runs the tram, coming to its natural end, just metres from the beach. Special too is the array of shops and I am never one to comment on matters like that. They are almost brand-less, still very much with their own identities, again a Britain of years gone by.

I love it, and the sunset is spectacular, as I predict it is every day of the year. Come to Glenelg, if you want to be at one with the world, and sit and contemplate. This is the beach to do it on.

Indeed, I am not surprised to learn from a plaque that the Queen docked here in 1977, though I doubt very much that it was her who chose to park up at this little gem along the coast.

These will be our last memories of Australia and we couldn't have got it more right. I shall never forget a pie shop, empty and closed down, with the typically Aussie note in the window, saying that 'the management apologises for any inconvenience caused but if you really cared about it that much then you would have bloody well come in when we were open.' I love it.

There's a brilliant theme park too called The Beachouse. Brilliant for kids and grown-ups, complete with amazing waterslides, stunning dodgems and mini-golf, a Ferris wheel, trains and arcade games and every time that you play you seem to win a prize, and I'm not joking when I say that grown-ups love it too. There's even a wedding taking place as we enter. After the photos, they go for a quick ride on the dodgems. Clearly, a messed-up family, who wanted to do something different to defy their parents!

The kids love it, and secretly I do too, and afterwards of course, everyone is starving which is a problem because we want to eat quickly, but there is an unbelievable choice of restaurants in the town. We so nearly dine at Scampis, a magnificent looking fish restaurant overlooking the beach, and I want to desperately, but I tell Nat that it is not right for the kids. Normally, we always eat where I want to. What am I thinking? What has happened to me? Why am I not putting myself first?!

Instead we pick the excellent 'Dublin,' and what a feast at what a price as we over-order excessively, and how fascinating to sit adjacent to the kitchen, watching chef Brian in action.

I know his name is Brian as he stars on all the posters on the wall. There is some sort of inter-restaurant chef challenge underway in South Australia, which I mention as he clearly is a hot talent, only for him to comically mess up Sam's ice cream. He is embarrassed over it, apologising on the way out, but I am embarrassed for embarrassing him, as finally the right flavour appears at the third attempt.

For goodness sake, he has cooked a feast, is trying to be recognised as the top chef in the region, and he has come a cropper over vanilla ice-cream. Brian, I hope you are over it. The food was perfect.

It was so good that on the way out I nearly invite our slightly eccentric waitress Becky to come and stay on her trip to Cornwall later in the year, but I don't think Nat will have it somehow! (Do you see what you learn in one small encounter - we have her entire itinerary for her big trip!)

Instead, I make sure that I pass to Dan (who seems to be in charge) all the restaurant vouchers that I collected from a tourism booklet at the campsite, and I ask him simply why he isn't in it, and tell him that he damn well should be as his restaurant is excellent and more people need to know about it. I feel happy though, as he hasn't seen the booklet before, and at the end of every meal, I always struggle mentally with the thought that I should leave a tip, but on this occasion I have given him the best tip in the world.

We're full, tipsy and happy – and sad. The campsite is dark, and as a way of re-entering ourselves into the world, we turn on the TV in the cabin.

Cat Deeley is on with an awful American import called *So You Think You Can Dance*. The same show that was on back at the site in between the highway and the airstrip, whose name I haven't remembered since.

Traralgon, I think.

Is this Australia's most popular show? I watch it all, like a man watching the television for the first time, staring and wondering what it is all about. I am clear. This is not entertainment and I don't need a TV. It's a surreal way of returning to the real world.

At 10pm, I ring my pals Chris Lees and Stonesy at home. I tell them that we have reached the end of the road. It is emotional speaking those words. Nat thanks me, and gives me a hug. That's two in four days, and a lifetime total of three!

We feel complete. Tomorrow we are up at four. We have no enthusiasm whatsoever to head for Hong Kong.

Day Forty-Seven

Today is officially the worst day of my life. We're leaving. That's obviously not true.

I was pretty gutted when Gareth Southgate fluffed the worst penalty ever at Euro 96, and though I don't remember it, I am sure the day that my mother kicked my Dad out in 1978, when maybe it should have been her going, was something of a shocker too, and there have been many other dark moments either side of those.

This one is different though in that I can actually do something about it. Behind me, the greatest trip of our lives, ahead the rat race and more of the same. I could get off if I wanted to.

I don't have the funds at this point to walk away and I have a broadcast contract for the next three and a quarter years but all this will have been wasted if it has not served as a vehicle to change my life. I am clear – we have to move to Australia.

For the moment though, we have to turn our back. We make the 4am alarm call, and whilst I tell myself that Qantas will do most of the work for me, the first bit is the hardest. I have to move nine bags about six hundred metres across the campsite to where our taxi should meet us, though who in the world, has ever expected an early morning airport taxi to show up on time?

It does, but so much luggage do we have that the boot is open, as we make the five mile trek to the airport, virtually adjacent to the campsite. Predictably, and as ever, we are there way too early.

Suddenly, without having left the country, we're dragged back to reality. The airport is swarming with Brits, many in common tracksuits. I am hearing that estuary Essex all around, and am grateful that *we* largely met Irish on our trip. Where have all these people been for the last two months, and why haven't we run into them? In an instant, my mood has changed, as though work-mode has been switched on. Hearing the Brit accent en masse means home and that means work and that means destroying all this.

Thankfully, there is still a piece of Australia to negotiate as we check in. What a contrast to the self-imposed stress of arrival in Cairns – they can't help us enough today. Perhaps Maui passed on the word, and they want us to leave.

Our baggage is way over, but they package up Sam's ball, and his cricket bat separately in see-through Qantas bags. Our allowance is a generous 32kg, plus you can take a laptop, a suit bag and one piece of hand luggage as well as your cases. They have no intention of charging us, just helping us. I have never been so warmly treated. But then they are getting rid of us.

We say goodbye to the bags. I hate that thing that people do at airports as in 'say goodbye to the bags, say goodbye to Adelaide, say goodbye to the campervan.' Obviously we have been on a countdown of goodbyes for the last few days from Auntie Celia, our last campsite, dumping the Maui, and now the big one, when we utter those finite words (and who hasn't said them?)

'Well, we won't see them again until Hong Kong.'

When you get rid of them, you feel so light, so unburdened, but missing a limb too, after all the stress of getting them ready. What do *you* normally do in these situations? Nat always goes straight off and wastes a tenner on fancy coffees and breakfast, even though she is going to get one on the plane. I like to wander round, people-watching, seeing where planes fly to. It's like a who's who of places that we have been through. In fact, it seems slightly bizarre, perhaps pointless that we are about to fly back on ourselves, and head to Sydney.

In a way, I think a look from the air is good, and continuing the theme, it will be nice to say goodbye to Sydney again, for the second time! When you think as well how long it takes to drive but knowing that we will be there in two hours, it rubbishes our hard, industrious driving, and of course, this is just a daily short hop for many of those onboard, perhaps a business trip to the heart and soul of Australia and back tonight. For us, it is just the first leg of a long, long journey home, and Hong Kong looms.

In the same way that you do all that 'say goodbye to the bags' nonsense, who hasn't added 'well, this is it then (deep breath) our last steps in Australia.' That moment finally comes with heavy hearts.

Normally people are emotional at boarding because they are about to put distance between a loved one and themselves. We are different but with the same intensity. We are about to put oceans between ourselves and an experience. The emotion perhaps harder to justify, but more real in that we are still together, not separating and not saying goodbye, and if anything were more needed by this family, it has been this trip, and just being together.

We board, resigned. Resigned to our departure, but also that it is absolutely hammering it down outside and we can see our rucksacks being loaded, already sodden it seems. Great, we will have to go naked in Hong Kong.

Soon we are off, trying to clock the campsite as we climb above the Adelaide skyline. It is funny how you can always spot a plane from the ground, but you can't spot what you are looking for on the ground from the sky. Hey, even Nat missed Ayers Rock with no obvious competition to vie for her attention.

Consequently you say patronising rubbish like '...oh look over there kids, that must be where Auntie Celia lives.' Of course, you are totally lying, just trying to sound informed and making the most of the view before you disappear up, up and away into the never-ending skyline, admiring as you go the seldom-imposing height-restricted Adelaide, emerging just under a couple of hours later on approach to Sydney.

I imagine the regulars no longer gasp as they circle around Sydney. There is no pleasure in a business commute, even if you are landing onto one of the most scenic descents on the planet.

For us though, we see brighter sunshine, and Watson's Bay, and Bondi, and it looks like a proper life, that surely we were all meant to enjoy. We were here a matter of a fortnight to three weeks ago, negative in our mind about the cost of the Rock, unsure about whether the kids could sit through a three hour musical in Melbourne, and with wine-tasting not really on our radar. It is strange to be back, but it helps summarise all the magic experiences in my mind.

As we approach, the Opera House seems old hat now. Once you've had these experiences, like seeing the Bridge for the first time, they never match that initial moment. I spy the road out of the city that we took on a one way ticket to nowhere-ville whilst trying to find the suburb of Mascot to fix the Maui on the day that the Pope arrived. I am happy today to just cruise alongside it, and of course, the great thing about landing at Sydney, is that to land over water, within a whisker of the beach, is always the best way. That feeling on approach that in the next ten seconds you are either in the sea or on the ground is one of those great 'take pleasure from danger' moments in life. Seconds later you land, questioning what all the fuss was about.

We have a long taxi, and then are dropped at a back door, taking us up through some rear corridors into emigration. Oddly, there is no advice, yet whilst the queues to leave are three rows back, nobody is actually pointing you the way of the forms along the left hand side of the room, which you must complete before your departure. Maybe they are having a bad day, but we only become aware of this by following the pack and from learning from the person in front of us. This, over the years, has become increasingly an irritation, filling in four forms with nonsense that they know anyway, like your birthday, or the flight number. It is all on computer anyway and they know by now that we are not carrying packages for Al Qaeda or marching powder for Columbians. They've got you covered before you even reach this far. Some people just like paperwork.

Eventually we are through. Frankly, I am not bothered. I quite like the idea of not being allowed to leave.

There's work underway behind the scenes at Sydney airport, so we have to follow our way through a makeshift corridor before yet another x-ray attendant is begging me to strip off again. The irony of my words is not lost on me, though truthfully the whole flying experience has been a nightmare since 9/11.

Forgive me, but I don't really believe anybody is going to kill you with their belt, but off it must come. If you really want me to take my shoes off, on your head be it. They began stinking about Cairns, some seven weeks ago.

What could I really have in my wallet that is dangerous, or are you just calculating how much you can fleece me for in the shops the other side?

I hate it when people say the extra checks are a price worth paying. I look at it like this. I once flew from Manchester to Heathrow – it took me about an hour. It then took about two to get to my gate for a flight to Addis Ababa. With everything available to all these people, if they think they can thwart major disaster as late as at the x-ray conveyor belt, then they ain't doing their job, because it is the entire surveillance process before you even step into the airport that counts, rather than leave it to a chance spot at the airport. Go watch *Spooks* if you don't believe me.

Even at 9/11 when intelligence knew that those people were even in the country, they still let them board the planes, so what on earth is the point of stopping Molly because she has the tiniest pair of scissors in her pencil case?

Tears follow. Then floods. Her lip is quivering.

'Auntie Helen got me that for my birthday,' she sobs.

There is no consoling her. I stare at the security worker. I don't believe for one moment that she believes that she has done her job properly there. Still, while these problems are the same the world over, it is part of the gentle phasing back into normal life.

Past security we spot our plane. Oh no, come to think of it, they are all Qantas. I begin my usual airport routine.

This consists of a two-pronged attack. On one side, I am the MI5 wannabe, on the other the drama queen. I weigh up the flight – who's on it, who is fat, who is likely to smell of spices, who has kicking-off kids, who looks dodgy, which air stewardess I fancy ...all that kind of stuff, checking out my options. Clearly I was joking about the air stewardess, there's normally three or four of them.

Except on BA where they tend to be a bit more scraggy. Plus there are the gay ones too. It's always a relief when you clock the first camp one.

Then there's the *me* bit. I have stared out of so many airport windows over the years, often very moved by an experience or people, from Lima to Addis, Antigua to Bogotá. Even if it has just been a business trip into London, I am always watching the world's population going about their business, each at different stages and different emotions in their life. Who are all these people, I always think?

Throw all that into a gaze across Sydney, a final nostalgic stare for a time that is so recent in the memory that I know I should turn back and grasp it forever. Of all the airports from which to dream that dream, Sydney airport is the best that I have come across yet. It seems right suddenly that we chose the odd route of coming back on ourselves FROM Adelaide into Sydney before flying onto Asia but hey, there's no fairytale Hollywood ending here, no slow-motion running back towards the gate with a big soundtrack playing, as we decide that we cannot leave Australia after all.

No, our flight is being called. We have to head to Hong Kong.

Day Forty-Eight

I came to Hong Kong at the beginning of 2005, or maybe 2006. I don't remember. I came for work to do a ridiculous outside broadcast for the Hong Kong Tourism Board and they didn't like it when I asked someone in government about China's human rights record ahead of the Beijing Olympics.

Now, I am back again and the Olympics are here. What a time to turn up. First the Pope in Sydney, now the Olympics in neighbouring China, and here in Hong Kong too.

My memory of that previous trip is what inspired me to make Hong Kong our return-leg stopover though I am aware that my memory is probably playing tricks.

There are only two good things about foreign OBs, as glamorous as it may sound. Hopefully you have a better time zone (we were on air at 1pm not 5am) and secondly you don't have to go in the office to deal with all the nonsense, but believe me, even though most of the radio industry love the freebie, they are hell, with intense travelling at either end, invariably resulting in a ten day trip away from home, plus the sponsor controls you. It is close to prostitution.

Most importantly the show is crap because when it is icy in January in Newcastle, nobody wants to hear you cracking open a beer in seventy degrees overlooking Victoria Harbour in Hong Kong. Though, that didn't stop us.

Nat was at home with the kids, virtually dying from some flu bug at the time, so that made things even worse. It was the time of bird-flu and SARS. If it hadn't have been for the laughs that I had with my producer 'Dogsbody' pretending not to take the piss out of some of the nonsense that we were forced to do like reflexology and dancing with a Chinese dragon, I would have lost my mind. Everybody, of course, hates you back at work for doing these trips, not that I care about that.

I think, therefore, I must have made some promise to Nat a couple of years back that I would take her to Hong Kong.

We landed with zero enthusiasm last night, constantly looking over our shoulder at our Qantas airline, the forgotten friend. It didn't feel right. In fact, for most of the journey, we were following the computerised map on our little screens, as we said goodbye (once again) to every place in Australia. It took forever to reach the tip at Darwin, and then it was gone. We watched intently as the airplane symbol on the screen moved from land to sea, and uttered the words, '...there it goes (sigh).'

We can't be the only people to have touched down in Hong Kong from the oh-so-laid-back land of Australia and straightaway noticed the gear change. Whether it is the smell, the noise, or the traffic. Whatever it is – it couldn't be more contrasting.

My first confirmation of this is at immigration. They couldn't be less friendly, and I couldn't be more certain that we have made a mistake. Oddly, I notice a specially manned check-in for Olympians taking part in the equestrian. It is empty, yet our queue is some way back. I resent the Olympian special treatment. I don't believe that countries should go broke funding a two week sporting event with all the other needs in the world, and as for the athletes, well – they get their own special desk, but we are the people who have paid for our tickets! Oh no, you can queue up with your javelins like everybody else.

Furthermore, with such a global event on its doorstep, the security is the worst of any major airport that I have been to. No questions, no searches, and you're in.

We only get accosted on the way out, and even though there

is an excellent train link to our hotel, the taxi driver is persuasive.

He seems bent, shepherding us through back exits of the airport where he flags his mate to pick us up. I have agreed a fare with him but notice there is no semblance of documentation in our eight-seater. This guy is no Kenny. In fact I am not sure he is even a taxi driver . Ah Kenny in Singapore... where are you now when we need you?

I booked our hotel principally on price. Some of the reviews said that it was a bit out of the way for Kowloon, but all seemed commutable. On approach, my emotions change rapidly as I am pleased to recognise the Happy Valley racetrack, but after that I just keep feeling that we are slipping down side-street after side-street, like on one of those chase scenes from a Bond movie, walking into a trap.

We're at the Harbour Plaza Metropolis. It is reasonable, though it takes about three calls to reception to change our pillows because of Nat's feather allergy. The building and facilities are fine, the view is obscured, the service very foreign. Already, it is clear. Hong Kong is a poor man's Singapore.

Suddenly, I am on a different trip with a different Nat.

'Well, you know Hong Kong, what is the plan?'

I bluff a response, and take us walkabout, on the basis that, like Sydney, the waterline is your map. I see some signs that are familiar like the Governor's House, and the Hong Kong Cricket Club, but I am lost instantly.

We wander, barely speaking for an hour or so, even getting lost in a mall from which there seem to be no exits. We have got off to an uncertain start, and I know already that we all wish the plane hadn't bothered stopping last night.

In a panic, to lay on some entertainment and to prove myself as tour guide extraordinaire, I hail a cab and ask to be dropped at the entrance to the Peak Tram train, a searing cable car that affords spectacular views across the water.

My belief that the driver hasn't understood a word that I have said is confirmed within minutes as that sinking feeling reaches my stomach with every bendy turn up the mountain. He is not dropping us at the bottom of the cable car, he is taking us all the way to the top and charging us a fortune. At this point, I look like the worst tour guide in the world.

My intention had been that we take the train up so that we could see the land slipping away behind us, but the stupid idiot has gone and dropped us at the peak.

This goes from bad to worse, but at least we are now at something with a view. Except Hong Kong is misty and hazy and there is no view. Nat is adamant that it is pollution from China and that they have wrecked the place. I certainly didn't remember it being this bad a couple of years back, but it looks awful. If this is the future then the view from the top of the Peak Tram is doomed, and it is on that which this particular tourist dollar is built.

It also seems busier than last time I was here, not in the sense that there are more people, but more outlets and more people on the streets selling you stuff you don't want like readings and fortune-telling, as though they are about to make it extremely tacky and wreck the place.

I saw it at night last time, which I think is better. Perhaps the mist had been here on that day. I just hadn't seen it in the dark. It is quite a clever place though, as essentially there is nothing to do at the top except stare, and then go back down again, so feeling that you have wasted your time particularly when the mist is high, you oblige yourself to eat or buy something. In so doing you can say when you embellish your tales, that you stayed, '...oh a good few hours.' This, we obviously did, only to rise from the restaurant table to then begin our descent. Approximate time at the top doing anything – five minutes.

We can clearly get the tram down, as it is obviously easier to locate at the top than at the bottom under the guise of a foreign taxi driver, and this really is where you begin to discover how obnoxious and rude the locals are, how simply Hong Kong *is* a poor man's Singapore.

I blame ourselves as a nation, just over a decade on from the handover; they clearly have cut loose, dispelling all imperialism and Britishness. There is no, '...oh I am sorry, after you, please. No, please, after *you*.' When that tram comes, it is every man for himself. Truly, it is obnoxious viewing.

A ride in a cable car is always something to be cherished – it reminds me of going to Hastings as a kid. There's something old-fashioned about it, and clearly this mode of transport goes back to the empire. Of course, because we are just the dopiest tourists in the world, we sit all the way down facing the wrong direction, and I was right by the way. It would have been much better to have climbed out of the city and see it peeling away behind you than it is to descend on it and be back at ground level, as ground level means chaos in Hong Kong.

I don't think the hustle and bustle can be passed off as 'just like any other city in the world.' It's the people, the speed at which they move and speak, the smells, the physical symbols of the written language, the searing buildings sweating off each other, so compact in the city skyline, and in its midst lies this mad but necessary strait of water, with fishermen and cruise ships both fighting for the sea, yet without this gateway to the ocean those on land would surely suffocate. Hong Kong, in short, needs to take a breath.

We take the legendary Star Ferry. Everybody who has been to Hong Kong has been on it. It is billed as a tourist attraction, though essentially it is the hop across the water for the locals. Sensing new vocabulary to be learnt and seizing on this belief that Hong Kong is a poor man's Singapore, Molly announces that the Star Ferry is a poor man's Manly ferry. And she is right. What, after all, is stunning, about a manky old vessel taking you on a choppy five minute trip across the water? Highly overrated, though key if you want to get back to Kowloon.

On arrival, Victoria Harbour opens into the bus terminus, so you can imagine the multitude of people in an already over-populated city. On the exit from the ferry, whilst the kids stuff themselves with ice cream, I am drawn instinctively to placards and newspaper cuttings mounted on boards detailing atrocious human rights, and imprisonment of journalists, who dared to investigate and speak out. Unfortunately, most people pass by, either disinterested or in the knowledge that this is old hat. And that of course, is the problem.

I don't recall seeing this last time that I was here, and I sense that the ante has been upped for the Olympics, and the more that the volume seems to have increased about the untold story, the more it seems to have fallen silent too.

I despise the Olympics, for all its cost, its corruption historically, and the excessive National Lottery funding at home, plus the fact that politics of the event meant that America got it twice in four games in Los Angeles and Atlanta. That said, I admire the mind of anybody who can spend four years preparing for something that, in the case of the hundred metres, can be won and lost in nine seconds. That's a life on a knife-edge and if you win that, particularly in a bygone pre-drugs era where amateur meant amateur, then you have my total respect.

Strangely, my best man Crossy is reporting for *The Mirror* from Beijing. We hardly see each other these days, and now he is just down the road – and we still don't see each other. I ring him as he is filing a report on the judo or something else from martial arts that we both know he knows nothing about! Perhaps he thinks it is judo but he doesn't know and nobody else will actually notice. He is after all, a football reporter!

We both agree that Hong Kong is a dump, and hang up, and then absent-mindedly we wander into the mini Olympic village on the water's edge. The equestrian is being held in the city.

I love the fact that, even though I despise the Olympics, I have now just casually sauntered into its history. The irony being that

I'll ignore it totally when it is on my doorstep in 2012, but half the way around the world, it suddenly does feel quite exciting.

There doesn't seem to be anything going on, just an exhibition, some sort of propaganda spreading the message, and as the sun begins to shine for the first time, a ridiculous mini musical procession files by, all of them sweating now as the temperature rises past thirty degrees. They seem to be dining out on the Olympic ticket, making more of a noise with ceremony and procession, rather than actually witnessing any sport. I smell tokenism. The real deal is over the border.

You have to keep moving though, or you get collared. Nat is tetchy already, as she seems a target for cowboy salesmen wanting to sell her a watch, all of them completely unaware that somewhat oddly, none of us ever wear one. For me, as long as I am up and in the radio studio on time, no other time-check ever matters. The last thing that I want is a watch, or a suit.

They're offering to measure me there and then in the harbour, but I blow them away, rebutting them with news that I have one from the publicity-shy Sam the Tailor. If you have never heard of Sam, he has fitted everybody from Pavarotti to Clinton. If you've ever watched the Michael Palin DVDs – he's on there as well. So predictably when I was on OB for the radio show last time I was here, he came to my hotel room and tickled my inner thigh too.

It is all rather annoying in its slightly unauthentic commercialism, like a fly that needs to be swatted. I say that, but Nat is suddenly interested when she sees Fiona's sunglasses for four quid. Fiona is our ex-next door neighbour. She is Fiona Weir, wife of Scotland football international David. I can tell you that Fiona is no wag, but she doesn't spend £4 on shades. Nat's estimation – a ton at least.

There's a sense that we're killing time before the inevitable. We have tomorrow to fill, and then it is Hong Kong Disneyland and home. So we hole up in a bar for a couple of hours just along from Hong Kong's Avenue of The Stars, their equivalent of Hollywood's Hall of Fame.

Nat is quite impressed but I'm lost once you've seen Bruce Lee and Jackie Chan, and I can't claim particularly to be a fan.

From the bar, it is quite pleasant to stop and watch this mad world pass by against the electrical background of all the flashing signs and boats charging up and down the water, but it is still chaos.

Food is a big problem, especially with the kids. Where can you trust to eat in this place, with so many people selling off the street and so much filth around, and what honestly will the kids stomach? We take the unadventurous option and head for the cafe restaurant at The Sheraton, thinking that you can't go wrong here, but how wrong can you be. Nat's salad, even at the third attempt, is pathetic and we refuse to pay. It was truly disgusting but at least with a high-class chain like The Sheraton they don't answer back when you complain. It seems they have bigger fish to fry anyway. Half of the British Olympian equestrians – those who are still in – are dining here.

On return to the hotel, we down a bottle of wine and retire to our room. I've been trying to sell them the free nightly sound and light show, which you can see far and wide along Kowloon, and just about pick up from the hotel, but they are not impressed. Come to think of it, I am not too bothered either second time around. I saw it last time and remember thinking how extraordinary that the council or the government or whoever would put on, to all intents and purposes, an electronic firework display every night of the year, but now I am tending to think it must be annoying if you live here, and if you are just passing through like us, it just serves to remind how commercial Hong Kong is, as essentially the light show is bouncing off all the logos of all the companies who grace the skyscrapers with their presence. In short, it is the world's most elaborated advert.

Nothing else to do – we watch The Community Shield on TV.

Day Forty-Nine

It's no straw Monday!

I know you are wondering what No Straw Monday is too. Never having been one for the delights of an oriental breakfast which just looks like an oriental dinner but colder, we have no hesitation at heading over to the public transport complex just behind the hotel for a McDonald's breakfast. They announce boldly at the till that every other Monday, they are encouraging you not to take a straw in a bid to save the planet.

I don't think that I have ever seen such a pathetic gesture from a major corporation. If they really meant it, it would be every Monday, or indeed every day or presumably if they can factor in getting rid of the straws for one day in fourteen then they surely would go the whole hog and get rid of the straws altogether.

What makes it even more bizarre, and for me, insincere, is the global picture. Here is one of the world's leading brands, encouraging people in Hong Kong not to have a straw to save the planet, yet on its very doorstep, China is opening up a new power plant every week, sometimes two. That, obviously is not Ronald McDonald's fault, but it does put this weak effort into context. I, therefore, take as many straws, as I can. To be bloody-minded.

Oh to get out of this place. It is pouring down. I decide that in the rain, we have to take a trip, and my fondest memory of my last trip was heading down to the out of town Stanley Market, so I take the group decision that today we will shop. Stanley is a place about half an hour out of Kowloon. It has nothing to do with cheap carton wine.

The blind leading the blind, and with no concept of the Hong Kong bus network, we hop across on the Star Ferry to Hong Kong Island to find the bus. Then an extraordinary thing happens, as we are walking from the ferry terminal to a big shopping centre, under which awaits our bus. Sam suddenly stops dead in his tracks.

'Oh no, it's them.'

The last people any of us want to see. I can't resist sneaking up behind them and shouting very loudly.

'Did you enjoy the train back to Alice Springs then?'

They answer on auto-pilot before, somewhat startled, they clock us. We have just run into the obnoxious Brummies from the Ayers Rock tour.

You remember these guys – they told us that our plane was going out of Melbourne not Adelaide, when in fact, it was total fabrication. These are the last people, of all those whom we have met, that I wish to see again, and I definitely do not want to get stuck with them. They are possibly the most unsophisticated people in the world, and if *we* don't like Hong Kong, there is no way that these guys can appreciate it.

Draped in jewellery, and always with the video camera rolling, they are from a different era and social spectrum. They seem like Harry Enfield characters. When one of the guys comments that there are a lot of elderly British men wandering around with young Oriental girlfriends and is adamant that that isn't right, more on racial grounds than age, I hasten our departure. That, broadly speaking, is their outlook on life.

It takes us about twenty minutes to decide which bus to board, principally because all the English people seem to be starting some rumour that the bus driver will not give you change, nor is there an exact fare. What madness. Eventually, we just go for it and throw some coins in his chute in exchange for a scowling glance, and begin the drive out of Hong Kong.

This itself is an education, travelling ten metres and braking sharply, watching the Hong Kong people go about their business, eyeing up the beautiful Happy Valley racecourse and Hong Kong cricket club, but equally, being disgusted by live markets in the street with blood from animals running down the road to the drain.

It is a relief to climb the hills and head out towards Stanley, with lots of beautiful little islands to witness on the way. Nobody is particularly sure where this bus ends, but eventually we all pile off at something resembling a terminus. Straightaway, it is not the Stanley that I remember. I recall it being a one street market with a really boring maritime museum that you pad out your trip with! Now, there is so much more, but I think this time, it is an improvement. There's some gorgeous looking restaurants and a McDonald's, whose sole purpose for us is that it is a free toilet stop. Who hasn't done that in any city in the world? When your little ones need the loo, and you don't know where to go, the Golden Arches is always the easiest option.

Nat is drawn to rather a curious little shop where they are selling little sheets of paper with your name on it, and the spiritual, oriental explanation of what it means. She buys one for our nephew Ben, though I predict that as he is just one, he will never read it. It is the kind of thing that you buy in the moment, then lose in a heap of junk at home, and they sell them everywhere too. It is either tradition out here, or a massive tourist trap.

The market itself is an extraordinary adventure. A little labyrinth of bargains, one store rolling into another, and covered too, to shield us from the downpour. The vendors ruin it of course, by hassling you. It is probably the norm here, but it is not something any Brit appreciates.

There's so much to pick from but can we realistically take anything else home? Silk, shoes, toys, rugby tops, bracelets, handcraft cigar boxes, and beautiful chess sets, but one question persists...is any of the label stuff genuine?

There is nothing tacky here, and the prices are reasonable without being exceptional. You need a good two hours to walk up and down browsing, then repeat the process knowing what you want to buy this time around and stopping only at that specific shop, to avoid being badgered. We buy something truly local that will always remind us of the Orient, an item that you can't get anywhere else in the world that says that we were in Hong Kong. A new pair of Crocs shoes for Molly.

As the usual scenario unfolds, I am left standing outside the shop – though it is more of a cupboard. Nat keeps telling me what great value they are and how Molly needs some anyway. Just buy the bloody things woman and stop your justification.

I fire off a text to Tim Jibson, the guy who brought us on the OB last time around. Sam is desperate for a replica Ronaldo shirt and I have assured everybody that we can get them for peanuts, but I can't for the life of me remember where. Knowing that Tim will remember, I await his response, only to be blown away by its content.

'Are you ready for the Maldives in the first week of September?'

What? Oh no, it is all starting again and how on earth do I break this to Nat?

I hadn't spoken to Tim since May when my boss Trevor decided to cancel an OB from the Maldives, only for him to disappear with Tim on a freebie to the Mediterranean the week after for our sister station Magic, despite the fact that Trev, by his own admission had no reason to be on the all you can eat and drink sun-drenched vacation!

My last words before I left for Australia were these: If the OB comes up again, then there is absolutely no way that it can be in the first two weeks of September. Everyone is getting back into their routine after August where the northeast still traditionally shuts, plus I am returning after two months off and I don't want to send the message that I am buggering off again. People will think that I am a knob.

Now you're reading this and you don't see the problem. Correct? Well, this will cause me immense problems at home. Secondly, I do not want to go long haul again for at least six months, and thirdly and most importantly, what is the value for the listener when they are driving into Newcastle with back to school and back to work on their mind? It is one of radio's great errors, so foolish in its conception.

Plus the first week of September is a no-no. Auntie Helen is getting married on the 6th.

This is going to be interesting. I feel myself tensing up before I have even returned, furious at people's inability to follow instructions combined with their deluded thought process. I am not back at work for another week and already I have battles to fight. Well tough, they have to work around me. I have put radio before my family every day of my life and *they* have got to learn 'not this time.' I couldn't be more cross. I am conscious of the fact that I am now slipping, regrettably, back into the real world.

It is the Ladies Market that we have to head for in search of counterfeit Cristiano, so it's back on the bus and into town, and back on another bus from Victoria Harbour out to the market. Again, it is guesswork knowing where to get off, and even then we can't find it. I remember this market principally for its smell. We came previously close to midnight when the smell was rife, though Tim assures me that it starts around four in the afternoon. The smell is of burning tofu, and second to what I can only imagine torched flesh must smell like, it has to be one of the worst smells in the world. It is the workers by the way, not the tourists who are responsible, cooking up on their stalls. After all, they are there all day long.

Now, if Stanley had a certain amount of class and mild restraint about it, this is tacky heaven. You can't move for being hassled. The question is do you want any of this stuff or are you just buying it because it is cheap? None of it genuine, I am sure.

Last time that I was here, I saw a Beckham shirt with Beckham spelt incorrectly, though famously he once did play for Manchester United in such a shirt. What I find extraordinary is that the Manchester Uniteds of this world are so keen to tap into the far east market that they inevitably have been out to places like Hong Kong and China on business trips, and probably with a few hours spare to explore, have wandered these very same streets, but return home, with merchandising so at the core of their business that they either turn a blind eye to what is being sold here or are powerless to prevent it.

Of course, as a westerner with a pound in his pocket, you play the game. And the game is to barter. I am not sure why we do this. Is it because we have been told that they expect it, and it is the custom? Do we bargain over small change because we are tight and times are hard? Or is it fundamentally because we are superior?

For me, it is the latter, and when I say superior, I mean craving to feel it. The whole experience brings out the worst of being patronising. You're in control all the time, chucking ridiculously low prices at the street traders, only to hear their pathetic tales of woe coming back at you with exasperated faces of distress and their stories of dying dogs and sick children and how you are offending their honour. This is the game, and it is mutual.

I smile, even laugh at them, and walk off. This is why it brings the worst out in you, because you play them over a matter of pounds, knowing that they will charge after you screaming a new price as the next trader tries to work on you.

Nat will ask occasionally if I feel bad. I can only answer no. I tell her that we are just passing through these people's lives, and their lives won't change because of us. After all, it is a government's problem, not a tourist's. Even Molly is pragmatic about the situation. Sensing that Sam is about to clean up here, she is studying an expensive gift, though somewhat knocked-down in price. I would quite like her to have it, and she would like it too, though she admits quite maturely afterwards that she didn't over-want it, she was just sucked in by the process. What a smart little girl.

Her brother has no such morals or thought process, leaving with Spiderman underwear, a Spiderman watch, Spiderman pyjamas, and that Ronaldo shirt. Total cost £4. It is relief in the end to leave.

We dine at TGI Fridays – something we would never do at home – but it has to be the safe option. The highlight of this is – wait for it– Sam's watch breaks. He is devastated. Nat and I shrug our shoulders. It only took two hours. Well, two hours according to that watch. This is morality come full circle.

Back at the hotel, I have to do some internet banking, paying some bills for this vast expense of a trip. The rate on my American Express card is so high that if I don't meet the deadline, I will be paying a third more. I am always nervous of using a public internet, though not as nervous as the guy before me should be. I am able to click on the previous sites and searches that he has left behind. What was the last thing that he googled? Gays in Hong Kong.

Well, whatever floats your boat. So I make excuses to Nat and disappear for an hour with his print-out in my hand.

Only joking, what do you take me for?

With just a few minutes left of my allotted pre-paid time, I decide to browse. I log onto one of the radio websites to see what is happening. I have no reason to do this and find myself there instinctively before I have even weighed it up as a thought. This is bad. I am slipping back into it.

Day Fifty

We had some loose change and some time to kill last night, so we broke with tradition. We went to another market, and cleared them out of Batman.

It's terrible, I know. You go to Hong Kong, and you buy something from Hollywood. Never mind the rights and wrongs of bartering, the morality to be questioned is the intellectual void that means you would rather buy a superhero in pants than a wok.

Today we're up for a quick swim. That is at least one of the good things about Hong Kong. The rooftop pool! It is never pleasant to be in amongst the mist of the city, or perhaps it is Chinese smog after all, but there's something mysterious, or perhaps luxurious, about being on the top of a skyscraper and being at the level where the mist kicks in and you can barely see. I can imagine this was once a great view.

I'm just killing time with the kids while Nat packs up. This is a standard Horne arrangement. She packs up, then I bring down wet swimming costumes, having tried to be helpful by occupying the kids for an hour.

We really are in the end zone now, and nothing symbolises the downbeat mood more than checking out at the Harbour Metropolis. They have me down for a porno on my account. I wouldn't mind but I had only just finished filming it.

No, I joke again of course.

I *am* incensed however, that they have charged me for the bottled water in the room. I think I am only really cross on two counts. Firstly, Hong Kong has been the least friendly place on our trip, second only to the woman in the bog at Eumundi markets so if you like I am pre-conditioned to confrontation; secondly either make me pay for the water, or give it to me all free. Apparently, on your first night, you don't pay. After that you do – with no hint of explanation in the room.

Often it is the little things that set you off, and this just drives me nuts. I've already made six calls to reception over the feathered pillows, which even though they eventually changed them on the first night, they took them all away again when they made up the room the next morning.

When I protest and tell the dolly on reception that it is typical of the rubbish service over the last couple of days, and that all this is going in the book, she calls me back, clearly about to refund the water, but I am so riled on principle that I will teach the hotel a lesson for charging me a few quid by telling as many people as I can, and that ladies and gentlemen is how customer service works! It is like being back at home already. Very little made me cross down under. Fact.

And so to our last journey...to Hong Kong Disneyland. Our psychology at booking had always been that if the kids didn't enjoy life in the van, this would be the carrot at the end of it – a trip to Disney to look forward to, or if misbehaving, to pretend to take it away, in that immature grown-up way that we threaten kids not to deliver on things that we have already paid for.

I can't think of anything worse than two days at Disney. In my mind, we should have left at Adelaide. Worse, the weather out of Kowloon is better. Yes, I actually mean worse. Too hot in fact at thirty-one plus degrees, in a stifling Asian way.

We're able to check in early, by a very handsome man who has for the benefit of westerners changed his name to Jim, just like when a call centre rings you in the UK, but it really is Jamal speaking, he will always say '...hello Mr Horne, this is Davey speaking.' Please tell me your real name, or I can't treat *you* sincerely. But then, this is Disney, the home of sincerity!

Our room is immaculate with Mickey Mouse everything everywhere, from soaps to wallpaper. It is way too tacky in an excellent-for-your-kids kind of way. Get this, there are even Disney sanitary towels. Is that the ultimate business model, or just insulting? I don't know. I am a man.

They're not daft, are they Disney? You can't get room service food – possibly the only hotel of this standard in the world where it is not available. I assume that they want you out of your room and down to the park and the restaurants to get you spending your dollar.

So, to the park we must head, on a two day pass, which is brilliant value actually as we're only checked in for the one night, and as customer service is truly everything for this brand, we can check out tomorrow, and they will store our luggage all day and give us a courtesy room for an hour in the evening as well as the second day ticket, which is kind, proper customer service, and actually the least that they can do, given that it is a sweat-fest out there and that most flights back to the UK leave around midnight.

You see, there is a lot of time to kill, or if you ask the kids, we're here about a week shorter than we should be.

I mean that too, because as we enter the park around 11am, I am already hearing Nat's words like a bad echo that we simply have to see the Disney parade and the Disney nightly firework show. I am doing the maths, you see, wondering if the kids can stay up and fresh until 9pm, and more importantly, if I can too.

Inside, it is all so perfect. I am sure they just employ pretty people to stand around and look helpful, answering questions or selling balloons, or whatever you need. No request is too small. We sense a hierarchy at play, all the way down from cleaner, to litter-picker, gate attendant, ride operator, extra in the parade, and the big one when you have finally made it – a fully fledged cast member, all of whom are available at regular intervals for photo sessions - queues annoyingly busy particularly as Snow White is quite hot! I will stop at a hug from Mickey and Goofy however.

In fact, these photo sessions generally can provoke some of the biggest queues, because of the excellent fast-track for the ride system which means that as long as you are not too greedy, you can line up for the Flying Dumbos, knowing that you are straight to the front for Space Mountain directly after. If you want some advice here, well...unless you are four, ignore the Flying Dumbos altogether.

I don't want to rave particularly about any of the rides actually, for fear of looking un-cool but Space Mountain is quite good. It's an indoor rollercoaster that scares the hell out of Sam. He's much happier shooting lasers at imaginary targets on the Buzz Lightyear Astro Blasters. It's a ride where even girls can look like they can aim. Much to my disgust, however, I am cornered on the way out, and appear to be having my picture taken with Buzz himself.

What on earth am I doing, and why am I the only person in Asia today who doesn't seem to know that here is a man in a costume! He is not real, kids! You can't get me with your Disney magic. Someone has been observing us though, because as we walk away to dump excess rubbish in the bin, the bin starts moving and begins a dialogue. This is like one of those Noel Edmonds or *Candid Camera* shows where somebody with a false beard and a camera crew emerges after twenty minutes of you talking to a bin.

I'm not playing. I walk away. It follows me. The kids think that this is hysterical, and want more. I refuse to laugh. Principally because I can see a man with a suspicious hand movement, away to my left – remote control at play. Ha, got you! Good trick though, and Disney's answer to Pambula's bacon-craving kangaroo.

The biggest queue for the day baffles me. It is for a rather naff car ride called Autopia, where after forty-five minutes, Molly and I drive an estimated ninety second circuit. Ah that's the Disney magic, isn't it? The wait! Imagine how bad it would seem if you didn't have to queue and you could hop on and off all day long. You would be round in an hour, and devoid of the expectation, which of course creates the thrill.

My favourite ride, if I am allowed to begrudgingly have one, is the Jungle River Cruise. In the mood for childlike adventure after climbing Tarzan's Tree House, we board for the ride of our lives. This is not exactly a get-wet ride, more a 'what's that in the water?' adventure. What's more, in a little ironic twist for humourless Hong Kong, we encounter the spitting image of Kenny our taxi driver from Singapore, who is 'driving' the boat. Life indeed, has come full circle. He's cracking gags, as though his life depends upon it, which is a remarkable feat because he probably makes about two hundred trips a day, repeating these gags every time. His job is to lure you into a false sense of security, as you ride the swamp, encountering hippos clearly on a timer or a sensor, and crocs closer than we got to them at Australia Zoo. Then I realise that they are not real!

Now that may seem a stupid thing to say, but on the first seconds of the ride, with the element of surprise, elephants are roaring and waterfalls are spurting high into the sky and I swear there is a large element of doubt. There's fire in the air too, all perfectly controlled. Sam is gripping me tightly. What he doesn't know is that I am curious to be on the ride on the day that it doesn't all come in together on time. Surely this ride can't operate flawlessly from now until the end of time?

Curiously, when the jungle cruise passes us by later with us safe on dry land, I hear Captain 'Kenny' cracking exactly the same jokes in exactly the same place. What a pro – and that's the Disney magic.

The heat is incredible, and not even the lunchtime water

parade can cool us down, leaving us drenched and stinking of damp sweat. It is, you will agree, a strange concept that crowds of people will pay to line the streets of the park, only to be hosed by a daft bunch of Disney characters. Worse, can you imagine being inside those costumes, and having to hold that smile and wave that wave for the entire duration of the route, several times a day. I'd rather be the queen.

There are no manners of course, the locals pushing you tightly and forcing you onto the road. It's worse at the entrance to the Magic Of The Lion King, itself an excellent half hour summary in the round of the amazing stage show that we saw in London a couple of years back. In fact, it is better for being in the round, the compact space removing some of the obvious elements of the longer version, such as characters emerging from the audience or the balcony, but it is even more intimate, and to be admired, given the chaos that it must be backstage.

I really don't know if the locals are in awe at all. When Wham! went to China in the eighties, I read a quote that the crowd sat there stone-dead, not knowing how to react. Here, they don't seem to know how to behave either, though they are at another extreme, photo-snapping impatiently during the show despite several warnings not to do so. Even at the end, Disney staff guard the props left in the centre for the next performance, as they try to clamber aboard for souvenir shots. This must be normal fare – hence the staff, ready for them. Nat and I have never seen such rude behaviour.

Unfortunately, after this we make the mistake of going to an Oscars type show, called 'The Golden Mickeys,' essentially celebrating Disney shows such as *Toy Story* and *Lilo and Stitch*. What a shame, that before we enter we omit to read the sign outside. This version wasn't in English.

By seven we are flagging and all I can think is that I can't be bothered to hang around for the fireworks show at nine. Nat is adamant, to the degree that she would have paid to enter the park just for that. Twenty minutes beforehand Sam is asleep and Molly is whingeing a tired whinge, only perked up by some food. I can see that they don't want any part of this, and I can see that Nat wants every part of it. Ah yes, here comes our last row on tour! She storms off towards the exit, when we are just minutes from it starting. I calmly suggest that after waiting for an hour, the compromise is to walk slowly, very slowly, towards the exits, with one eye on the sky, and by the time that we get there we will have a clear view up above, *and* be first for the buses. I am sure that I am not the only Dad to have walked out of these gates, carrying two children.

It turns out to be a stunningly good Disney waste of money! These people must have budgets, but everything about their message radiates 'whatever it takes,' which is rare, so rare in any walk of life these days. It is perfectly delivered too, with a magic mix-up of colour, pyrotechnics and of course, the perfect Disney tunes to accompany.

As Molly tells me that she hates fireworks, and Sam piles in to agree, *A Whole New World* spins permanently around my head. They even put it on in the bus back to the hotel. I hate it in a sickly admiring kind of way.

And we have to do it all again tomorrow. Our last day.

Day Fifty-One

The kids passed out last night like two angels that could sleep forever. Little did they know that Molly's best friend's Dad, my mate Chris, had left a message on the answerphone saying that little Edie had been in hospital but he didn't want to be in touch, because he knew that we would worry.

Not true at all, we are in Hong Kong, what could we possibly do about it!

We were shocked though – everybody hates that call on holiday, don't they? What did we do before we couldn't get hold of people, just over a decade ago? We haven't wanted to be in touch with a soul really on this trip, bar the odd drunken text and Nat's parents. We sought to disappear, but one thing that is as sure as night follows day is that if you want to inflict pain on somebody that you care about, put an ocean between you. I am definitely from the did-I-turn-the-gas-off school of traveller, despite the thousands of miles that I have done over the years. I always fear the worst.

We have had the adventure of all adventures and poor Chris couldn't even get past Exeter. His summer holiday is over at exactly the same time as ours. For totally different reasons. Perhaps, we shouldn't invite him round just yet to view all of the seven hundred plus photos!

Yes, home is not just on our mind, it is our sole thought, and like a lot of people on their last day, we just to want to go. First things first, fill up at breakfast. Our diet over the next day may be rubbish, or as we are flying British Airways, probably worse than that. We decline the option of the character breakfast. Any parent will tell you that there goes your hope of children eating, when stupid Goofy is at your table. We go conventional for a bog-standard American buffet, declining all of the Oriental delights on offer. Yes, you *can* have rice for breakfast, if you so wish.

Checkout is wonderful. An extraordinary thing to say, I know. Nat is panicking about the number of bags that we have. Oh yeah, we have about five too many but the Disney staff are all prepared for this, storing them for a few hours. It makes such a difference when you don't fall out at check-in or out. Thanks Jeremy, or Jemima, or whatever your name wasn't really this time.

We're back in the park for a half-day. One night gets you two days, and that's good value, though psychologically for a Disney park of this size, it might not be smart. It depends, I suppose, on whether you are racing to do it all again or a second day is a traipse too far. It's the old question of leaving you wanting more, or smothering yourself in every last drip of Disney.

I can't be a lone adult in thinking this, especially with the night flights back to the UK.

Time to kill can damage memories, and in fact, it can't be the same as the very first day, because, you're second-guessing the time at every opportunity with 'how long do you think we have left,' or 'shall we think about making a move?'

The heat is a concern. We're sweating instantly, not the kind of conditioning that you require before boarding a long night-time flight. There's relief though in the shape of a horrendous twenty minute downpour, which leaves us soaked but refreshed, in that Caribbean style of a short, sharp downpour, the kind that you associate with end-of-the-world floods, only for it to all be fine again, moments later. You never see that at home. It just drizzles all day. It is exhilarating, almost sexy. Certainly very

335

exciting, and not at all uncomfortable. After the rain, and partly because he is wet, but principally because he is white, pale and thin, Sam becomes *the* tourist attraction.

It starts with two girls, then a group follows, all asking politely. In the end at least ten join in. They want his photo. He's laughing and milking it. I feel sorry for Molly, who is obviously too quirky, being too ginger. Nat is laughing. I'm embarrassed, and disapproving. I just don't think you do this kind of thing in the modern era. I mean, who are these people, and of course, on what social networking sites is my son now plastered? He is turning on every pose going, announcing that he is famous, still not quite sure what the fuss is. Nat says I am overreacting. It is, of course, racist. Can you imagine, when I had been in Ethiopia, if I had gone up to well, anybody, and said these words.

'I'd like to take your picture – because you have a lovely tan.'

Exactly, racist, I tell you.

Sam doesn't want to go back to Space Mountain, instead preferring a few last trips on the It's A Small World ride. I must warn you about this. Well, it is not really a ride. More a gentle snail's pace boat trip, but excellent nonetheless for its content, most of which you don't fully appreciate until your second or third visit. Lucky me then for enduring five circuits.

The problem is that the music is so hypnotic that it takes control of you so that with no pleasure at all, you are humming it for no obvious reason at any given moment thereafter. It is the same hook all the way round, except that it is made worse by the detail. So, if you know the It's A Small World music, imagine it with a Mexican twist, or a gay French trot, or a sleeping Latin panpipe. The same tune all the way round with all the linguistic nuances and musical key changes from all corners of the globe. That is the Disney detail that is both exceptional and bloody annoying.

Around four we decide that enough *is* enough, even though we still have what most people would consider an honest day's

work between now and our flight – a whole eight and a
hours. I am ashamed to say that yes, we do part with our mo
in the Disney store. I recall how early in the trip we encourag
the kids to hold onto their money as there would be lots o
chances to buy presents on the way. Yet now, with the trip fading
before us, who hasn't been in that situation where any gift will
do, as long as it says Hong Kong Disneyland on it? Sagely, I advise
everybody that there is an excellent Disney store at the airport,
when we will be free of our bags, so it may be worth picking some
stuff up there. I know this, of course, because I was so
disorganised last time that I was here that I went one better and
bought those last minute souvenirs some thirty minutes before
the flight.

The problem is that I don't think that the kids want anything,
but I think that they know that they can have something so they
are looking at everything whether they want it or not. Or, if you
like, a bit like Christmas.

Poor little Edie gets a Mickey Mouse. Nat and I allow this
one through because we know how much her Dad Chris will
disapprove. He would rather have a eucalyptus tree he is such a
bloody hippy. Sam walks off with a Donald – another one. Molly
buys a purse, the irony of which, of course, is that she now has no
money to put in it, so fleeced has she been by the Disney store.

I am doing that man thing of pacing up and down, then
removing myself to stand outside and tut. At this rate, with all
the cuddly tat in our possessions, I clearly haven't booked enough
seats for the plane back.

As we leave the gates of the park, it is time for another
farewell. Very soon, there will be nothing left to say goodbye to.

We take a last look across the water from the gardens of the
hotel while the light is good. On our way back inside, the Disney
promise is broken. Nat is very much up on these things. She
always reminds me that the rumour is that every employee is
called a cast member and that behind every door there is

supposed to be a sign reminding you to smile. I don't know if this is true, but we both laugh as though we have landed a sensational scoop when we see one of the characters being chaperoned back into a quiet part of the hotel, just down from the diner, and yes, we see him begin to remove his costume! It makes not a jot of difference to us. It would, of course, devastate every kid in the park if they had seen it!

At reception, the staff are brilliant. We're allowed into a secret room to access our luggage, and we have a spare room for an hour to freshen up. How kind, considering that we are basically going to trash it.

It is much needed too after the heat of the day and the prospect of the journey ahead. Just think, of all the hotels that you have stayed in across the world, how many would do this for you at 6pm? You see Disney may be a sickly sweet annoying sister, but it is also a very kind, caring, wealthy uncle.

At just after seven, Nat and I are very conscious that we have to drag dinner out for as long as we can. Suddenly, China versus Cuba at the Olympics in the women's volleyball looks a cracker.

We delay ordering food as long as possible to string this thing out, and then deliberately order everything stodgy, uncertain of what rubber delights the great chef in the sky will serve. It's pizzas all round here.

With the flight due at 00.35 (that's past midnight), we bail out at 9pm – still hours to go before we fly.

At the airport, it is chaos. Not because there is a multitude of people, but because all the equestrian toffs are here from the Olympics checking in extra baggage that comes with being a show-jumper. Horses, I can only assume, and whips too!

The queue is filled with the worst of British, upper-class accents looking down on people, talking about a world only the elite and the aloof can relate to, still flying BA, because it is in their imperial blood to do so, though as we are about to be reminded, BA disappoints us every time.

We're checked in by a trainee, and we have Sam's football and cricket bat still in their transparent Qantas bag. We explain that their affiliate airline had sent them through without a fuss, in fact with great delight, and the checkout girl duly obliges, only for her supervisor to storm over and berate her in front of the waiting passengers in one of the worst pieces of customer service that I have ever witnessed, and I expect no less from BA. I have had problems with them since flying back from the States in the early nineties. A humourless, difficult experience for me every time.

The supervisor has Sam in tears, saying that the Qantas bag is not satisfactory to transport his bat, and that his Australian football must be deflated at security. There is no need, and even if someone from BA reads this and replies that 'it is standard policy, Sir' then I counter by saying that a partner airline couldn't do enough to get the bat and ball on board so where is the consistency?

Inside the terminal, eventually, we locate the Disney store, though just as we are about to enter, it closes. I find this disgusting – there are so many late British flights out of Hong Kong, and I can count at least three – that surely this problem occurs every night, and you would imagine that the British would be more likely than most nations to part with their dollar, us being America's poodle and all that.

Surely though, if your busy time is late night, the shops in the airport, especially one of the world's leading brands, must remain open. Furthermore, I think Mr Disney would be very unhappy at hearing that his store was locking up and turning away two kids with tears streaming from their eyes. Disney don't do tears.

It is indicative of the airport, from the casual nature of security at arrival, to the sternness, humourless souls of those working immigration, and our last experience on Hong Kong soil is complete when they call the flight, but call everybody at the same time. Frankly, a stupid thing to do and a disservice to those waiting for the 'people travelling with young children' call.

I am enraged both with the airline *and* the other passengers to such an extent that I march to the front of the queue to demand precedence, which is duly granted, albeit somewhat late and somewhat blushingly.

I shouldn't have bothered. It is a furnace inside the plane. Neither the video screens nor the air-con are working. We've come from thirty-one degrees to hotter.

This is going to be the flight from hell.

Day Fifty-Two

The air-con fails for two hours, by which point there is no point as dry sweat clings to you and that never goes away. The best worst explanation that I am given is that the plane has been on the ground in Hong Kong for much of the day and they don't start up the air-con until the engine starts up, hence the delay in it kicking in.

I am afraid, as I point out to the stewards, that BA's operational procedures and cost-saving measures are none of my business and I really don't care if the plane was shot at while it was landing. I have paid to have a certain level of comfort and service, and this doesn't come near the minimum, and presumably this is the norm, as thirty-one degrees on the ground in Hong Kong is pretty standard.

Every time I fly back from anywhere with BA, my national airline, I find that there is something cold and unsatisfactory. You can have the trip of a lifetime, and they literally bring you back down to earth. It prepares you beautifully for the depressing life that is England.

We take no pleasure in landing at the crack of dawn in London. You notice instantly that it doesn't feel right. The temperature is bland; the air quality has no depth to it. The people are cold, the skyline depressing. London isn't a great city. It is full of individuals struggling to survive financially, unable to express themselves emotionally. There isn't a single person I would like to talk to.

Even when Australian immigration were hassling us for the missing apple some forty days or so ago at Cairns, the tone in their voice was still very much that even though I am a criminal, I am still their best mate. At Heathrow, you can hear the silence of the workers, and the British passengers depressed to be arriving, and the never-ending lines of security, now taking multiple photos. It feels foreign to be home.

There's still a flight to Manchester to take, which surprisingly is called early even though I have sent Nat to the shops, on the assurance that no domestic flight leaves early. It is due to go at 7.50, and for that I read about 8.10, but then I had been browsing a leaflet which, clearly in a bid to boost Terminal Five confidence, offers you extra air-miles if your flight doesn't leave on time, where, 'on time,' is defined as within fifteen minutes, so obviously there is some sort of effort thing going on here.

It doesn't make its fifteen minute window. In my head the complaint email is already being composed. This tendency to compose my letter of objection is a past-time that had been dormant. Since Adelaide, it was coming back fast.

On the plane, I try and chat to a couple of people, but nobody is interested. We are a miserable bunch of bastards, aren't we, and I have broken that spell in the last two months. Me, of all people, looking to be a friend amongst strangers. I can't get sucked into this again. I have to cling to the positivity that I have felt during the last two months. There is another world out there, at a different pace, and you can rediscover your family and why you liked them in the first place. I feel closer to them now than ever before, but isolated too being back in England. We no longer belong in this struggling vacuum of being British in Britain. Whatever that means these days.

Already we are thinking about the next trip.

Work, though I am grateful for three and a quarter years money already lined up, is no longer a priority. I have a job that many would crave, but I have seen a lifestyle, that I can't have until I free myself of that burden. I know that it is time to stop chasing that dream of being some world famous radio personality, and time to start pursuing that other concept of being a real person and chasing quality time. How long before we go back to the kids asking me a question, and the answer is a grunted '...hang on a sec.' That was the old me, and the new one has to prevail.

If there was one moment of symbolism that represented the juxtaposition of the frustration of living in this country against the delight of exploring time and space in a land where all dreams seemed possible, it comes at the baggage carousel at Manchester Airport, where our name is being called even before any bags have arrived.

The cricket bat hasn't made it. Spectacularly all the others have. I can only assume that it was that nasty woman in Hong Kong. Sam is in tears again. The ground staff assure me that it is on the next flight in the next hour.

There is no pleasure in joining the rush hour traffic. Turning into our street feels like an outsider, like a Sunday afternoon snooper pretending to purchase your house. Opening up the house is a sobering experience. Nat's parents have managed the post, but I chuck most of it in the bin. They will come back for me if it is urgent. I have eleven thousand emails, which I just delete. The house feels horrible. Too big. Way too big. We don't even turn on the TV for the first two hours, and it is normally on all the time at home. We're preserving the stillness, savouring the last drops if you like.

I ring something resembling a BA baggage line, and get to speak to someone in Scotland. He couldn't help me less, but claims he has done me a favour by locating the missing bag. I point out to him that he hasn't done me a favour at all, in that he has only told me what I knew already, and that he can't start claiming the moral high ground when they lost the thing in the first place. Then brilliantly, he tells me that I can't have the number for the baggage desk at Manchester Airport and I quote, 'that number's not for the public.'

Oh spectacular, so who is that number for then – the staff, whose baggage is…well, presumably at home because they are in some crap call-centre job not helping me.

This is the epitome of where we are at as a country. Yes, there is a number, but no, I can't have it. No, I can't speak directly to the guy to whom I had been speaking face to face a couple of hours ago. The number exists, the phone line is active, and the people that need to ring it are not allowed to.

By contrast, and in despair, I ring a Qantas number in London with a view to reclaiming my air-miles for my BA account as our flight to Ayers Rock is part of an affiliate scheme. To my delight, I am diverted to a guy in Tasmania, who, even though I have none of the information required is able to provide me with my unique passenger reference and give me the precise information that I need. I am chatting to him for about twenty minutes, I would say. He asks me if I made it over to Tazzy. Regrettably, we didn't, I tell him, though I did once know David Boon, which delights him. He couldn't, of course, have been more helpful, more proud of his country's heroes and heritage, and more keen to represent his nation, even though I had just left it and it didn't need selling.

Like the tour guide in the Barossa Valley who gave us a tour about everything before the actual tour, like the guy at Noosa who apologised for the cow at Eumundi, like the immigration officer who just got the Tipex out when Nat presented the wrong entry documentation, like the man at Maui who urged me to take compensation when I didn't want any, like Karl Kennedy and the magnificent Irwins, it was in their DNA, and I wanted a piece of it and more.

The thought of returning to work on Monday was killing me. I wanted to get started straightaway on planning New Zealand. This had to be the beginning, and not the end of the Hornes Down Under.

After The Van

How quickly one reality slipped into another. The cricket bat never turned up and I gave up ringing, settling instead for twenty thousand free air-miles, safe in the knowledge that it is still going round the carousel at Terminal Five.

Nat got stung for the fines in Sydney and we paid up for fear of it complicating re-entry in the future.

Trailfinders refunded the money from the hotel in Adelaide, after I pointed out just how silly they would look in the book if they had sold a hotel to a family of four in the red-light district. Furthermore, Woolies UK went bust and the guy in the Townsville honeymoon murder was finally extradited.

Back at work, a retired sportsman was making my life hell in something that dragged on for three months and caused me an unbelievable amount of stress that I nearly quit the whole thing, and only the knowledge that I wouldn't chuck away what I had personally spent years building up kept me going.

I had to leave my sister-in-law's wedding early to be sent on an outside broadcast to the Maldives, which was a total farce with only three and a half shows making it to air forcing me to take the decision to cancel the last show myself after discovering that the OB man Tim had failed to organise the appropriate transport for us off the island, resulting in a forty hour trip home, which left me ill for the next two weeks. Delayed, and vomiting, spending a Friday night in Colombo airport just hours after city-centre bombings wasn't the new life that I had envisaged. Predictably nobody at the radio station was on hand to help – other than to sign on return my £1500 expense bill for four and a half utterly disastrous days.

The ratings crashed in my absence and our show had gone to number two for the first time in my life, and Nat was ostracised by almost everyone at the school gate. Frankly, I was glad that she was out of that fake-bag party, false laughter, two-faced world.

In a bid to be positive, I did something to make me feel like a man. I ordered a skip.

I had cleaned out my soul, now it was time to do my house, and rid myself of many material possessions which, like my mind, had just been gathering dust for many years.

Little did I know that much of the stuff that I was throwing away I would soon regret saying farewell to.....

Because then came the bombshell that I had craved, but rocked my world the day that I found out.

There was one little surprise left that I hadn't been expecting despite all our joking all summer long, which meant that Nat's book might be slow to see the light of day, that we wouldn't be travelling anywhere the following summer, and that the earliest that we could return to Australia or embrace New Zealand would be Christmas 2010, and this time there would be five of us in the van...